A Public Speaking Guide

FOURTH EDITION

Penny Joyner Waddell, EdD

Kendall Hunt publishing company

Cover designed by Cassandra West

www.kendallhunt.com
Send all inquiries to:
4050 Westmark Drive
Dubuque, IA   52004-1840

Printed in the United States of America

"You do not have to be GREAT to START,
but you have to START to be GREAT!"

Zig Ziglar

LET'S GET STARTED!

"Start by learning about
the foundations of public speaking,
the types of speeches,
and methods of delivery."

Table of Contents

Presenting a speech may be frightening, like standing on a dock and being afraid to jump into deep water. However, once you learn the basics of public speaking, you can become an expert.

UNIT 4   CREATING VISUAL AIDS   235

UNIT 5   PRESENTING THE SPEECH   275

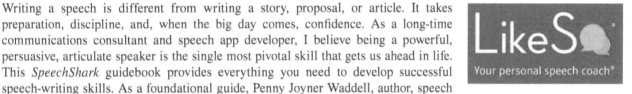

Foreword

Penny Waddell's newest book, *SpeechShark*, guides novice and experienced speakers to create a professional presentation in a quick and organized way. This book and the *SpeechShark App* are practical tools to prepare you for success! Whether you are planning a speech for a special occasion, group presentation, or an informative talk, Penny's advice will help you feel more confident by giving a well-structured presentation and knocking it out of the park or, perhaps I should say, knocking it out of the water!

Nick "Sunshine" Tokman, a former four-year cast member of the hit show **Deadliest Catch** is now a professional speaker, empowering others to conquer negative influences and connect with their voice to create their own definition of success.

Website: www.nicktokman.com **Facebook:** NickSunshineTokman
Instagram: NickTokman **Twitter:** NickTokman

Writing a speech is different from writing a story, proposal, or article. It takes preparation, discipline, and, when the big day comes, confidence. As a long-time communications consultant and speech app developer, I believe being a powerful, persuasive, articulate speaker is the single most pivotal skill that gets us ahead in life. This *SpeechShark* guidebook provides everything you need to develop successful speech-writing skills. As a foundational guide, Penny Joyner Waddell, author, speech coach, speech program director, and instructor, provides an easy-to-follow method for both novice and experienced speakers. The bundled SpeechShark app is the best on the market, provides templates and prompts for creating speeches from a variety of genres, and is a great way to prepare. Simply brilliant.

Audrey Mann Cronin
Co-founder/President, Say It Media, Inc. (creators of LikeSo app), Founder/President Mann Cronin PR, Inc.

Drawing inspiration from her effective public speaking app, Dr. Penny Joyner Waddell's newest book, *SpeechShark: A Public Speaking Guide*, goes right to the heart of the issues that most determine communication success or failure. Readers will come to understand that public speaking intimidation is not a permanent state and can be overcome with preparation and practice. There's no doubt *SpeechShark* can help public speakers turn their biggest fear into their greatest strength.

Joel Schwartzberg
Public Speaking Coach and Author of "Get to the Point! Sharpen Your Message and Make Your Words Matter"

SpeechShark Logo, Book Cover Design, Shark Bites and SpeechShark Terms Design
created by
Cassandra West, Graphic Artist
E-mail: West.Cassandra@gmail.com

Preface

Several years ago, I had the inspiration to develop a speech writing app that would help students and business leaders plan and write speeches. Through my many years as a speech instructor and speech coach, I learned that when people say they have a fear of public speaking, it is more a fear of not knowing what to say. Speakers who have a clear message and a plan for the clear points they will cover, take time to rehearse, and incorporate trained tech support to make the presentation shine, realize they have cured their own fear of public speaking or speech anxiety. The SpeechShark app was developed to be a tool for speakers to help organize thoughts and put content into a package that would be well received by any audience.

Speakers are not sharks, like vicious man-eaters; instead, they are a focused species with a key role to share a message with an audience. Instead of an ocean, SpeechSharks navigate stages and platforms. Instead of sharp, pointed teeth, they use their intelligence and problem-solving skills to strategize and create a calculated plan for success. To a speaker, the audience is not a large, deep abysmal pit. The audience is an opportunity for the speaker to go deeper!

With the help of a talented App Design Team, SpeechShark was born! Charles Hardnett, project manager, worked closely with Maurice McFarlane (iOS Specialist) and Marcus Smith (Android Specialist). Cassandra West (Graphic Artist) designed the SpeechShark icon, logo, and colors used within the app, along with the cover for this book. My job was to provide the idea storyboards, the plan that a speech should follow, and troubleshoot content issues that would rise to the surface.

You've heard the saying, "It takes a village to raise a child," and I can tell you that it takes a dedicated team to build an app. This is not as easy as it looks and I am sure this team became quite frustrated with me on many occasions as I was asking them to help develop the app while all of them were working other full-time jobs! True to the SpeechShark theme, they threw themselves one hundred percent into the turbulent waters and assumed the sharky attitudes that made this dream a reality. Over the past few years, I have lovingly referred to my friends as "The Sharks." Before this project, I might have considered sharks as cold, blood-thirsty predators in the ocean. Now, I have a true respect for a species that remains in constant motion, never vulnerable, with armor plated skin, and with a reputation of power and skill not held by many!

Did you know that a group of sharks is called a shiver? Have you ever walked on to a stage to make a presentation and felt a shiver of excitement or anxiety? Now, perhaps you understand why we have taken on the title of SpeechShark for the app and also for the book. This companion guidebook was requested by Kendall Hunt Publishing Company. They realized that an app as effective as SpeechShark would also benefit the public if an accompanying guidebook were available.

For anyone old enough to remember the television show *Happy Days*, the main character Fonzarelli, also known as Fonzie or The Fonz, was waterskiing in the ocean and decided to jump over a shark to prove just how cool he really was. This is where I first heard the term, "jumping the shark." To do this means that you are doing something so amazing that everything after that event pales in comparison. I'm reminding you of this story because I hope that it will let you know that overcoming the fear of public speaking is just like Fonzie jumping the shark. Sometimes, you just have to take a deep breath, believe in your own abilities, and go for it! Or, to quote The Fonz, "Heyyyy!"

Having a good plan and a strategy for crafting an effective speech allows you to say, "Bite me!" to speech anxiety. Stay out of the water? Not you, because you will put on your shark skin suit, better known as thick skin, and walk confidently to the stage because you are no longer the guppy in the shark tank! You are a SpeechShark and this public speaking guidebook was designed just for you!

Meet the SpeechSharks!

Penny   Marcus   Maurice   Cassie   Charles

Dr. Penny Joyner Waddell, author of *SpeechShark: A Public Speaking Guide* and designer of the SpeechShark app, has years of experience as a public speaking coach and a reputation for providing students with a practical step-by-step approach to public speaking. SpeechShark has just the right amount of instruction along with easy to use guides and worksheets to help you begin thinking like a professional speechwriter. This guidebook coupled with the SpeechShark app will have you speaking like a pro in record time.

Marcus Smith is the key coder and developer for Android versions for the SpeechShark app development team. As a software engineer and with a background in game development, Marcus has worked on several group projects creating mobile platforms and web APIs, as well as principles of software designs. He is especially talented with identifying software defects and recommending improvements.

Maurice McFarlane is the key iOS coder and organizer for the SpeechShark app development team. As an accomplished applications developer, Maurice also works with Tier 1-2 retailers creating the Point-of-Sale system customizations, building custom APIs for payment devices, and implementing P2Pe/EMV solutions.

Cassandra (Cassie) West is the graphic designer for SpeechShark. Her expertise includes brand identity, corporate presentations and campaigns, web collaboration, UI design, package design, book cover/layout designs, and more. You'll see her beautiful design on the cover of this guidebook and she created the brand, icon, and page displays used for the SpeechShark app.

Charles Hardnett is the project manager and senior developer for the SpeechShark app. His career includes a vast array of experiences as a computer science professor and researcher, software developer, educational administrator, and software architect. Charles has worked on projects involving the development of compilers for high performance computing, access and switching for telecommunications, web applications for a variety of domains, and mobile applications for entertainment, productivity, and education.

How Do I Use the SpeechShark App?

Using the app means you are on your way to creating effective and exciting speech presentations for your audience! Click on your SpeechShark app and let's get started!

Here are steps to follow:

1. Open the SpeechShark app.
2. Select "Home" to see options to create speeches, manage speeches, or select preferences.
3. If you want to create a NEW speech, select "Create Speeches."
4. A page will open that asks about the purpose of your speech. Read through each type of speech and choose the type that works best for your purpose. If you need more information about each type of speech, simply "LONG PRESS" the speech type to receive a brief tutorial regarding the speech. A "SHORT PRESS" of the speech type will take you directly to the next step in creating a speech.
5. Answer each prompting question using a complete sentence. Use correct grammar and spelling as this information will automatically begin building a speech outline.
6. Take your time and work through each step—one at a time—answering each prompting question and when finished touch the "Continue" bar.
7. SpeechShark takes all of the guesswork out of crafting an effective speech, but it is up to you to answer the prompts, keep the purpose of your speech as your goal, and consider who will be listening to your speech. What does your audience need to know? What does your audience WANT to know? What can you do and say to connect with the audience and engage them?
8. As you have answered all of the questions, you will notice that SpeechShark will then deliver a full written outline that you can print, share, or e-mail. Additionally, you will see that SpeechShark will automatically generate three note cards that can be used for notes on your phone or tablet/iPad. This will make you a Card Shark because instead of standing in front of your audience with awkward note cards, your notes are easily accessed using your electronic device and are available with a simple swipe.
9. Once the speech has been written, you can always retrieve it by going back to the "Home" file on the SpeechShark app and selecting "Manage Speeches." Every speech you craft will be stored there in a file with the "TITLE" that you give to the speech.
10. You, too, can be a **SpeechShark!**

Acknowledgments

Deep appreciation is extended to the following: the dedicated members of the SpeechShark app design team, Charles Hardnett, Maurice McFarlane, Marcus Smith, and Cassandra West; personal editor, Ruth Rowell Joyner; and Kendall Hunt Publishers. I am most grateful for the support of my husband, Bill, our children, Katie, Steven, Maggie, Marc, Halie, and Nick, along with our grandbaby sharks, Will, Bailey, and Hunter.

SpeechSHARK™

Unit 1

Foundations of Public Speaking

Public Speaking

Speaker and Audience Responsibilities

SpeechSH▲RK.™

Key Terms to Know

Chapter 1—Public Speaking

- Active Listening
- Appreciative Listening
- Asynchronous Meetings
- Communication
- Critical Listening
- Decoding
- Empathetic Listening
- Encoding
- Feedback
- Hybrid
- HyFlex
- Informative Listening
- Noise
- Public Speaking
- Synchronous Meetings
- Virtual Meeting Etiquette
- Virtual Meeting Platforms

Chapter 2—Speaker and Audience Responsibilities

- Active Listener
- Appeal to Action
- Attention Step
- Connectors
- Conversational Tone
- Empathetic Listener
- Empathy
- Establish Credibility
- Establish Relevance
- Imagery
- Shark-o-licious Treat
- Startling Statement
- Thesis
- Transitions

Chapter One
Public Speaking

In this chapter:

Have you ever felt like a guppy in a shark tank?

Do you need help finding your voice?

What is the difference between communication and public speaking?

What should I know about public speaking through a virtual meeting platform?

Why are listening skills important?

HAVE YOU EVER FELT LIKE A GUPPY IN A SHARK TANK?

One day, I approached a client who was scheduled to present his first informative speech and he looked terrified! He was sweating, had almost no color in his cheeks, and his hands were shaking. I sat with him in the corner of the room for a few minutes and tried to help calm his fears. Following my instincts, I told the client that I was confident he would do a great job! For weeks, I watched this same man present impromptu speeches and he clearly had no trouble communicating his ideas to others. Yet, here he was looking quite frazzled. After a few minutes of "pep talk," I asked him to take a deep breath and then tell me exactly how he felt. He looked directly at me and said with a shiver, "Have you ever felt like a guppy in a shark tank?"

Truthfully, we can all say that we have felt like a guppy in a shark tank when faced with presenting a speech! We feel like ALL eyes are on us and that we are the tender morsel of the day. We believe the audience members are staring at every part of our bodies, evaluating every piece of clothing, shoes, even judging the fact that we brought note cards to the lectern. They are listening to every word and hearing every unplanned pause, every stutter or stumble, and are critically judging us and finding fault with the information we are trying to share. Yes, we know what it feels like to be the guppy in a shark tank!

You don't have to feel like a guppy any longer—YOU are the Shark! Using the information in this book, along with the SpeechShark app, you can maneuver your way through murky waters and move confidently and fearlessly toward your goal! So, grab your device, click over to your speech notes, and walk to the stage area prepared to knock your audience out of the water! Make your points clearly because you wrote the speech with the end purpose and your audience in mind! No longer are you a guppy, you are a SpeechShark!

DO YOU NEED HELP FINDING YOUR VOICE?

Have you ever been asked what you think about an issue? Were you able to answer immediately? Did you feel confident with your answer? Did you feel like your answer was delivered effectively? Since before the time of Aristotle, it was evident that speaking and sharing opinions and facts are important to our society.

We all have opinions and the right to voice those opinions. Becoming a competent speaker is a goal that most of us have, but many of us are not entirely sure how to find our own voice, to exercise the freedom of speech, and to use our voices to bring about societal change.

Quite often, you will be asked to participate in group presentations or to make solo presentations. The higher you proceed in a college education and the more you advance in your company or organization, the more often you are going to be challenged with the prospect of public speaking. Since this is going to be an ongoing reality in your life, why not take time now to find your voice and learn to speak professionally and eloquently?

WHAT IS THE DIFFERENCE BETWEEN COMMUNICATION AND PUBLIC SPEAKING?

When going into the ocean or into a business meeting, many things can go wrong. *Sharks* can be the changing business climates, creative investment strategies, communication opportunities, or problem-solving strategies. You might ask yourself, "Why do we keep swimming in spite of calculated risks that we can't always navigate?"

My plan to avoid a shark attack is to not resemble the seal! Understand your strengths and weaknesses. Become informed. Learn the difference between communicating and speaking in public! Just as sharks maximize water safety, SpeechSharks maximize stage safety. Become an educated communicator, focus on your goals, and swim confidently toward your prize!

Communication is defined as a process in which ideas or information are transmitted, shared, or exchanged. In other words, you can communicate through various methods that are verbal and nonverbal: writing, speaking, art, music, movement, food, clothing, e-mails, videos, gifts, and the list goes on.

Public Speaking is a communication process in which speakers and listeners participate together. Public Speaking operates with the intention that speaking will be done in a public setting and with an audience. This type of speaking integrates theory and practice. While theory is important, speaking situations demand that content should be adapted to the speaking situation and to the audience for which the speech is intended. The speaker will share content, which can be received by the listener. In turn, the listener communicates to the speaker through verbal or nonverbal cues to indicate understanding or the lack thereof. In other words, communication is a *transactional* process.

With public speaking, there is participation between the sender (speaker) and the receiver (audience). This diagram shows how the communication process might look.

First, the speaker decides to send a message. Before sending the message, the speaker encodes the message and content to send. **Encoding** is a process by which a person derives meaning and understanding. It may involve finding a common understanding to develop a deeper understanding of the point or topic. Many speakers find that conducting research or speaking to someone with experience about the topic will help them develop a deeper understanding of the topic.

Once the speaker has a good understanding of the content, **the speaker delivers the message** to the audience. Each rhetorical situation is different; therefore, the speaker needs to consider many factors when deciding how to deliver the message. Finding common ground between the speaker and the audience, emphasizing the sharing of an idea with the audience, and determining an effective approach will help the speaker achieve the intended goal.

The audience receives the message, but the message may be distorted according to distractions in the surrounding area or by preconceived ideas and opinions of each audience member. As the audience receives the message, they decode what they have heard and understood before sending verbal and/or nonverbal feedback to the speaker. **Decoding** is a process by which we translate or interpret the content into meaning. The decoding process can be altered depending upon "noise" in the environment. **Noise** can be defined as distractions in the speaking environment, but also can include preconceived notions, opinions, and ideas. Sometimes **feedback** is verbal, but many times feedback is nonverbal. Feedback helps the speaker know if the content delivered has been effectively decoded and received. In order to have feedback, the receiver (audience) will need to listen.

What should I know about public speaking through a virtual meeting platform?

Prior to COVID-19, we thought of public speaking as delivering a message in a public setting with a face-to-face audience. Most of us in the education and business world were already using online meeting opportunities occasionally, but most meetings were in physical spaces. We grew light-years during that time and quickly adapted to conducting meetings and classes online with the use of technology. Years from now, historians will talk about the way our use of technology grew at a mind-boggling rate. For those of us who have experienced this growth, it was a method of survival. Much like sharks who focus on the goal move quickly and push through obstacles which might interfere, we plunged into the deep waters with one goal in mind. The goal was to effectively communicate online. To do this, we had to learn, adapt, and swim confidently toward the new normal. The information in this section will help you navigate public speaking through virtual meeting platforms.

Virtual meeting platforms are applications and software designed so that we can meet remotely online. There are many different types of virtual meeting platforms. Some are free to users for a basic package price, they will charge a monthly fee for packages that include more functions. Others limit the number of people who can be on the video call and might also limit the amount of time spent on the call. Various functions are quite different for each platform. Some allow the user to record the meeting and share links to the recording and others include virtual backgrounds, sharing privileges, whiteboard, chats, instant messaging, emojis, and permission to monitor microphones and cameras. Platforms may be presented for synchronous or asynchronous meetings as preferred by the user and the attendees.

Synchronous meetings are scheduled and happen through real-time interactions by phone, video conference, or in person. This type allows attendees to experience a more in-depth exchange and actively participate in the meeting. Not only will the speaker be able to deliver content, but in this case the speaker can involve the audience to brainstorm, address issues, invite feedback, or solve problems.

Asynchronous meetings happen on your own time and are accessed through a video recording, e-mail, letters, text messaging, or direct messaging. Both types of meetings are needed, but asynchronous meetings do not require everyone to be present at the same time. This type of meeting is often preferred because the attendee manages when the meeting starts and can pause the meeting to resume it at another time that is more convenient. Since there are pros and cons to both types of meetings, the speaker might choose to offer both options.

Meetings that include virtual and face-to-face at the same time are *hybrid* meetings. *HyFlex* is a new buzzword in the virtual meeting world. These are meetings where the participant can choose to attend in person or attend at a time that is best for their own personal schedule. They may choose to bounce between options as it suits them. Since they may choose online one day and F2F another, we call this HyFlex since it is hybrid with a flexible option for the participant.

The most commonly used types of virtual meeting platforms are Google Meet, Microsoft TEAMS, Calendly, SKYPE, Join.me, Highfive, Pexip, XTalks Meetings, Evia, Adobe Connect, ZOOM, GoToMeeting, Digitell, Intrado, Aventri, On24, Livestorm, WebEx, BlueJeans, and ClickMeeting. Which one is best? This is where your sharky skills come in handy. Feel free to research the different platforms to find out which one works best for your needs and budget. Keep in mind that some platforms work best within a specific software ecosystem or browser. Others might have great looking video, but do not offer functions you might need. Most of these are fairly intuitive. If you are comfortable using one type of virtual meeting platform, you should have no trouble using another.

VIRTUAL MEETING PLATFORM RULES AND EXPECTATIONS

Speakers who communicate clear expectations of virtual meeting room basics experience less distractions and develop a positive environment so that audience members feel respected, focused, and engaged. Behaviors valued should be demonstrated throughout the meeting by the speaker and formally established during the beginning of the virtual meeting transmission.

Virtual meeting etiquette is an expectation of how meeting leaders and participants should behave during virtual meetings. Professional expectations for face-to-face meetings should also be observed during virtual meetings. This includes arriving on time, dressing appropriately, listening while someone else is talking, showing respect for others' ideas or questions, showing appreciation (clapping) following a speech, and avoiding disruptive behaviors to avoid being shark bait when meeting online with techno-sharks. Whether you are the speaker or an attendee, here are some basic rules:

VIRTUAL MEETING PLATFORM EXPECTATIONS

1. **Find a quiet space** to join the virtual meeting without interruptions and free of background noise.

2. **Check your technology** to confirm the meeting platform you will need. Download any software or apps prior to the meeting to make sure you are ready to begin on time. This includes setting up your username and password if needed. Charge or connect your device so that you have enough power to last the full meeting and run a sound and video check to confirm functionality.

3. **Check the lighting in your meeting area.** Experiment with different colors and forms of lighting to make sure your light does not cast shadows, glare, or interfere with your audience's view of you.

4. **Mute the microphone (mic) and close the video camera** to have a stronger Internet connection. Since many speakers prefer to see and hear their audience members in the beginning and at the end, the speaker may mute all participants when content is being delivered and will unmute all during the question-and-answer session. Be aware that any sights or sounds in your virtual meeting area will be seen or heard by others.

5. **Frame your face and shoulders for the camera view.** Focus eye contact on the camera and not on the window with your image or the image of others on the call. This is hard to do since you are tempted to look at the person speaking; however, it will be obvious that your eye contact is not where it should be.

6. **Be aware of the background view of your meeting space.** Clutter, people, and pets can be distracting. Choose a professional looking space and avoid using high traffic areas for virtual meetings. Think about what your audience will see or hear before you turn on the camera and the microphone. Simple is best.

7. **Avoid eating or drinking during virtual meetings.**

8. **Dress, sit, act, and communicate professionally** while the camera is on. Nonverbal cues are always present whether you are in person or meeting through a virtual meeting platform. Guard your facial expressions during virtual meetings so that you do not send the wrong message and be on your best behavior. If using the chat feature, use full sentences, correct grammar, and correct spelling. You never know who will be reading what you write, so make it count. Good manners are always in style.

9. **Sign into the virtual meeting platform ten minutes prior to start time.** Be familiar with the device and meeting platform, download relevant files, turn off notification alerts, silence phone, and have notetaking materials. Treat this meeting the same way you treat a meeting that is face-to-face. You'll never regret taking the extra time to be prepared.

10. **Sign off and close the video window after the meeting is over.**

ADDITIONAL TIPS FOR THE HOST

1. **Be prepared for the meeting.** Create a meeting agenda, manage the meeting time, and demonstrate respect for others during a meeting. Planning and managing effective meetings are appreciated anytime regardless of whether they are face-to-face or virtual. Your audience will also appreciate receiving the agenda prior to the meeting.

2. **Set the stage for a great meeting.** Remove anything in the background that could distract from the purpose of the meeting. Select and use a professional virtual background if your home office background is not appropriate. Here is an example of a user-friendly background where you can position yourself against the blank wall. Most platforms have an option for choosing virtual backgrounds.

3. **Start the meeting on time.** Everyone appreciates good use of their time, but they do not appreciate wasted time. Stay on target and stick to the agenda. Announce a specific time to answer questions and ask audience members to hold questions until that time.

4. **Create a warm and inviting atmosphere.** Welcome audience members and introduce the participants to each other. Suggest that attendees use their emojis and hand-raising options on the virtual platform to share their thoughts as topics are discussed. Request for attendees to type their questions into the chat box so they can be answered during the meeting or brought up during the final Q&A session at the end. Remind participants of virtual meeting platform expectations and request for them to mute microphones when not speaking. Instead of asking over and over, don't forget that the host can mute all participants' microphones if that is needed to solve the problem. Encourage attendees to be positive, engaged, responsive, and collaborative during planned portions of the speech.

5. **End the meeting on time.** Plan to end the meeting several minutes early so that you have time to summarize meeting accomplishments, answer questions that were not addressed, and thank the audience for their time. Since you are the host, stay online until everyone else leaves the meeting. This allows attendees to leave at their own pace and to offer any final words before disconnecting.

Public speaking is still public speaking, regardless of whether the speech is presented in a face-to-face or online environment. Throughout this book, tips will be shared to help as you enter the world of public speaking.

WHY ARE LISTENING SKILLS IMPORTANT?

Consider how sharks find their prey. They do this using sensory receptors found along the sides of their bodies. These receptors perform much like our ears. They can feel vibrations or movement in the water around them with these receptors and respond to the message received.

SpeechSharks (that is you) also use sensory receptors to navigate communication waters to detect and gather information from that which we hear. **We listen!** Some of us are better listeners than others. You will also find that at times, you may be a better listener than you are at other times. What we hear often is determined by the amount of distractions that interfere with content being delivered. Instead of hearing a full sentence spoken to us, we might only hear bits and pieces of that sentence and decode the message into something that is not what the speaker intended. It happens all of the time. Business deals, marriages, and friendships are often broken because of this breakdown in communication. Become a better listener and you will be a more effective employee, a better marriage partner, and a more reliable friend.

Listening is quite different from hearing. Without any effort, you can hear something; however, it takes a conscious effort to listen. Hearing is a physical process that occurs as sound waves vibrate against eardrums and then that sound moves to the brain where it is decoded into a message or response. Perhaps this table will make this clearer for you:

Listening vs. Hearing

Listening	Hearing
Activity	Process
Learned Skill: can be taught and learned	Response to stimuli: involuntary
Active: requires the listener to be engaged, encode/decode, and respond	Passive: requires no action on the part of the listener
Choice: requires focus and attention	Continuous: if no hearing loss, hearing is ongoing
Message or content is consciously received and message gets a response	Sound is received, but will not always elicit a response

Effective speakers are great listeners! They must listen to find out what is needed by their potential audience and then go the extra mile to research main points within the content to provide the audience with credible information.

What keeps us from being good listeners?

In the section above we discussed "noise" that can be distractors during communication. Let's spend time now discussing these distractors in more detail. They include things we hear, see, do, know, and perceive/feel. These distractors are all prevalent whether we are in a public speaking situation or a private conversation. I'm sure you will be able to relate to all of these.

Things we hear: Have you ever tried to talk to someone in a crowded restaurant and the environmental noise surrounding you was so loud that you couldn't carry on a cohesive conversation? This could be anything from background music, other people's conversations, dishes rattling, glasses clinking, to chairs scraping on the floor. Extraneous noise can make it difficult to enjoy the person with whom you are sharing dinner. Do unusual accents cause you to reflect on how the speaker is pronouncing or saying a certain word resulting in misunderstanding content that was being shared? Perhaps you are visiting with friends during a play date with your children, and you are trying to listen while your friend tells you about an issue she is having with her phone company, but you are also trying to tune in to the chatter going on with the children. Chances are you didn't hear your friend's entire story and you also did not gather the full meaning of the tug-of-war going on with the children. You may be hearing lots of sounds, but are you really listening?

Things we see: Often, we have trouble focusing on a message if things we see are interfering with the message. It could be a glare off the windshield of a car parked outside, the speaker's choice of clothing, decorations on the stage, or other people in the audience. I am sure this distraction is something with which all of you can identify.

Things we do: What are your own listening habits? Do you have a tendency to tune out conversations while you check your text messages, Facebook, Instagram, or Twitter? Are you completing a sentence on your computer while a colleague is trying to tell you about a problem they are having in their department? Does the heavy cologne worn by the speaker distract you from listening to the content? Do you anticipate how you will respond before your speaker finishes the sentence? What poor listening habits do you have that might keep you from actively listening?

Things we know or don't know: Have you ever been confused by meanings of words and spent the next few minutes trying to decide the meaning of the word or correct pronunciation of the word instead of listening to the message? Do you wonder, "How is that spelled?" or look up the meaning on your phone? Do you find yourself pondering over incorrectly cited research or questioning facts offered by the speaker? Too many facts presented during a speech can also cause us to miss the speaker's main point because we are too focused on details. These things can prevent us from active listening.

Things we feel or perceive: Illness, pain, hunger, anger, extreme happiness, or exhaustion can keep us from hearing all that is being said. Negative attitudes, prejudices, beliefs, or feelings toward a topic can cause us to lose our desire to actively listen as a topic is presented. We are more critical of speakers who have views which differ from our own. Consequently, we will receive less of the intended message that we would have heard had we listened with an open mind. Likewise, we might listen closer to those who speak about a topic with which we agree. To become better listeners, resist positive or negative distractions, focus on verbal and nonverbal messages, try to see the speaker's point of view, take notes, and concentrate on active listening.

What are the types of listening skills?

Active Listening: Listen to understand. Determine if nonverbal cues being sent by the speaker mirror the speaker's message. Position your body so that your shoulders are facing the speaker, body posed forward, and use positive head nods and smiles to send a nonverbal cue that you are actively listening to the speaker.

Critical Listening: Resist outside noises and distractions to use critical listening skills. This involves looking past a speaker's distracting behavior and the environmental distractions that are around you. Avoid concentrating on yourself and your own feelings or perceptions. Instead, concentrate on the speaker and message being delivered.

Empathetic Listening: Try to see the speaker's point of view, even if you do not share the speaker's views. We often find ourselves in diverse audiences and it is imperative that we actively try to understand the speaker's message and offer positive nonverbal cues in support for the speaker.

Informative Listening: Taking notes during a speech will help you to use informative listening skills. Make notes of the main points, research, or data presented, and examples that are especially interesting to you. Even if your colleague is speaking to you about an issue, take notes about the issue and show active listening skills with strong body posture.

Appreciative Listening: This is my favorite type of listening skill. As we show enjoyment of a speaker and their content, we exhibit appreciative listening. Send nonverbal cues that you are listening and enjoying the speech. This is important and also helps the speaker to be less anxious due to the positive nonverbal cues sent during the speech.

WHERE CAN YOU PRACTICE YOUR PUBLIC SPEAKING SKILLS?

Many people enjoy belonging to professional development organizations that encourage public speaking presentations and provide opportunities to improve leadership skills. Take public speaking courses through your local college's continuing education program. Find organizations in your area that provide a public forum to practice your skills. Options to consider are Toastmasters International, National Speaker's Association, National Communication Association, Church or Religious Organizations, College Clubs, Meet-ups, Civic Organizations, Community Functions, Sports Events, Political Organizations, Book Clubs, Craft Clubs, and Business Networking Events. Speak at every opportunity to improve your communication skills, and you will become a more effective listener, communicator, and leader!

The key to being a good speaker is to speak so that others can understand you and your message! Every time you speak, give your audience something wonderful to remember. Make it a pleasant experience and they will ask you to speak again. Speak again and you will get more experience. The more experience you have the better speaker you will be.

The key is . . .

WHAT TYPE LISTENER ARE YOU?

Instructions: Evaluate the following by answering the question truthfully as you are at this time. Later, take the same evaluation to see if you can notice improvements. When finished, tally your score using the key found at the end of the evaluation.

Questions:	Never 1	Rarely 2	Sometimes 3	Often 4	Always 5
1. I pay attention to the speaker.					
2. I can ignore distractions during the speech.					
3. I can listen to a speaker's ideas without letting my ideas/opinions get in the way.					
4. I can ignore distracting personal habits of the speaker (Throat clearing, movements, note cards).					
5. I take notes to organize the speaker's main points.					
6. During the speech, I am thinking of questions to ask about ideas I do not understand.					
7. I can understand the meaning of unknown words from the balance of the speaker's message.					
8. I can separate fact from opinion, without it being verbally cited.					
9. I can tell the difference between important and unimportant details.					
10. I listen to hear the speaker support points with research or personal stories.					
11. I agree and respect that others have differing points of view.					
12. I evaluate the speaker and the content of the speech.					
13. I identify specific words or phrases that impress me as I listen.					
14. I get caught up in the story or poem the speaker shares.					
15. I put what I hear into my own words so that I can recount it to others.					
16. I listen to what the speaker is saying and try to feel what the speaker feels.					

Questions:	Never 1	Rarely 2	Sometimes 3	Often 4	Always 5
17. I find hidden meanings revealed by subtle verbal and nonverbal cues.					
18. I use good listening skills and resist the urge to multi-task by listening to a speech and checking my cell phone.					
19. In a small group setting, if the speaker is struggling to explain something, I want to step in and assist.					
20. When people speak to me, I give head nods and verbal confirmations like, "OK" or "Yes."					
Calculate Score by Adding Points MY SCORE IS: _____					

Due to many different types of situations and speaker variables, responses to this questionnaire may not always reveal the same results. However, this assessment should give an idea of your average listening skills. **Circle the evaluation that corresponds with your score.**

15–30 — POOR — Continue work to improve your listening skills.

31–74 — AVERAGE — But, you need to set your goals higher

75–100 — GOOD — Never stop working to be a better listener

Public Speaking

After reading this chapter, you will be able to answer the following questions:

1. What is the definition of communication? _____

_____

_____

2. What is the definition of Public Speaking? _____

_____

_____

3. What are the six steps found in the communication process? _____

_____

_____

4. What happens through the encoding process? _____

_____

_____

5. Why should the speaker find common ground with the audience? _____

_____

_____

6. What happens during the decoding process? _____

_____

_____

7. What is noise? _____

_____

_____

8. Describe feedback. _____

_____

_____

9. Is listening an activity or a process? _____

_____

_____

10. Is hearing an activity or a process? _____

_____

_____

11. Is listening a learned skill or an involuntary response? _____

_____

_____

12. What distractors can keep us from receiving communication signals sent our way? _____

_____

_____

13. List the five types of listening skills: _____

_____

_____

14. What is active listening? _____

_____

_____

15. What is critical listening? _____

_____

_____

16. What is empathetic listening? _____

_____

_____

17. What is informative listening? _____

_____

_____

18. What is appreciative listening? _____

_____

_____

19. What type listener are you (Poor, Average, Good)? _____

_____

_____

20. When is your next speech? Are you prepared? _____

_____

_____

21. What is a virtual meeting platform? _____

_____

_____

22. What is the difference between synchronous and asynchronous meetings?_____

    _____

    _____

23. What is your favorite virtual meeting platform and why?_____

    _____

    _____

24. What is involved with virtual meeting etiquette?_____

    _____

    _____

Shark Bites

IMPROVING LISTENING SKILLS

Let's work on our bad habits and explore cures!

Bad Habit: Often it is hard for me to concentrate on things people are saying because I tend to focus on their speech patterns, posture, clothes, or appearance.

Example: Last week while attending a church service, the pastor was explaining a Bible verse that was particularly hard to comprehend. I was so distracted by the number of filler words the pastor was using that I completely quit listening to the content and began counting the filler words.

Cure: _____

_____

_____

Here is another one:

Bad Habit: Sometimes I may pretend to be listening, but my mind is on other things. I will often look directly at the speaker, smile and nod like I am listening to them, when actually I am thinking about something else.

Example: Last week, my co-worker friend was telling me all about her weekend away with another set of friends. I am sure the plans must have been fun for her, but my mind was on a work deadline that I had to meet by that afternoon. I was smiling, head nodding, and acting like I was truly listening to her, but in reality, I was thinking about how I was going to meet the deadline. When I came back around to hearing her conversation, she was asking me if I wanted to join them next weekend. I had no idea what she was wanting me to join!

Cure: _____

_____

_____

Chapter Two
Speaker and Audience Responsibilities

In this chapter:

What are the speaker's responsibilities?

What are the audience's responsibilities?

SPEAKER RESPONSIBILITIES

Speakers have a responsibility to the audience. It is your job to know who will be in your audience and to plan your speech for them! Just because it is your opportunity to deliver the speech does not mean that you can stand on your soap box and use the time with a captured audience to share just exactly what you think about anything and everything. No, you will need to provide content that the audience needs and it is your responsibility to present it in a way that is effective, clear, and to the point. Prove you are a competent speaker by the content that you provide and the manner in which you provide the content.

Audiences are a wonderful combination of learners, personalities, educational levels, backgrounds, cultures, religions, political affiliations, and expectations. Set the tone for a positive, constructive event with a friendly attitude, whether you are meeting face-to-face or online. Virtual class meetings may fall into the category of distance education, but it is the speaker's responsibility to make sure the meeting does not feel distant. Stress and logistical challenges from the pandemic continue to filter into our communication efforts. However, we can still target positivity through strategic and intentional actions.

A public speaking opportunity presented through a virtual meeting platform will involve more thought and planning than a face-to-face speech. Engaging an audience of 20, 200, or 2,000 can be more challenging because audience members will be signing in from different locations. Presenting a speech online involves reacting positively to challenges and having the confidence to know you can overcome any difficulty that may surface. This might include technical issues with sound, connectivity, and actively engaging an audience online. If you are not confident with your own personal technical skills while presenting an online speech, arrange to have a friend, classmate, or co-worker nearby to trouble-shoot technical issues that may surface. Face-to-face speaking opportunities have their own set of challenges. Keeping a positive mindset is an integral element of success which influences our initial reaction to challenges and the way that we handle them.

Speak to your audience using a conversational tone. Your speech should not sound canned or rehearsed. It should sound as if you are sitting with one person in your audience at your kitchen table and discussing the topic over a nice cup of hot tea! Audiences do not want to be talked at. They want a conversation between you and them. This is the type of interaction you want on a small scale between you and another person. This is also the type of interaction an audience desires with a speaker. Talking *with* someone, sharing information, feelings, convictions are so much more enjoyable than having someone talk *at* you! It is a more intimate transaction. Just remember, the same type of interpersonal communication skills that work on a one-on-one or in a small group setting will also work beautifully between a speaker and an audience.

Show the audience that you care about them with the content you provide. Mention their names or the town where you are speaking. Say something positive about their local sports team, mayor, or director of the business where you are speaking. This will help your audience to feel like you wanted to be there with them enough to know what is important to them. It will help you to get the audience in your corner and will also make your speech so much more effective! Consider yourself as a host or hostess at a gathering. Your job is to make your audience comfortable and to supply their every need. Serve them a *Shark-o-licious* speech!

SERVING UP A *SHARK-O-LICIOUS* TREAT?

My daughter brought home a bag of gummy treats yesterday that were shaped like sharks! Isn't that fun? Sharks are everywhere! These fun shark treats made me think about great speeches and how they have a lot in common with a great meal. Since you might be presenting a speech soon, I wanted to share this with you so that you can serve a *Shark-o-licious* treat to YOUR audience.

Every memorable meal begins with an appetizer and then moves to a second dish before leading to the main course which usually includes a protein dish, starch, and vegetable before concluding with a delicious dessert.

Memorable speeches should follow the same type of menu as I will explain in the following table:

Memorable Meal	Memorable Speech	Similarities
Appetizer	Attention Step	Just as you arrive at a meal hungry and ready to eat, your audience will arrive anxious to hear your speech. This is where you set the stage, get the audience's attention, and provide your audience with a "taste" of what is to come.
Soup	Establish Relevance for the Topic Establish Credibility to Speak About the Topic Preview of Main Points (Thesis)	The soup prepares your palate for the main course of a meal, but it is this step in the speech that prepares your audience for the topic. First, explain why it is important that the audience hear about the upcoming topic. Then, tell your audience why YOU are credible to speak to them about the topic. The next thing that you will do during this phase is to clearly state the three main points that you will cover. This prepares your audience and allows them to anticipate the "main course"!
Bread	Transitions	Bread during a meal is often used to cleanse the palate and is enjoyed between courses. For the speech, transitions, also called connectors, are essential as they transition the content from one thing to the next. A great speaker will use clear transitions to move from the Introduction Step to the Body of the speech, to each Main Point, and then finally into the Conclusion.

Main Course:
  Protein
  Starch
  Vegetable
	Body	The main course is the purpose of the meal and the body is the purpose of your speech! The body of the speech contains three main points that support the topic. Often the main points include research, stories, and examples that further define the topic.

Dessert	Conclusion	All great meals culminate with a sweet treat! The dessert that concludes the memorable meal is my favorite part of the meal because it leaves a sweet taste in my mouth! A great speech conclusion should leave your audience wanting more! Signal that you are concluding the speech, re-state the three main points, and then provide closing statements or an appeal that will make your audience wish the speech could last just a little longer! Now, isn't that sweet?

It is time to start cooking, or should I say, writing the speech! How are you going to make sure your next speech is *Shark-o-licious*? Plan, Prepare, and Persevere! Keep these tips in mind and your next speech is sure to be a crowd pleaser with your audience having an appetite that will have them demanding an encore!

Plan

Even the simplest things need to be considered as you prepare for your presentation. And, yes, there are still more questions:

- What can you say or do to get your audience's attention from the very beginning?
- How can you get your audience to relate immediately to your topic?
- Why are YOU credible to talk to an audience about this topic?
- How can you conclude the speech so that your audience continues thinking about your speech topic even after your speech is over?

Answering these questions will help you prepare an introduction step that introduces the topic to your audience and will have them in the palm of your hand before you actually begin speaking about the topic. A strong introduction step (appetizer and soup) is important for an effective presentation, but this step cannot be written until AFTER you have planned the body (main course) of your speech (topic and three main points). This will also help you to prepare a conclusion step (dessert) that ends your speech with a BANG!

Prepare

The speaker has a responsibility to begin the speech with an attention step or opener that will get their attention within the first few seconds of your presentation. Consider how you would feel if you were one of the audience members sitting and waiting to hear a great speech from YOU. Start strong with an engaging attention step. Here are some suggestions and why they work:

1. **Questions:** This works because a well-designed question is just begging to be answered. Be careful that your question leads directly to the topic you will be covering and remember that presentation is everything. A great question with a weak delivery will not make for a memorable attention step.
2. **Empathy:** This allows you to connect with your audience on a personal level. This starts the feeling of an intimate relationship between you and the audience in the first few seconds of your speech. Ask, "Have you ever thought about why. . .", "I'll never forget the moment when", or "Just like YOU, I was brought up to believe. . .".
3. **Announcement of a NEW Policy or Procedure:** While this might not always be met with full cooperation, it does get the attention of your audience and they will be very interested to see how this change will affect their own area or their lives.
4. **Secrets:** Everyone loves a secret! Start your speech by saying, "I want to let you in on a little secret—this is a secret that not even my husband knows. . ." Doing this provides you with the opportunity to promise something to your audience that they simply cannot refuse. They want to know the secret!
5. **Startling Statement:** Beginning your speech with a shocking statement that makes your audience feel like they may be making a huge mistake about something will certainly give them reason to sit up straight and listen to what you have to say!
6. **Warnings:** If you start your speech by saying, "There are three warning signs to look for when. . .", then your audience will want to hear you identify the three warning signs.
7. **Quotes:** This is always a good strategy, but can get a bit boring if every speaker that day begins with a quote. If you are going to use a quote, make sure that it is a quote that will make the audience want to sit up and take notice! Also, make sure you have the name of the person correct who is cited with the quote.

8. **Imagery:** You can start by saying, "Imagine, if you will. . ." People love imagery and they will enjoy an attention step that begins with imagery!

9. **Stories:** Everyone loves a good story. Start by saying, "Do you mind if I share a story with you? Last week when I was a XYZ, I heard about. . ." Now, they want to hear about it, too!

10. **Choices:** If I were to ask you to choose between this donut and an apple, which would you choose? Wait for the answer? Of course, you are hoping they will choose the apple, but you notice that more than half of your audience raised their hands saying they would choose the donut! Give them a choice! Then, allow that choice to help shape the direction of your speech topic.

Don't introduce yourself in the opening words of your speech. Save your introduction for the portion of your introduction step where you will establish your own credibility as a speaker for the topic. Here is an example:

Introduction to the Speech:

Attention Step:

Establish Need/Relevance for the Topic:

Establish Credibility: For the past twenty years, I have been a public speaking coach helping young people to prepare for interviews and competitions. Hello, my name is Dr. Penny Joyner Waddell and I am happy to be here with you today to discuss the importance of dressing for success when giving a speech presentation.

Thesis:

Just as we open a speech with an attention step, the speaker has a responsibility to end the speech with a review of the main points and final closing statements. The closing statement is often referred to as an appeal to action. The speaker should look carefully at the speech and choose a method of closing the speech that will leave audience members thinking about the topic or anxious to ask questions about the topic. Here are some suggestions and why they work:

1. **Answer the question asked in the Attention Step:** This works if the speaker did not provide the answer to the question as the speech began. Also, it helps for the speaker to continue making short references to the question throughout the speech. The speaker could begin the closing statement by saying, "Do you remember the question that I asked at the beginning of this speech? Would you like to know the answer?" This should have the audience primed and ready to hear the answer and will keep them thinking about the topic.

2. **Startling Statement:** End your speech with a shocking statement that makes your audience feel compelled to find out more about your topic.

3. **Warnings:** This is effective for persuasion speeches when the speaker offers a warning of things to come if the problem is not resolved.

4. **Quotes:** The speaker could end with a reminder of the quote used in the beginning of the speech or the speaker could offer a different quote as the ending. Make sure the quote is relevant and adds value to the topic; otherwise, it will not be effective.

5. **Imagery:** This is effective for persuasion speeches as the speaker closes the speech by saying, "Imagine a world where this problem no longer exists. Now, imagine that you helped eradicate this problem!"

6. **Stories:** This is effective if the speaker designed the attention step to begin a story but did not finish it. The speaker could begin the closing statement by saying, "Remember the story that I told you in the beginning? Now, it's time for the rest of the story!" The audience will be happy to hear the rest of the story and will continue to think more about the topic you presented. This is also effective as a closing statement if your story clearly sums up the topic you have chosen.

Persevere

Using the speech writing formula that we have presented in this book, we want you to begin thinking like a speech writer. You are on the right path—you are a SpeechShark swimming easily toward your target! Take a deep breath. It's almost time to meet your audience!

AUDIENCE RESPONSIBILITIES

Audiences have a responsibility, too! As the speaker enters the stage, please show appreciation for the speaker by giving your undivided attention and clapping until the speaker has taken his/her place on stage and is ready to begin the presentation! Your next task is to LISTEN to the speaker. Put away cell phones and electronic devices that would cause distractions and position your body to face the speaker. Using your nonverbal cues, show the speaker that she has your full attention and that you are anxious to hear her message. Smile at the speaker, nod your head in agreement, and show support with your face and body posture.

Prepare yourself to hear the speech. Listen carefully to identify the message delivered. Get plenty of rest and a good meal prior to the presentation. Just as the speaker has to prepare for you, it is your job to prepare yourself. Not enough sleep? You could be tempted to take a short nap during the presentation. YES, your speaker will know you are napping and that sends a negative nonverbal cue that you are bored and what the speaker is saying is of no consequence to you. If you are hungry, your stomach may growl or you could spend her speech thinking about what you might eat just as soon as the speech is over. Here are some tips to help you be a great audience member:

1. **Be an active listener** by showing appreciation for the speaker. Sending positive nonverbal cues such as smiling, head nods, leaning forward toward the speaker, and establishing eye contact, will show the speaker that you are glad to hear the speech. Just using the active listener posture will help you focus more on the speaker and become a better audience member.

2. **Resist distractions** and use your critical listening skills to focus in on the speaker and the message.

3. **Practice empathetic listening** and try to see the speaker's point of view, even if it differs from your own.

4. **Focus on verbal and nonverbal cues** being sent by the speaker. Are the speaker's verbal and nonverbal cues matching with the content of the speech?

5. **Take notes and create a presentation outline** during the speech. Informative listening is used during this time of the speech. Write down questions you may have so that you can ask them after the speech is over. Never interrupt the speaker to ask a question. Always save the questions to ask during a question and answer session or to pose privately to the speaker after she leaves the stage area.

Whether attending a face-to-face speech or an online speech through a virtual meeting platform, it is the audience member's responsibility to behave professionally, use good manners, send positive nonverbal cues, smile, nod your head at the speaker, and show support.

Speaker and Audience Responsibilities

After reading this chapter, you will be able to answer the following questions:

1. What is the speaker's responsibility to the audience? _____

   _____

   _____

2. What type of tone should be used when speaking to an audience? _____

   _____

   _____

3. When should the speaker introduce themselves? _____

   _____

   _____

4. What audience responsibilities should be expected? _____

   _____

   _____

5. What is the difference between an active listener and an empathetic listener? _____

   _____

   _____

   _____

6. What are six ways to close a speech:

   (1) _____

   (2) _____

   (3) _____

   (4) _____

   (5) _____

   (6) _____

7. What is the audience's responsibility when attending an online speech? _____

   _____

   _____

Shark Bites

Consider how you might plan your next Shark-o-licious Speech using this table:

Memorable Meal	Memorable Speech	What are YOUR plans?
Appetizer	Attention Step	
Soup	Establish Relevance for the Topic Establish Credibility to Speak About the Topic Preview of Main Points (Thesis)	
Bread	Transitions	

Main Course:
  Protein
  Starch
  Vegetable
	Body
	
	Three Main Points
		1.
		
		2.
		
		3.

Dessert	Conclusion End with a BANG!	

SpeechSH🦈RK™

Unit 2

Types of Speeches
and
Methods of Delivery

Types of Speeches

Specialty Speeches

Methods of Delivery

SpeechSHARK.™

Key Terms to Know

Chapter 3—Types of Speeches

- Attitudes
- Behaviors
- Beliefs
- Central Idea Speech
- Ceremonial Speeches
- Demonstration Speech
- Entertaining Speech
- Ethos
- Group Presentation
- Informative Speech
- Key Idea Speech
- Logos
- Moderator
- Motivational Speech
- Pathos
- Persuasion Speech
- Question and Answer Session
- Questions of Fact
- Questions of Policy
- Questions of Value
- Sales Presentation
- Social Occasion Speeches
- Special Occasion Speeches
- Values
- Work-Related Speeches

Chapter 4—Specialty Speeches

- Competition Speeches
- Debates
- Humorous Speeches
- Improvisational Speeches
- Oral Interpretation
- PechaKucha Presentations
- Specialty Speeches
- Storytelling
- TED Talks

Chapter 5—Methods of Delivery

- Extemporaneous Speaking
- Impromptu Speaking
- Manuscript Speaking
- Memorized Speaking

Chapter Three
Types of Speeches

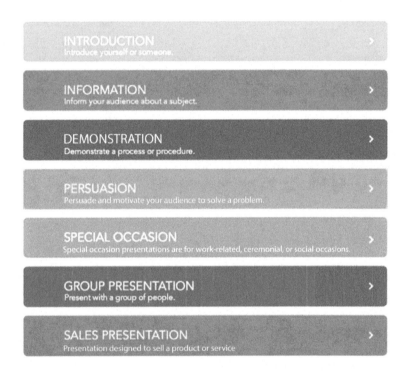

INTRODUCTION
Introduce yourself or someone.

INFORMATION
Inform your audience about a subject.

DEMONSTRATION
Demonstrate a process or procedure.

PERSUASION
Persuade and motivate your audience to solve a problem.

SPECIAL OCCASION
Special occasion presentations are for work-related, ceremonial, or social occasions.

GROUP PRESENTATION
Present with a group of people.

SALES PRESENTATION
Presentation designed to sell a product or service

In this chapter:

What are the different types of speeches?

How do I use brainstorming worksheets to plan my speech?

What plan should my speech outline follow?

PURPOSES AND TYPES OF SPEECHES

Speeches can be categorized into three basic *general purposes:* informative, entertaining, and motivational. Some speeches will address just one purpose, but there are many that will include elements of all three.

Informative speeches are designed for the speaker to provide interesting and useful information and to add knowledge to the listener's existing understanding of the topic. For this type of speech, the speaker takes on the role of an instructor and will teach, instruct, explain, report, and/or describe.

Entertaining speeches are enjoyable speeches. Some organizations list this type of speech as a humorous speech. Although not all speeches are categorized as entertaining speeches, it is possible for all speeches to contain entertaining aspects. Audiences enjoy speeches that are light-hearted, incorporate humor, and provide entertaining factors within the speech. Storytelling is considered one strategy for delivering an entertaining speech. Special occasion speeches usually include entertaining aspects. Due to the nature of this type of speech, speakers are able to build relationships, bond with the audience, and enhance networking possibilities.

Motivational speeches are designed to inspire the audience to act on information. Most often, persuasion and special occasion speeches will incorporate motivational strategies. Speakers who have the purpose of motivating the audience will need to consider incorporating information, research, and stories which will influence the audience's values, beliefs, attitudes, or behaviors. More information about this is covered in the Persuasion Speech section of this book.

The *specific purpose* of a speech determines the type of speech that will be presented. For example, if the *general purpose* of the speech is to motivate the audience, the *specific purpose* will be to motivate/persuade audience members to volunteer for a community-wide food drive. Realizing this, the speaker will need to organize and design a speech that follows a persuasion speech plan.

Before you decide which type of speech to present, determine the purpose of the speech and ask:

- What must you say to the audience to provide content they want to hear?
- Is your purpose to introduce yourself or someone else?
- Do you need to inform your audience about a specific topic?
- Will you need to demonstrate a process, product, or procedure?
- Do you want to persuade your audience to solve a problem?
- Is this a special occasion and will require a roast, toast, or presentation about the occasion? Is it a ceremony, work related, or a social event?
- Are you making a group presentation or trying to sell a project?
- Are you taking part in a fun PechaKucha event?
- Are you competing in a debate, oral interpretations, improvisation, or story telling competition?

Unsure about writing a speech? This chapter breaks down the various types of speeches; gives explanations of each speech type; and provides brainstorming worksheet pages, outline templates, example outlines, and grading rubrics to submit to your instructor prior to the speech. Help is also available through the ***SpeechShark*** app that was created just for you! Select the type of speech you need, answer the intuitive questions in full sentence format, and ***SpeechShark*** will do the rest.

Introduction Speech

In your personal and business life, you will have plenty of opportunities to introduce yourself or others. Whether your introduction is planned or unplanned, understanding the tips below will help you complete the introduction with ease. Introduction Speeches are informative in nature because the purpose of the speech is to provide your audience with information about you or the person you are introducing.

Usually, introduction speeches are not very lengthy and last between two and three minutes. This isn't much time, so you will need to consider specific points to include, but without too much detail.

When introducing yourself, choose a theme and plan the introduction around the theme. If the setting is casual or informal, then you could introduce yourself with a theme about your hobbies, work, or family. Personal introductions on an informal scale will often include a handshake along with eye contact and a smile.

If the setting is business or formal, then you should introduce yourself by including information about your work, innovative ideas, experience in the field, and future goals. In both cases, consider the setting and provide information you think the audience would like to know. Avoid giving so much information that your introduction becomes tiresome! It should be light and positive.

One safe rule of thumb for an introduction speech is to follow a chronological or time-ordered sequence to introduce yourself or someone else. Begin your speech by briefly covering the **past**, then move to the **present**, and finally, share your hopes for the **future**.

If you are using the SpeechShark app to create this speech, then you can begin now to craft the speech. If you are not using the app, you may want to use the Introduction Speech Brainstorming Worksheet to get your thoughts together and prepare to write your presentation outline. Remember that all speech writers follow the **Standard Outline** procedure for creating a speech outline. We will only show you this type of outline in this book so that you will begin thinking like a professional speech writer!

Consider your audience and the speech making situation so that you know what type of information to include. **Answer the following questions:**

- What is your ultimate purpose for the introduction?

- Are you speaking to a room full of people or to one person?

- Is the introduction in a formal or informal setting?

- What information do you need to share?

- How much time do you have for the speech?

- What can you do to make the introduction relevant to the audience?

Brainstorming Worksheet

Speech Category: Introduction Speech

Speech Title: Give your speech a clever title. _____

Specific Purpose: Write a full sentence to show what you plan to accomplish by introducing yourself or introducing someone else.

Introduction:

Attention Step: Consider how you will get your audience's attention. Write all you plan to say using full sentences.

Establish Need/Relevance: Explain why this introduction should interest the listener. Write all you plan to say using full sentences.

Establish Credibility: Explain why YOU are credible to introduce yourself or another person. Write all you plan to say using full sentences.

Thesis (Preview) Statement: Write a complete sentence and clearly state the three points you will cover:

Point 1: Past _____

Point 2: Present _____

Point 3: Future _____

Body:

Transition Sentence: Write a full sentence to transition from the Introduction Step to the first main point.

    I. First Main Point—Past: (Share information about your past—stay with a theme.)
        A. First Sub-Point
            1. First Sub-Sub-Point (Not all points will require sub-sub-points.)
            2. Second Sub-Sub-Point

B. Second Sub-Point
    1. First Sub-Sub-Point
    2. Second Sub-Sub-Point

Transition Sentence: Write a full sentence to transition from the past to the present.

II. Second Main Point—Present: (Share information about your present—stay with the theme.)
  A. First Sub-Point
    1. First Sub-Sub-Point (Not all points will require sub-sub-points.)
    2. Second Sub-Sub-Point
  B. Second Sub-Point
    1. First Sub-Sub-Point
    2. Second Sub-Sub-Point

Transition Sentence: Write a full sentence to transition from the present to the future.

III. Third Main Point—Future: (Share information about your goals for the future—stay with the theme.)
  A. First Sub-Point
    1. First Sub-Sub-Point (Not all points will require sub-sub-points.)
    2. Second Sub-Sub-Point
  B. Second Sub-Point
    1. First Sub-Sub-Point
    2. Second Sub-Sub-Point

Transition Sentence: Write a full sentence to transition from the third main point to the conclusion.

Conclusion:

Summary: Write in full sentence format a summary of your three main points.

Point 1: _____

Point 2: _____

Point 3: _____

Appeal to Action: Leave your audience thinking about your introduction. End with a **BANG!**

(NOTE: Place the Works Cited Page on a page separate from the outline).

Works Cited

*Note: If you use visual aids, please include a Visual Aid Explanation Page
as a separate page following the Works Cited page.*

Visual Aid Explanation Page

Outline Template

First Name/Last Name
Introduction Speech
Day Month Year

Speech Category: Introduction Speech
Title:
Purpose:

Introduction:
Attention Step:
Establish Need/Relevance:
Establish Speaker Credibility:

Thesis: Today, I want to share three points about (Topic): (1) _____,

(2) _____, and (3) _____.

Body:

Transition/Link: First, I will start at the beginning by sharing a little about (Point 1).
    I. First Main Point
        A. Sub-point
        B. Sub-point

Transition/Link: I've shared (Point 1) with you, now I'd like to tell you about (Point 2).
    II. Second Main Point
        A. Sub-point
        B. Sub-point

Transition/Link: You've heard about (Point 1 and Point 2), now I'll cover (Point 3).
    III. Third Main Point
        A. Sub-point
        B. Sub-point

Transition/Link: My purpose today was to (insert purpose and add a statement about the topic).
Conclusion:

Summary: Today, I shared with you three points: (1) Point 1 _____,

(2) Point 2 _____, and (3) Point 3 _____.

Appeal to Action: As I conclude this speech, (End with a BANG).

(NOTE: Place the Works Cited Page on a page separate from the outline).

Works Cited

*Note: If you use visual aids, please include a Visual Aid Explanation Page
as a separate page following the Works Cited page.*

Visual Aid Explanation Page

Penny J. Waddell
Introduction Speech
30 June 2017

Speech Category: Introduction Speech

Title: A Penny Saved Is a Penny Earned

Purpose: The purpose of this speech is to introduce myself to the readers of this book.

Introduction:

Attention Step: Benjamin Franklin, one of the most famous Americans in our history, once said, "A penny saved is a penny earned" (*Benjamin Franklin Quote*s 1).

Establish Need/Relevance: My father would say this quote every time he introduced me to someone because he loved my name. Since we will be spending time together this fall, it is important that you get to know a little about me. Through the years, my name, Penny, has become a way to start conversations with complete strangers and so I wanted to share this quote with you and a few tidbits of information to let you know how a person's name can help that person build a life.

Establish Speaker Credibility: Hello, my name is Penny and I am credible to introduce myself to you because I know myself better than anyone else in this room, unless of course, it is my father!

Thesis: Today, I want to share three points about my life as a speech coach: (1) Past Speaking Experiences, (2) Present Speaking Experiences, and (3) Future Speaking Experiences.

Body:

Transition/Link: First, I will start at the beginning by sharing a little about my past speaking experiences.

    I. Past Speaking Experiences
        A. Learning Public Speaking Tips
        B. Not a Penny to My Name
        C. College Experiences Worth Every Penny

Transition/Link: I've shared past speaking experiences with you, now I'd like to tell you what is going on presently.

    II. Present Speaking Experiences
        A. Not a Bad Penny, But a Good Penny
        B. Turning a Penny Postcard into a SpeechShark Postcard
        C. Developed a SpeechShark app for Speech Writing and Author of the *SpeechShark* textbook

Transition/Link: You've heard about my past and present speaking experiences, but the best is yet to come!

    III. Future Speaking Experiences
        A. Throwing a Penny Over My Shoulder into a Wishing Well
        B. A Good Penny is Worth a Pound of Cure
        C. A Penny for your Thoughts

Transition/Link: My purpose today was to introduce myself to you and to help you know a little more about me. Do you think you might be able to remember my name, if we met again somewhere along the way?

Conclusion:

Summary: Today, I shared with you three sweet points—you might call them Penny Candy: (1) Past Speaking Experiences, (2) Present Speaking Experiences, and (3) Future Speaking Experiences of a new friend named Penny.

Appeal to Action: As I close this speech, the next time you see me at a meeting or in a crowd, I hope you will remember that I am not a "bad penny." I am a "good penny" and a speech coach that can help you "Save" face when asked to speak in public and "Earn" the respect of those in your audience. Remember, "A Penny Saved Is a Penny Earned" (*Benjamin Franklin Quotes* 1).

(NOTE: Place the Works Cited Page on a page separate from the outline).

Works Cited

Benjamin Franklin Quotes. Your Dictionary. Lovetoknow.com 2017. Accessed 12 March 2017.

Note: If you use visual aids, please include a Visual Aid Explanation Page as a separate page following the Works Cited page.

Visual Aid Explanation Page

INTRODUCTION SPEECH EVALUATION WORKSHEET
Instructor's Copy for Grading the Speech

Speaker's Name: _____   Title of Speech: _____

Time of Speech: _____   Date: _____

Grade: _____

Speech Performance 100 possible points	Excellent 5 points	Good 4 points	Average 3 points	Fair 2 points	Poor 1 point	N/A 0 points
Introduction Step Attention Step						
Establish Need/Relevance Establish Credibility						
Thesis (Preview 3 Points)						
Body Point 1—PAST Direct Support of Point						
Point 2—PRESENT Direct Support of Point						
Point 3—FUTURE Direct Support of Point						
Transitions (4) To First Point To Second Point To Third Point To Conclusion						
Conclusion Summary (Review 3 Points)						
Closing Statements						
Language Skills Vocabulary Filler Words Sentence Structure Grammar Usage						
Vocal Delivery Skills Voice Volume Rate Vocal Variance						
Enthusiasm for Topic Passion/Energy						
Gestures						
Eye Contact						
Poise						

Speech Performance 100 possible points	Excellent 5 points	Good 4 points	Average 3 points	Fair 2 points	Poor 1 point	N/A 0 points
Confidence						
Professional Appearance						

Movement
  Entrance to Stage
  Exit from Stage
  Movement on Stage						

Time of Speech
  Meets Minimum Time
  Exceeds Maximum Time						

Handling of Notes/Note Cards						

Suggestions/Comments

Informative Speech

What is an **Informative Speech**? It is an opportunity to share something of value with your audience. You may choose to provide information about a hobby, career, politics, religion, or something that is happening in your school, college, or community. The purpose of an informative speech is to share knowledge with your audience. Often, the audience may already have a good understanding of the topic, but you will then be able to expand their knowledge by providing credible research, data, and personal stories to support your main points.

Conducting research will allow the opportunity to provide a strong attention step and conclusion for the informative speech. You may choose to begin the speech with a great quote or startling statistics that will get your audience's attention and will also lead to the informative speech topic you will present. Research can also provide options for the conclusion to keep your audience thinking about the information you shared. Supplementing your informative speech with credible research and personal experiences will make the topic come alive for your audience and will help your audience to remain more attentive.

Once you know who will be in your audience, consider choosing a topic that will be interesting to those in your audience. Also, consider a topic that interests you. Remember, enthusiasm is contagious! If you are enthusiastic about your topic, then your audience will enjoy your speech so much more.

Don't be afraid to share a topic that may be personal in nature. Audiences truly enjoy hearing personal stories and your experience with the topic will help support the points in the speech. Let us see your personality and passion for the topic.

An **Informative Speech** is often called a **Key Idea Speech** or a **Central Idea Speech**. You will hear these titles interchangeably because you begin with one general topic idea, but find it necessary to narrow your topic down to one key or central idea. From that point, you will have a better chance of informing your audience about the topic you have chosen.

The best informative speeches have titles that lead to the information the speaker wishes to share. Most of these titles will begin with *"How to. . .", "Why You Should. . .", Did You Know. . .", "Tips for. . .", "The Pros and Cons of . . .", "Examples of. . .", and "The Problems With. . .".*

Here are some examples of informative speech titles:

Informative Speech Topics	
How to Make Brownies	How to Choose a Church That Is Right for Your Family
How to Start a College Club on Your Campus	Where to Go on Your Next Vacation
Why You Should NOT Text and Drive	The Problem with an HOA (Home Owners Association)
Why Homeowners Should Have an HO3 Insurance Policy	Examples of GMOs (Genetically Modified Organisms)
How to Hang Glide	Time Management Skills
Tips for a Winning Interview	How to Name Your Child
The Pros and Cons of Being a Stay-At-Home Mom	The Problem with Sugar
What are the Symptoms of Alcohol Addiction?	How Do I Handle a Fire Alarm at My School
Is Vaping Safe?	What's So Wicked about WIKIs?
What Are the Pros and Cons of Artificial Insemination?	My Favorite Vacation
How I Learned about Attention Deficit Disorder	How to Change a Tire
How to Be GREAT at Bargain Shopping	How to Ask for a Date
Have You Considered Carpooling?	What is FERPA?
How to Feed Your Family for $100.00 a Week	How Do I Appeal a Grade?
Why You Should Recycle	Why Should I Register to Vote?
How Much Television Is Too Much?	What Is SkillsUSA?
Choosing a Child Care Facility for Your Family	How to Pack for a Trip Abroad

What are your Informative Speech Goals?

Now that you've started thinking about an informative speech topic, it is time to consider a plan. Set goals that will enhance your audience members' understanding of the topic while creating interest and focusing on a message that will be remembered long after your speech has ended. These goals may seem lofty, but your job is to define the topic, provide clear examples, and elaborate in such a way that your audience members clearly interpret the intended meaning of the message.

Avoid turning your informative speech into a persuasion speech. Informative speech topics are meant to inform about a topic, but the presentation takes a neutral stance. The closing remarks for an informative speech are not meant to be a call to action as found in a persuasion speech; instead, they are meant to leave the audience thinking and hopefully encouraged to learn more about the subject you shared.

What are the different types of Informative Speeches?

As we began this chapter, you learned about the different types of speeches, but informative speech topics can also be divided into different types: objects, procedures, people, events, and ideas. The *purpose* and *content* of the speech varies by the type.

The *general purpose* of an informative speech is to inform, and the *specific purpose* is to explain, define, describe, or demonstrate. Having a clear plan of the purpose strategy will guide the content and organization of the speech. In many cases, you may cover one or more of the purpose strategies as you assume the role of an instructor and share knowledge using the informative speech as a platform. More information regarding the purpose of the speech and the way it should be organized can be found in Unit 3 of this textbook. The following will help you understand five informative speech types and help with the process of narrowing the topic for your audience.

Objects: Informative speeches about objects cover items that can be seen or touched. The *general purpose* will be to inform your audience about the object. The *specific purpose* will include describing or explaining the object. If possible, consider showing it as a visual aid. If the object is small, post a picture in your Power-Point presentation. Audiences enjoy seeing the object that is being introduced because it creates interest and speakers report they feel less nervous when holding or showing an object as they speak. Using an object for the informative speech will incorporate a strategy of organizing main points chronologically, spatially, or topically.

Procedures: Informative speeches about a process or procedure will include a definition, description, or demonstration of a specific skill. This type of speech will usually have a title that begins with "How to . . ." The *specific purpose* of the speech is to show how something works. Visual aids are important for this type of informative speech because it allows the audience the opportunity to visualize themselves completing the process or procedure. Organization for this type of speech most often follows a chronological path but could also follow the cause–effect or problem-solving method depending upon the complexity of the process or procedure.

People: An informative speech that introduces a person, culture, or group of people is often considered biographical. It is very important to narrow the topic for this type of informative speech so that you stay within your *general purpose* and do not go over the time limit allowed. The topic could be one person or a group of people, it could cover someone you have not met or someone that you know very well. In any event, audience members are more inclined to retain interest if the speaker highlights key information regarding the person, culture, or group of people. Personal stories hold the audience's attention and appreciation for the topic. Chronological organization is usually chosen for this type of informative speech as you introduce the person, culture, or group at the beginning and move in order toward the end.

Events: An informative speech that describes an event the audience has experienced will most certainly gain attention, but you could also cover an event that has great historical significance. What if the event you are introducing does both? Mention COVID-19 and your audience will be able to relate. Your *general purpose* will be to inform your audience about COVID-19, but the *specific purpose* will be to explain, define, or describe a specific aspect of the pandemic and how it will be talked about in years to come. Personal stories and pictures shown as a visual aid will bring the topic to life. The organization of this speech will be suited for chronological, cause–effect, problem-solving, or spatial.

Ideas: Informative speeches that describe or explain ideas are more abstract in nature and more difficult to present. The general purpose is to inform; however, the specific purpose may branch into ideas that include theories, concepts, or principles. Consequently, it is more difficult to keep the audience's attention for this type of informative speech. Conducting a more intense audience analysis is a good idea so that you do not offend others who may not agree with the concepts presented. To organize this type of speech, consider the complexity of the concepts to determine if a cause–effect or problem-solving strategy should be followed.

Visual aids are often used during informative speeches to help the audience visualize content being shared by the speaker. If you are not familiar with creating effective visual aids for a speech, please refer to Unit 4 of this textbook to learn more.

An important visual aid tip to remember for an informative speech is to keep it simple and show one slide per main idea. Too many slides and too much information will be distracting, but a visual aid that is effectively designed will help the audience to visualize the speaker's points. No murky waters here for SpeechSharks who know how to combine quality research, personal experience, and visual aids to paint a clear picture of the speech topic!

Whether you are informing your audience about people, places, careers, hobbies, objects, procedures, or events, you can be sure that the more time you spend crafting a speech FOR your audience, the more successful you will be communicating that information TO your audience. Use the Informative Speech Brainstorming Worksheet to help craft your next informative speech.

Brainstorming Worksheet

Speech Category: Informative Speech
Speech Title: Give your speech a clever title. _____
Specific Purpose: Write a full sentence to show the purpose of your speech.

_____

Introduction:
Attention Step: Consider how you will get your audience's attention. Write all you plan to say using full sentences.

_____

Establish Need/Relevance: Explain why this informative speech topic should interest the listener. Write all you plan to say using full sentences.

_____

Establish Credibility: Explain why YOU are credible to speak about this topic. Write all you plan to say using full sentences.

_____

Thesis (Preview) Statement: Write a full sentence clearly stating the three points you will cover:

_____

Point 1: _____

Point 2: _____

Point 3: _____

Body:

Transition Sentence: Write a full sentence to transition from the Introduction Step to the first main point.

    I. First Main Point:
        A. First Sub-Point
           1. First Sub-Sub-Point (Not all points will require sub-sub-points.)
           2. Second Sub-Sub-Point
        B. Second Sub-Point
           1. First Sub-Sub-Point
           2. Second Sub-Sub-Point

Transition Sentence: Write a full sentence to transition from the first main point to the second.

    II. Second Main Point:
        A. First Sub-Point
           1. First Sub-Sub-Point (Not all points will require sub-sub-points.)
           2. Second Sub-Sub-Point
        B. Second Sub-Point
           1. First Sub-Sub-Point
           2. Second Sub-Sub-Point

Transition Sentence: Write a full sentence to transition from the second point to the third point.

    III. Third Main Point
        A. First Sub-Point
           1. First Sub-Sub-Point (Not all points will require sub-sub-points.)
           2. Second Sub-Sub-Point
        B. Second Sub-Point
           1. First Sub-Sub-Point
           2. Second Sub-Sub-Point

Transition Sentence: Write a full sentence to transition from the third main point to the conclusion.

Conclusion:

Summary: Write in full sentence format a summary of your three main points.

Point 1: _____

Point 2: _____

Point 3: _____

Appeal to Action: Leave your audience thinking about your speech. End with a **BANG**!

(NOTE: Place the Works Cited Page on a page separate from the outline).

Works Cited

*Note: If you use visual aids, please include a Visual Aid Explanation Page
as a separate page following the Works Cited page.*

Visual Aid Explanation Page

Outline Template

First Name/Last Name
Informative Speech
Day Month Year

Speech Category: Informative Speech
Title:
Purpose:

Introduction:
Attention Step:
Establish Need/Relevance:
Establish Speaker Credibility:

Thesis: Today, I want to share three points about (Topic): (1) _____,

(2) _____, and (3) _____.

Body:
Transition/Link: First, I will start at the beginning by sharing a little about (Point 1).
    I. First Main Point
        A. Sub-point
        B. Sub-point

Transition/Link: I've shared (Point 1) with you, now I'd like to tell you about (Point 2).
    II. Second Main Point
        A. Sub-point
        B. Sub-point

Transition/Link: You've heard about (Point 1 and Point 2), now I'll cover (Point 3).
    III. Third Main Point
        A. Sub-point
        B. Sub-point

Transition/Link: My purpose today was to (insert purpose and add a statement about the topic).
Conclusion:

Summary: Today, I shared with you three points: (1) Point 1 _____,

(2) Point 2 _____, and (3) Point 3 _____.

Appeal to Action: As I conclude this speech, (End with a BANG).

(NOTE: Place the Works Cited Page on a page separate from the outline).

Works Cited

*Note: If you use visual aids, please include a Visual Aid Explanation Page
as a separate page following the Works Cited page.*

Visual Aid Explanation Page

Example Outline

Penny J. Waddell
Toastmasters International Meeting
30 June 2017

Speech Category: Informative Speech
Title: How to Dress for An Interview
Purpose: The purpose of this speech is to inform my audience how to dress for an interview.

Introduction:
Attention Step: (Show pictures on a PowerPoint slide of different people dressed in different ways. One person is dressed in jeans, flip-flops, and a T-shirt; another is dressed in a short minidress with tattoos showing on her arms and legs; another is dressed business casual.) Take a look at the pictures of these three candidates who are about to interview for a job position at a Fortune 500 Company. Which candidate do you think will get the job?
Establish Need/Relevance: The truth is that any one of these candidates MAY get the job. The secret is knowing with which company the candidate is interviewing. If interviewing for a position at GOOGLE, the jeans and T-shirt may be appropriate. If interviewing for a position with The Coca Cola Company in Atlanta, the candidate dressed business casual may get the job. Before interviewing for a job position, be sure to know what type of dress is expected.
Establish Speaker Credibility: I am credible to speak to you today about dressing for an interview because I have recently interviewed for a job position and got the job! For the position, I needed to dress in an upscale suit, very little jewelry, and I needed to project extreme professionalism.
Thesis: Today, I will cover three points to inform you how to dress for an interview. (1) Research the company, (2) Understand the culture of the company, and (3) Put your best foot forward.

Body:
Transition/Link: Let's begin with the first point, research the company.

    I. Research the Company
        A. What type of business does this company do?
        B. For this position, what type of work responsibilities are expected?

Transition/Link: I've shared the importance of researching the company with you, now I'd like to tell you how to understand the culture of the company.

    II. Understand the Culture of the Company
        A. Make a trip to the company prior to the Interview (Quast).
        B. Watch to see how other employees dress.

Transition/Link: You've heard how to research the company and how to understand its culture, now I want to show you how to put your best foot forward.

    III. Put Your Best Foot Forward (Smith)
        A. Choose clothing, shoes, and accessories that mirror how other employees in this company dress.
        B. Always err on the conservative side, but don't forget to show your personality.

Transition/Link: Now you should understand a little more about how to dress for an interview.

Conclusion:
Summary: Today, I shared with you three points: (1) Research the company, (2) Understand the culture of the company, and (3) Put your best foot forward.
Appeal to Action: As you interview for what might very well be the most important interview of your life, be sure to remember that "You never get a second chance to make a first impression" (Quast). With this quote, I want to challenge you to dress for success and make sure this interview is the one that will help you get your dream job!

(Note: The Works Cited page is a separate page from the Outline).

Works Cited

Quast, Lisa. *"8 Tips to Dress for Interview Success." Forbes.* (2014). Accessed 12 March 2017.

Smith, Chris. "Dress to Impress: what to wear for a job interview." *The Guardian.* Guardian Careers. (2017). Accessed

12 March 2017.

(Note: The Visual Aids Explanation page is a separate page from the Outline and the Works Cited page).

Visual Aids Explanation Page

PowerPoint Presentation:

Slide 1:   Title of Speech—How to Dress for an Interview

Pictures of Three People Dressed Differently

Slide 2:   (Point 1): Research the Company

Bullet Points:

- Type of Business
- Type of Work Responsibilities

Slide 3:   (Point 2): Understand the Culture of the Company

Picture of Business with Employees Entering the Door

Slide 4:   (Point 3): Put Your Best Foot Forward

Picture of Professionally Dressed Employee

Slide 5:   "You Never Get a Second Chance to Make a First Impression" (Quast)

Picture of a Group of Professionally Dressed Employees

INFORMATIVE SPEECH EVALUATION WORKSHEET
Instructor's Copy for Grading the Speech

Speaker's Name: _____   Title of Speech: _____

Time of Speech: _____   Date: _____

Grade: _____

Speech Performance 100 possible points	Excellent 5 points	Good 4 points	Average 3 points	Fair 2 points	Poor 1 point	N/A 0 points
Introduction Step Attention Step Establish Need/Relevance Establish Credibility Thesis (Preview 3 Points)						
Body Point 1—PAST Direct Support of Point						
Point 2—PRESENT Direct Support of Point						
Point 3—FUTURE Direct Support of Point						
Transitions (4) To First Point To Second Point To Third Point To Conclusion						
Conclusion Summary (Review 3 Points) Closing Statements						
Language Skills Vocabulary Filler Words Sentence Structure Grammar Usage						
Vocal Delivery Skills Voice Volume Rate Vocal Variance						
Enthusiasm for Topic Passion/Energy						
Gestures						
Eye Contact						
Poise						
Confidence						

Speech Performance 100 possible points	Excellent 5 points	Good 4 points	Average 3 points	Fair 2 points	Poor 1 point	N/A 0 points
Professional Appearance						
Movement Entrance to Stage Exit from Stage Movement on Stage						
Research Number of Sources Verbally Cited ❑ ❑ ❑						
Research Verbal Citations Supported Topics ❑ ❑ ❑						
Visual Aids Types Used: _____ Setting up Visual Aids Handling Visual Aids Design of Visual Aids Visibility of Visual Aids Management of Tech Team						
Time of Speech Meets Minimum Time Exceeds Maximum Time						
Handling of Notes/Note Cards						

Suggestions/Comments

Demonstration Speech

Sometimes the audience needs to see a **Demonstration Speech** in order to fully comprehend the process or procedure needed to complete a task. Demonstration speeches are informative type speeches, but will include a demonstration to complete the purpose. Usually this speech is a bit longer than the central idea (informative) speech and involves audience participation. This type speech also includes an entertaining aspect. Perhaps that is why this type of speech is so popular! Audiences are able to retain and comprehend information better when they actively take part in the demonstration and can visualize how the process or procedure works. It is because of this fact that demonstration speeches often appeal to diverse audiences and to people with varying learning styles. To summarize, the audience will hear the information, see the demonstration, and participate in the demonstration to retain the information much longer.

As with any speech topic, the speaker will need to choose a topic tailor-made for the intended audience. This is a great speech to incorporate your creativity and bring an element of entertainment to the speaking arena. Make it informational and useful so that you can add value to your audience's knowledge of the topic. Topics may include crafts, sports, hobbies, food preparations, horticulture, home or automotive repairs, but can also include how to budget, create a will, or participate in stock trading. If you have more time, your topic could involve the process of flipping a house, starting a business, or designing a website. Again, the topic you choose needs to be a topic that will be interesting and useful for the audience that will hear your speech. Demonstration Speech titles almost always begin with, "How to. . .". The title lends itself to the purpose of the speech.

Here are examples of good demonstration speech titles:

Demonstration Speech Topics	
How to Arrange Flowers	How to Organize Your Closet
How to Bake a Cake	How to Pack for a Trip
How to Clean a House	How to Paint a Room
How to Tie a Bow Tie	How to Play Dominoes
How to Change a Diaper	How to Wrap a Gift
How to Use Twitter	How to Write a Resume
How to Make Egg Rolls	How to Fold a Flag
How to Make a Picture Frame	How to Perform CPR
How to Set a Table	How to Find a Good Roommate
How to Choose Jewelry for a Formal Event	How to Make Pizza
How to Choose Wines for Dinner	How to Meditate
How to Deliver a Great Speech	How to Plan a Vegetarian Meal for Guests
How to Make Donuts	How to Start Running
How to Organize a Fund-Raiser	How to Fold a Napkin
How to Compete in SkillsUSA	How to Create an e-mail Address

The best plan to follow for a demonstration speech is to: (1) describe the history of the process or procedure you will demonstrate, (2) list and describe the materials needed for the demonstration, and (3) demonstrate the process or procedure. This plan may seem simple, but it truly is the clearest way to present demonstration information in such a way that will make sense to the audience.

Handouts and visual aids are important for a successful demonstration speech. The visual aids can help with the actual demonstration and handouts are given to audience members following the demonstration as a reminder of the process or procedures followed.

Understanding the setting of where the speech will be given may help you choose the topic and visual aids. Where will you be giving the demonstration speech? Will it be inside or outside? Will it be in a traditional classroom setting or in a public hall?

Rehearsals for a demonstration speech are different from rehearsals needed for other types of speeches. The demonstration speech will incorporate more visual aids than an informative speech. You might have a PowerPoint or Prezi Slide Presentation to illustrate steps in the process or procedure, but a table display is almost always used for a demonstration speech. The speaker stands behind the table and uses the props on the table display to demonstrate the process or procedure while speaking. It is for this reason that rehearsals should always include the actions that will be taken during the speech. Rehearse using the PowerPoint or Prezi Slide Presentation, but also using the props on the table display. Rehearse completing the steps needed to demonstrate the process or procedure. You'll notice that your speech time will actually last longer when you are giving the speech using the props to demonstrate than when you rehearse the speech without the props. This speech will involve using a Tech Team to help set up and break down the demonstration stage. Rehearse with your Tech Team so they know exactly what you want them to do and when you want them to do it.

Brainstorming Worksheet

Speech Category: Demonstration Speech
Speech Title: Give your speech a clever title. _____
Specific Purpose: Write a full sentence to show the purpose of your speech.

_____

Introduction:

Attention Step: Consider how you will get your audience's attention. Write all you plan to say using full sentences.

_____

Establish Need/Relevance: Explain why this demonstration speech topic should interest the listener. Write all you plan to say using full sentences.

_____

Establish Credibility: Explain why YOU are credible to demonstrate this topic. Write all you plan to say using full sentences.

_____

Thesis (Preview) Statement: Write a complete sentence and clearly state the three points you will cover:

Point 1: The history of _____

Point 2: Materials needed for the demonstration: _____

Point 3: Demonstration of _____

Body:

Transition Sentence: Write a full sentence to transition from the Introduction Step to the first main point.

_____

    I. **First Main Point:**
       A. **First Sub-Point**
          1. **First Sub-Sub-Point** (Not all points will require sub-sub-points.)
          2. **Second Sub-Sub-Point**

      B. Second Sub-Point
          1. First Sub-Sub-Point
          2. Second Sub-Sub-Point

Transition Sentence: Write a full sentence to transition from the first main point to the second.

   II. Materials needed
      A. First Sub-Point
          1. First Sub-Sub-Point (Not all points will require sub-sub-points.)
          2. Second Sub-Sub-Point
      B. Second Sub-Point
          1. First Sub-Sub-Point
          2. Second Sub-Sub-Point

Transition Sentence: Write a full sentence to transition from the second point to the third point.

   III. Demonstration
      A. First Sub-Point
          1. First Sub-Sub-Point (Not all points will require sub-sub-points.)
          2. Second Sub-Sub-Point
      B. Second Sub-Point
          1. First Sub-Sub-Point
          2. Second Sub-Sub-Point

Transition Sentence: Write a full sentence to transition from the third main point to the conclusion.

Conclusion:

Summary: Write a full sentence summary of your three main points.

Point 1: The History of (Product or Process) _____

Point 2: Materials needed: _____

Point 3: The Demonstration _____

Appeal to Action: Leave your audience thinking about your demonstration. End with a **BANG**!

(NOTE: Place the Works Cited Page on a page separate from the outline).

Works Cited

*Note: If you use visual aids, please include a Visual Aid Explanation Page
as a separate page following the Works Cited page.*

Visual Aid Explanation Page

Outline Template

First Name/Last Name
Demonstration Speech
Day Month Year

Speech Category: Demonstration Speech
Title:
Purpose:

Introduction:
Attention Step:
Establish Need/Relevance:
Establish Speaker Credibility:

Thesis: Today, I want to share three points about (Topic): (1) _____,

(2) _____, and (3) _____.

Body:

Transition/Link: First, I will start at the beginning by sharing a little about (Point 1).
    I. First Main Point
        A. Sub-point
        B. Sub-point

Transition/Link: I've shared (Point 1) with you, now I'd like to tell you about (Point 2).
    II. Second Main Point
        A. Sub-point
        B. Sub-point

Transition/Link: You've heard about (Point 1 and Point 2), now I'll cover (Point 3).
    III. Third Main Point
        A. Sub-point
        B. Sub-point

Transition/Link: My purpose today was to (insert purpose and add a statement about the topic).
Conclusion:

Summary: Today, I shared with you three points: (1) Point 1 _____,

(2) Point 2 _____, and (3) Point 3 _____.

Appeal to Action: As I conclude this speech, (End with a BANG).

(NOTE: Place the Works Cited Page on a page separate from the outline).

Works Cited

*Note: If you use visual aids, please include a Visual Aid Explanation Page
as a separate page following the Works Cited page.*

Visual Aid Explanation Page

Example Outline

Penny J. Waddell
SkillsUSA Culinary Arts Demonstration
25 April 2017

Speech Category: Demonstration Speech
Title: Manners Matter
Purpose: The purpose of this speech is to demonstrate how to set a table for dinner.

Introduction:
Attention Step: Two weeks ago, I went to a formal dinner that included several courses. The young lady seated to my left was quite nervous, so I asked her how she was doing. She told me that she was terrified because she had no idea which fork to use for each course. As she said this, she looked down at the place setting in front of her that had four forks, two knives, and two spoons. Have you ever been in this type of situation? Do you know which fork to use?
Establish Need/Relevance: Emily Post, whose name has become synonymous with etiquette and manners, said in her article, "The Table Setting Guide" that "Setting a proper table is not as difficult as it seems."
Establish Speaker Credibility: At a young age, I learned how to set a Basic Table Setting and a Formal Table Setting. As I grew older and had daughters of my own, I taught them to do the same. As they were growing older, I taught a course called, "Oops Your Manners are Showing." In that course, I was able to teach young people about table setting etiquette; therefore, I feel credible to share this information with you.
Thesis: Today, I will share three points about setting a proper table. (1) First, I will tell you about the history of setting a table. (2) Second, I will list the materials needed to set a table, and (3) Third, I will demonstrate the proper setting of a table.

Body:

Transition/Link: Before you learn how to set a proper table, let's first look at the history of setting a table.
    I. The history of setting a table
        A. How it Began
        B. Origins of Cutlery

Transition/Link: I've shared the history of table setting with you, now I'd like to tell you the materials needed to set a basic table.
    II. Materials needed to set a Basic table ("Table Setting Guide")
        A. Dinner Plate, Bread Plate
        B. Drinking Vessels, Cutlery and Napkin

Transition/Link: You've heard about the history of setting a table and learned the materials that you will need. Now, please allow me to demonstrate how to set a basic table.
    III. Demonstrate the setting of a table
        A. Step 1—Placement of Plates
        B. Step 2—Placement of Drinking Vessels, Cutlery and Napkin

Transition/Link: My purpose today was to show you how easy it is to set a basic table.
Conclusion:
Summary: Today, I shared with you three points: (1) First, the history of setting a table. (2) Second, materials needed to set a table. (3) Third, the proper setting of a table.
Appeal to Action: Do you remember the young lady that I told you about in the beginning of this speech? She did a great job that night at the formal dinner party. She just watched others around her and then picked up the fork she saw them pick up. We learn by watching. Be careful because your manners are showing!

(Note: The Works Cited page is a separate page from the Outline.)

Works Cited

"Table Setting Guide." *The Emily Post Institute.* 2017. Accessed 2 April 2017.

(Note: The Visual Aid Explanation page should be placed on a separate page from the Outline and Works Cited page.)

Visual Aid Explanation Page

PowerPoint Presentation:

Slide 1: Title of Speech

Picture of a Table Setting

Slide 2: History of a Table Setting

Picture of a Table Setting

Slide 3: List of Materials Needed

Picture of Materials

Slide 4: Demonstration of a Table Setting

Picture of a Table Setting

Slide 5: Conclusion Slide—Picture

Table Display:

Table with a tablecloth and dishes arranged in a Basic Table Setting *(*"Table Setting Guide"*)*

DEMONSTRATION SPEECH EVALUATION WORKSHEET
Instructor's Copy for Grading the Speech

Speaker's Name: _____   Title of Speech: _____

Time of Speech: _____   Date: _____

Grade: _____

Speech Performance 100 possible points	Excellent 5 points	Good 4 points	Average 3 points	Fair 2 points	Poor 1 point	N/A 0 points
Introduction Step Attention Step / Establish Need/Relevance / Establish Credibility / Thesis (Preview 3 Points)						
Body Point 1—History of the Process or Procedure / Direct Support of Point						
Point 2—Materials Needed for the Demonstration / Direct Support of Point						
Point 3—Demonstration of the Process or Procedure / Direct Support of Point						
Transitions (4) To First Point / To Second Point / To Third Point / To Conclusion						
Conclusion Summary (Review 3 Points) / Closing Statements						
Language Skills Vocabulary / Filler Words / Sentence Structure / Grammar Usage						
Vocal Delivery Skills Voice / Volume / Rate / Vocal Variance						
Enthusiasm for Topic Passion/Energy						
Gestures						
Eye Contact						
Poise and Confidence						

Speech Performance 100 possible points	Excellent 5 points	Good 4 points	Average 3 points	Fair 2 points	Poor 1 point	N/A 0 points
Professional Appearance						
Movement Entrance to Stage Exit from Stage Movement on Stage						
Research Number of Sources Verbally Cited ❑ ❑						
Research Verbal Citations Supported Topics ❑ ❑						
Visual Aids Types Used: _____ Setting up Visual Aids Handling Visual Aids Design of Visual Aids Visibility of Visual Aids Management of Tech Team						
Handout Type Design Distribution of Handout						
Time of Speech Meets Minimum Time Exceeds Maximum Time						
Handling of Notes/Note Cards						

Suggestions/Comments

Persuasion Speech

We use persuasion strategies all day long as we inspire or motivate others to do something. It begins in the morning when you are persuading your child to get dressed for school; it continues as you go to work and try persuading your co-workers to embrace a new policy or procedure at the office. Then at night when you go home, you are still using your persuasion strategies to motivate your family to get outside for a little exercise after supper. Just face it, we will use this type of skill more often than any other. Not only are you attempting to persuade others to think of something in a different way, but they will also be attempting to persuade you to think another way.

Did you sit with friends or family members after the last presidential election and try to persuade them to think like you? Were they trying to change your mind about the way you think about politics? These types of interactions happen quite often. Sometimes we actually stop to consider another way of thinking. What strategy motivates you to think of things in a different way? What strategy motivates you to action?

The key word here is—motivate! That is because as we attempt to persuade someone to consider the view we present, we are actually motivating or influencing their values, beliefs, attitudes, or behaviors. Let's look at an explanation for each one of these areas.

Area to Influence (Motivate):	Explanation
Values	Do you think something is right or wrong? Do you consider something is good or bad?
Beliefs	Do you perceive the topic to be true or false?
Attitudes	Do you look at the topic in a favorable or unfavorable light? What is your attitude toward the topic?
Behaviors	Behaviors are a combination of your personal values, beliefs, and attitudes. We behave a certain way when we are reacting to these different areas.

What type of appeal is effective to persuade an audience?

Aristotle, a Greek philosopher, developed a method of reasoning known for the power to persuade. His theory centers on the fact that audience members' disposition (*pathos*) will be influenced more if the speaker has character (*ethos*), and if the content of the message is supported with logic (*logos)*. Using this method helps us to communicate and persuade others to action. By the way, this is where we get the term, **Appeal to Action**, found in the conclusion of a persuasion speech.

Would you like to know more about Pathos, Logos, and Ethos?

Pathos: Appeal to someone's emotions and you will be using the strategy that Aristotle defined as *pathos*. This can be done by sharing examples or stories that tug at your heart. Depending upon the topic, you might choose to appeal to the audience's disposition for empathy, anger, humor, fear, sympathy, or frustration using verbal and nonverbal communication.

Ethos: Prove to the audience that you are qualified to speak about your chosen topic and your audience will perceive you as the authority. Share credibility for the topic by sharing personal stories or by explaining research you conducted. Persuading your audience will be an easier task if they see that you are professionally presenting information for which you have experience and using appropriate language skills to share your message.

Logos: Appeal to our sense of reason or logic and you will help us make connections between ideas and data that supports them. Referring to credible research that is historically significant or to facts that support your argument is another way. Your instructor will be listening closely to make sure you are offering support for each of the main points that you present and if you are presenting them in a logical manner.

To summarize, influencing values, beliefs, attitudes, and behaviors begins with appealing to the audience's emotions (pathos), their perception of the speaker's credibility (ethos), and connecting the message with supporting logic (logos). Now, all you need is a really great topic!

When choosing a topic for a persuasion speech, avoid choosing topics that are too controversial. Topics that are overly controversial can alienate your audience and you might find yourself in an unpleasant and hostile situation. In the few short minutes you have been given to present a Persuasion Speech, you will never be able to persuade an audience to completely change their way of thinking. Remember, people spend years deciding how they feel about things, whether it is religion, politics, personal rights, or simply things they like and dislike. Since people have very strong feelings about things, your topic will automatically be met with support or with opposition. Most speakers do not choose to cover a topic that would make most of the audience members angry. Even if your topic is not overly popular, you can motivate your audience to think about your topic in a different way.

Titles are important; especially when your audience sees the title of your speech projected on a screen before they see you. The title sets up an expectation of the content, so give your speech a clever title. Persuasion speech titles should involve the action you hope to influence. While informative and demonstration speeches often begin with "How to . . .", the persuasion speech will begin with a verb. For example, if you want to motivate your audience to manage time more effectively, title the speech, *Unlock the Clock*. Do you want your audience to dress more appropriately? Title the speech, *Dress for Success*. Are you concerned that no one in your class is recycling plastic water bottles? Title the speech, *Recycle, Reduce, and Reuse*. Making sure your audience knows what you are expecting them to do will influence the outcome of your persuasion speech.

One strategy for being persuasive without sounding preachy or gimmicky is to follow **Monroe's Motivated Sequence**. Perhaps you would like to know a little more about Monroe's Motivated Sequence, especially if you have never heard of this term before. According to Frymier and Shulman, authors of the article, "What's in It for Me?" published by the *Communication Education Journal*, one way to truly motivate someone to do something or to think differently about something is to show the benefits or "What's in it for me?" This allows the speaker the opportunity to make the content relevant to the listener and to increase their motivation toward a solution.

The person who developed the Motivated Sequence Theory was Alan H. Monroe, a professor at Purdue University and well known for his theory of persuasion. **Monroe's theory involves five steps:** begin with a strong attention step, describe a problem showing a need for change, introduce a realistic solution which includes having the listener help solve the problem, help the listener visualize the results of solving the problem, and finish by challenging the listener to solve the problem.

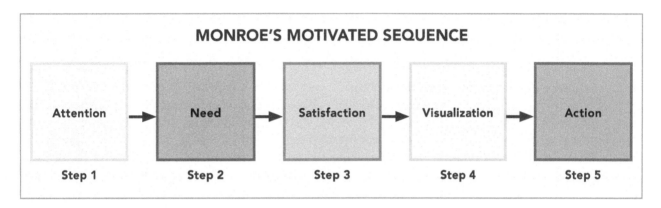

Step 1: The speaker should describe the problem using examples that will get the attention of the audience and will cause the audience to agree that there is, indeed, a problem.

Step 2: Credible and experiential research should be used to support the problem, which Monroe identifies as the need for a change. Show how the problem directly impacts the listener. This step allows the audience to relate to problems described so they are motivated to take part in the next step.

Step 3: The speaker should propose realistic solutions to solve the problem. The solutions should be something that every person in the audience can do to help solve the problem. If the solution is too difficult, the listener will not be motivated to help with the solution. It is imperative that the speaker present steps toward solving the problem and uses research to prove this solution is effective and doable. Using this strategy does not sound preachy because you are not blaming the audience for the problem, but enlisting their help to solve the problem. It is not gimmicky because the solutions are realistic and attainable.

Step 4: The speaker should help the audience visualize the results of solving the problem, whether it is the benefits of successfully solving the problem or consequences if the problem is NOT solved. This strategy involves connecting with the audience so they can see the vision of solving the problem as something that actually can happen.

Step 5: The speaker will need to challenge the audience to become an integral part of the solution. The *appeal to action* portion of the persuasion speech is the moment where the speaker challenges the audience with such passion and enthusiasm that the audience members are motivated to begin work that very moment to solve the problem that has been described. If the speaker has indeed influenced the values, beliefs, attitudes, and behaviors of the audience members, they will feel compelled to help the speaker solve the problem and they will want to begin immediately!

During a persuasion speech, the speaker should provide useful information and credible supporting research that will motivate the listener to action. When crafting a persuasion speech, the speaker will answer questions of *fact, value,* and *policy.* Let's take a moment to look at these:

Questions of Fact: During the problem statement, it is important to answer questions of fact by using credible research for support. Choose one side or the other as your topic. This is not a good time to "sit on the fence." If your speech is titled, "Don't Text and Drive," then you will want to motivate your audience to never text and drive—ever! If you say it is allowed to text while you are at a traffic light, then you are defeating your point. Your audience needs to know you are 100% committed to the topic you are covering; otherwise, you will destroy your credibility as a speaker for the topic and will not be able to motivate the audience to help solve the problem you describe.

Questions of Value: The problem statement will also need to cover questions of value. For most of us, this involves whether something is moral or immoral, whether it is just or unjust, whether it is good or bad. Choose the moral argument to cover and then offer appeals that will tug at the hearts of your audience members. A good strategy for this is to use arguments that will strengthen the audience's attitudes or beliefs toward the topic.

Questions of Policy: The questions of policy are answered during the portion in the speech where you offer a realistic solution to solve the problem. Solutions often involve changing laws or enforcing existing laws or revising procedures that are not working effectively. The speaker should focus on offering solutions that are something that any person in the audience can do. Audience members will not be able to change a law and many of them are also not in the position to enforce an existing law. Many of us are not in the position to revise procedures that are no longer working. So, what can we do to solve a problem? We can talk to those in our circle of friends and family about the problem. We can volunteer to help in areas that will impact the problem. We can contact or write the mayor, Governor of our state, County Commissioner, or State Representative. We can let those people know that we want to see a solution to the problem, a change to laws, or the enforcing of existing laws. THAT is something we can do and this will answer questions of policy.

With a topic that is relevant for your audience, a title that follows the action you hope to influence, and using methods and strategies to effectively persuade, you are ready to brainstorm ways to organize and develop your topic.

Conduct credible research to support your points and gain confidence in knowing you will be speaking about a subject that could have a far-reaching positive impact. Through the years, I've had students say they were moved to get involved with a cause they never considered before, and it was all due to hearing one life-changing persuasion speech. Personal stories of tragedy and triumph have brought us all to tears when we realized we have the power to bring about a positive change by solving a problem following realistic solutions that anyone can do. Remember, every great persuasion speech involves a cleverly designed appeal to action. What will you do to motivate others to recognize a problem, become part of the solution, and impact the future?

Brainstorming Worksheet

Speech Category: Persuasion Speech
Speech Title: Give your speech a clever title. _____
Specific Purpose: Write a full sentence to show the purpose of your speech.

_____

Introduction:
Attention Step: Consider how you will get your audience's attention. Write all you plan to say using full sentences.

_____

Establish Need/Relevance: Explain why this persuasion speech topic should interest the listener. Write all you plan to say using full sentences.

_____

Establish Credibility: Explain why YOU are credible to speak about this topic. Write all you plan to say using full sentences.

_____

Thesis (Preview) Statement: Write a full sentence and clearly state the three points you will cover:

_____

Point 1: Description of the Problem: _____

Point 2: Proposed Solution to the Problem: _____

Point 3: Visualization of the Results of Solving the Problem or the Consequences if the Problem Is NOT

Solved: _____

Body:

Transition Sentence: Write a full sentence to transition from the Introduction Step to the first main point.

   I. **The Problem:**
      A. **Discuss the problem you are covering.**
         1. **Support the problem with research.**
         2. **Support the problem with a personal example.**
      B. **Why is there a need for change?**
         1. **Who or what is negatively affected by this problem?**
         2. **Use logical and emotional Appeals.**

Transition Sentence: Write a full sentence to transition from the first main point to the second.

  II. **Solution to the Problem:**
      A. **Offer a realistic, detailed solution which solves the problem.**
         1. **Explain how the audience can help to solve the problem.**
         2. **Provide personal examples and research to support your solution.**
      B. **Answer questions of policy.**
         1. **The solution affects values, beliefs, attitudes, and behaviors.**
         2. **Use logical and emotional appeals.**
         3. **Support points with credible research.**

Transition Sentence: Write a full sentence to transition from the second point to the third point.

 III. **Visualization of Results**
      A. **Benefits of Solving the Problem**
         1. **Does it answer questions of value?**
         2. **Use descriptions to help audience members visualize benefits.**
      B. **Consequences if the Problem is Not Solved**
         1. **Use imagery to show the consequences of not solving the problem.**
         2. **Use personal examples and vivid descriptions.**

Transition Sentence: Write a full sentence to transition from the third main point to the conclusion.

Conclusion:

Summary: Write a full sentence to summarize your three main points.

Point 1: The Problem _____

Point 2: The Solution to the Problem _____

Point 3: Visualization of Results _____

Appeal to Action: Leave your audience challenged to help solve the problem. End with a **BANG**!

(NOTE: Place the Works Cited Page on a page separate from the outline).

Works Cited

*Note: If you use visual aids, please include a Visual Aid Explanation Page
as a separate page following the Works Cited page.*

Visual Aid Explanation Page

Outline Template

First Name/Last Name
Persuasion Speech
Day Month Year

Speech Category: Persuasion Speech
Title:
Purpose:

Introduction:
Attention Step:
Establish Need/Relevance:
Establish Speaker Credibility:

Thesis: Today, I want to share three points about (Topic): (1) The Problem with _____,

(2) Possible ways to solve the problem _____, and (3) a Visualization of the world if

this problem is solved _____.

Body:

Transition/Link: First, I will start at the beginning by sharing a little about (Point 1).
     I. First Main Point—Problem
        A. Sub-point
        B. Sub-point

Transition/Link: I've shared (Point 1) with you, now I'd like to tell you about (Point 2).
     II. Second Main Point—Solutions
        A. Sub-point
        B. Sub-point

Transition/Link: You've heard about (Point 1 and Point 2), now I'll cover (Point 3).
     III. Third Main Point—Results
        A. Sub-point
        B. Sub-point

Transition/Link: My purpose today was to (insert purpose and add a statement about the topic).

Conclusion:

Summary: Today, I shared with you three points: (1) Point 1 _____,

(2) Point 2 _____, and (3) Point 3 _____.

Appeal to Action: As I conclude this speech, (End with a BANG).

(NOTE: Place the Works Cited Page on a page separate from the outline).

Works Cited

*Note: If you use visual aids, please include a Visual Aid Explanation Page
as a separate page following the Works Cited page.*

Visual Aid Explanation Page

Example Outline

Penny J. Waddell
Political Rally
30 June 2017

Speech Category: Persuasion Speech
Title: Support America
Purpose: The Purpose of this speech is to persuade my audience to support America.

Introduction:
Attention Step: Arnold Whittaker, Tom Malcolm, Buck Brownlee. What do these three men have in common? They all are from Georgia and they all are World War II Veterans who defended our country's freedom and came back home to raise families and make an impact on their communities, their state, and their country! But, there are also differences.
Establish Need/Relevance: At a time in our country where the political parties are at odds with each other, it is important for us to realize that we are all members of one country. Regardless of our political beliefs, regardless of whether we are Democrat, Republican, or Independent, we are ALL Americans!
Establish Speaker Credibility: As an Independent American, I am credible to speak to you about how importance it is for our countrymen and women to stand together first as Americans. Also, the three men that I mentioned in the beginning of this speech were all very dear to me. I loved them, all.
Thesis: Today, I plan to share with you (1) the problem of a country divided, (2) solutions to this problem, and (3) help you visualize a future where we all stand together as one country.

Body:

Transition/Link: The first point that I'll share is about the problem we have with divided political parties.
    I. The Problem: Divided Political Parties in America (Pennock 203)
        A. Democrat Party
        B. Republican Party
        C. Independent Party

Transition/Link: I've shared with you the problem of divided political parties in our country, but there is a solution.
    II. The Solution:
        A. One Country: Bi-partisan Solutions (O'Neil 158)
        B. Working together as one country

Transition/Link: You've heard about the problem of divided political parties in our country, and you've heard about a solution where we all choose to work together to find bi-partisan solutions to a divided problem.
    III. Visualization of Results:
        A. Results: See other party's views and work together for a solution (Dalton 191)
        B. Consequences: Continue divided

Transition/Link: My purpose today was to motivate you to consider a world where we all work together to find the best solutions for America.
Conclusion:
Summary: Today, I shared three points: (1) the problem of a country divided, (2) solutions to this problem, and (3) a future where we all stand together as one country.
Appeal to Action: As I close this speech, the three WWII heroes that I mentioned to you did have ONE thing in common. They are all Americans. They also had differences. One was a Democrat. One was a Republican. One was an Independent. However, they did not let that stand in their way when they stormed the beaches of Normandy and fought to preserve the freedoms that so many of us hold dear. All three men have recently passed away. The last one, Mr. Brownlee, just passed away this year. They all three left behind families and friends who are enjoying the freedoms we have every day simply because they chose to overlook differences and worked together to make sure YOU are free. Free to worship, work, and live the way you choose. You can do the same. Will you stand with me today as an American? Not as a political party, but as an American? God Bless America!

(Note: The Works Cited page is a separate page from the Outline).

Works Cited

Dalton, Russell J. *Citizen Politics: Public Opinion and Political Parties in Advanced Industrial Democracies.* 6th ed.

Washington DC: CQ Press, 2014.

O'Neil, Patrick H. *Essentials of Comparative Politics.* 5th ed. International Student. 2015.

Pennock, James, Roland. *Democratic Political Theory.* Princeton: Princeton University Press, 2016.

(Note: The Visual Aid Explanation page should be placed on a separate page from the Outline and Works Cited page).

Visual Aid Explanation Page

PowerPoint Presentation
Slide 1: Introduction—Title of Speech and pictures of the three men
Slide 2: The Problem—Pictures of each Political Party
Slide 3: The Solution—Picture of an American Flag
Slide 4: The Results—Picture of American Flag with Citizens
Slide 5: Conclusion—Picture of Soldiers and Their Families with American Flag

Handout
Tri-Fold Brochure—American Flag on the front
Inside Left—Definition of Republican Party
Inside Center—Definition of Democratic Party
Inside Right—Definition of Independent Pary
Back—Center—Research Citations for Further Reading

PERSUASION SPEECH EVALUATION WORKSHEET
Instructor's Copy for Grading the Speech

Speaker's Name: _____ Title of Speech: _____

Time of Speech: _____ Date: _____

Grade: _____

Speech Performance 100 possible points	Excellent 5 points	Good 4 points	Average 3 points	Fair 2 points	Poor 1 point	N/A 0 points
Introduction Step Attention Step / Establish Need/Relevance / Establish Credibility / Thesis (Preview 3 Points)						
Body Point 1—The Problem / Direct Support of Point						
Point 2—The Solution / Direct Support of Point						
Point 3—Results of Solving the Problem / Direct Support of Point						
Transitions (4) To First Point / To Second Point / To Third Point / To Conclusion						
Conclusion Summary (Review 3 Points) / Closing Statements						
Language Skills Vocabulary / Filler Words / Sentence Structure / Grammar Usage						
Vocal Delivery Skills Voice / Volume / Rate / Vocal Variance						
Enthusiasm for Topic Passion/Energy						
Gestures						
Eye Contact						
Poise and Confidence						
Professional Appearance						

Speech Performance 100 possible points	Excellent 5 points	Good 4 points	Average 3 points	Fair 2 points	Poor 1 point	N/A 0 points
Movement Entrance to Stage Exit from Stage Movement on Stage						
Research Number of Sources Verbally Cited: ❏ ❏ ❏						
Research Verbal Citations Supported Topics: ❏ ❏ ❏						
Visual Aids Types Used: _____ Setting up Visual Aids Handling Visual Aids Design of Visual Aids Visibility of Visual Aids Management of Tech Team						
Handout Type Design Distribution of Handout						
Time of Speech Meets Minimum Time Exceeds Maximum Time						
Handling of Notes/Note Cards						

Suggestions/Comments

Special Occasion Speech

EVERYBODY LOVES A PARTY!

See how happy they are! This group of students just finished toasting each other and you can tell how much fun they had! There is always an abundance of laughter and mouths frozen into happy smiles as friends come together to celebrate! This is why we have special occasion speeches. Although there are many reasons and occasions for special occasion speeches, not all of them are the happy celebration that you see above. Some are more formal and subdued. Others are informal and spontaneous. Whether formal or informal, it is always a great opportunity to share your expertise at presenting a special occasion speech as long as you understand the occasion and make a presentation your audience will remember fondly!

Most special occasion speeches are not very lengthy. They are usually short and to the point, so they need to pack a punch! The words used during this type of speech need to be carefully chosen and precisely delivered to achieve the results that you want. Tribute speeches are delivered with dignity, grace, and sincerity. Ceremonial speeches will involve pomp and circumstance. Roasts and toasts can be delivered with humor. All special occasion speeches will take on the personality of the occasion. With this in mind, it is important that you understand the different types of special occasion speeches so you can choose the right one for your special occasion.

The three basic types are (1) work-related speeches, (2) ceremonial speeches, and (3) social occasion speeches. Most of these speeches will last three to seven minutes. A keynote address, eulogy, commencement, or commemoration could last between twenty to forty minutes. As with any speech, you should always check with the host who invites you to speak and ask for the time frame the host requires. A good rule to remember is that you should always end your speech before the final time that you are given. A three- to seven-minute speech should last five minutes. A twenty- to forty-minute speech should last no longer than thirty-five minutes.

Work-Related Speeches

- **Keynote Address:** Consider yourself a good speaker if you have been chosen to deliver the keynote address of a meeting or conference. This honor is usually reserved for established speakers with an impressive résumé. The first order of business is to establish a connection or bond with the audience and then welcome them to the event. Make sure that you thoroughly research the event, audience members, and organization sponsoring the event so that your speech will reflect the values, attitudes, beliefs, and behaviors of audience members. Choose a topic that will set the tone for the meeting or conference. Realizing the participants at this meeting or conference are already quite knowledgeable about the purpose for the gathering, your topic will need to be on-point to add to their existing knowledge and create value for each participant.

- **Announcement:** Regardless of the organization, you can bet there will be announcements delivered at each meeting. If asked to make the announcement, plan to deliver a brief explanation and address the announcement in a speech that is short and to the point. Having notes for this speech is a good idea so you do not leave out pertinent information which might lead to the need for a second announcement.

- **Public Relation:** This type of speech is made to inform the audience about aspects that are designed to improve a problem. It may deal with attendance, insurance changes, policy, procedure adjustments, or changes in protocol. This speaker will need to establish goodwill and a positive atmosphere prior to delivering the required information. It is important to set a stage that will encourage the audience to accept the information you are sharing. Public relation speeches are not always met with approval; therefore, it is important that you have the audience in your corner before giving the information needed.

- **Report:** The purpose of presenting a report is to communicate information to the audience. This information will not be entertaining and usually involves numbers, charts, and data as a vehicle for the information. Audience members will appreciate a visual aid to see a visual report in the form of charts or graphs as you provide the information. Keep your visual aids simple, but include all necessary material for a complete report. This report is short, to the point, and detail oriented.

- **Nomination:** Corporations and clubs that follow Roberts' Rules of Order will allow formal nominations to nominate people for positions or to make a motion to consider a change or alteration of a policy or procedure. This is usually not considered a formal speech, but will need to be treated as such as the person making the nomination will need to offer verbiage that is concise, clear, and complete.

Ceremonial Speeches

- **Installation:** Installations usually take place during a ceremony, but are also delivered in workplace situations. The purpose of this type speech is to install a person into a particular office or position. Once installed, the person who is installed will usually offer a few, well-chosen words of thanks to those who might have made the decision for the installation. This speech usually lasts two to three minutes.

- **Presenting an Award:** The actual presentation of an award is an extremely short speech. This involves referring to the occasion, acknowledging the contributions of the recipient, and then presenting the award with dignity and grace. This is a solemn presentation and care must be made to correctly name the award and to pronounce the recipient's name correctly.

- **Accepting an Award:** Often, the recipients of the awards will not know ahead of time that they are receiving an award. In this impromptu type situation, it is important that the recipient understand the gravity of the honor and accept the award in such a manner that the presenter of the award feels they made a good choice. The recipient should show sincere appreciation for receiving the award, delivering the acceptance speech with dignity and grace and should acknowledge the organization presenting the award. If advance notice is given, the recipient could add personal stories that led to the award and could thank individuals who contributed to the presentation of the award.

- **Dedication:** Dedication ceremonies happen at the birth of new babies, and for the opening of new buildings, parks, or monuments. This type speech is short and to the point. The person or object being dedicated is the focal point of the speech and allows those gathering to honor the occasion. The person chosen to present the dedication speech is usually someone quite close to the child being dedicated or to the organization or person who initiated the building, park, or monument. The speaker will need to establish a connection with the audience in the beginning before completing the formal dedication service.

- **Eulogy:** A eulogy is a ceremony delivered with the purpose of honoring or paying tribute to the deceased. Some people say they are *paying respects* to the person. Culture dictates how this speech presentation will be handled. The length of the speech will vary according to the culture of those attending and the circumstances for which the group has gathered. Often the speaker who has this task will recount personal experiences and stories of times spent with the person being honored.

- **Commemorative:** This type of ceremony is appropriate when a group wishes to celebrate a person or event and is most often delivered as a tribute speech. The speaker will need to emphasize people or history involved with the subject being commemorated. Accurate data and stories are necessary to present the information with dignity and honor. The speaker will need to correctly pronounce the person's name or the subject of the commemoration.

- **Commencement:** Everyone enjoys attending the graduation of a loved one, but no one enjoys a commencement speech that is long and boring! Therefore, it is important that the speech focuses on the actual event and those who are graduating, offers words of encouragement and motivational stories for the graduates, and keeps the speech short and to the point. It is a good idea to include research data and facts of positive employment trends that will give hope and encouragement to the graduates and their families.

I would like to propose a toast to all the SpeechSharks in our world!
To those of you who said you would never give a speech
and to those of you who are great at sharing your thoughts and feelings with others,
I invite ALL of you to raise your glasses high as I wish you ***oceans of success***.
May you be as stealthy and goal driven as a shark
and may all of your speeches be delivered with ease and finesse.
Cheers!

Social Occasion Speeches

- **Toast:** While not everyone at your event may drink alcohol, a toast is a wish that can be shared with everyone. Always make sure the glasses are filled prior to making the toast. Raise your glass to eye level as you present the toast. Plan your toast ahead of time making sure to put a great deal of thought into the sentiment so that it truly means something to the person you are honoring. Memorize the toast (it isn't cool to read notes at a toast). Acknowledge those present in the room and those who are not there to share the moment. Show emotion and passion for the moment. Keep

the toast short, light, and meaningful. As you finish, raise the glass above your head as a symbol of extending the wish.

- **Welcome:** This is another speech that could easily move over to the work-related speeches; however, it is also appropriate to list it with the social occasion speeches. The welcome speech is presented at the beginning of a social event. This should be used as a point to welcome those who are attending the event and should be short, light, and to the point. This also may be the time to introduce the agenda for the day and to introduce the next speaker or event on the agenda.

- **Farewell:** There are two different ways to offer a farewell speech. It can be presented by someone who is leaving or it can be presented by a person who is remaining and chooses this opportunity to honor the person who is leaving. It can be work-related or socially-related. Again, this is a speech that is offered in less than two minutes and offers regards with kindness, grace, and dignity. The farewell can also be delivered as a toast. There are lots of options here, but it is always important that it is brief and that every word is carefully chosen to say the things that need to be said.

- **Retirement:** There are distinct similarities with the farewell and the retirement speech, in that the speech can be presented by the person who is retiring or by a person from the organization who would like to honor the person who is retiring. This should be a short presentation that highlights the accomplishments of the person retiring and is delivered with kindness, grace, and dignity.

- **Roast:** Full disclaimer about this type of speech . . . we saved this one for last because it truly is one of our favorites. Also, this type speech is BEST when combined with a toast at the end of the roast. This type of speech has become quite popular recently and creates a stand-alone event where people attend just to hear and participate in the roast. Usually this type of gathering begins as a dinner and ends with the roast as the after-dinner entertainment. A traditional roast will involve several speakers and might focus on just one person or can focus on many people. Each speaker will take three to five minutes to roast the guest of honor and the purpose is to have lots of laughter. Research is not always necessary for this type of speech, but if research is used, please make sure that you correctly cite the source in the outline and include a Works Cited page to show the complete citation. My speech class always ends the semester with a roast followed by a toast. During the assignment, the students are asked to roast the people who are in their class. Often, they will roast the three or four people in their speech groups providing one funny item about each person; however, they can also choose to roast one person in the class and include three areas of humorous events about that one person. We tell the students that they have a full semester to gather material for the roast that is held the last day of class. The result is three hours of non-stop laughter and an opportunity for the classmates to bid farewell to each other. They all conclude their speech by ending with a well-designed toast to the person or persons that they just roasted.

Each special occasion speech should be planned according to the occasion where the speech will be presented. Since the roast and toast is our favorite special occasion speech, we will provide an example to help as you plan your next roast and toast! Use the Brainstorming Worksheet as you plan for your own special occasion speech!

Brainstorming Worksheet

Speech Category: Special Occasion Speech

Identify whether your speech will be work-related, ceremonial, or social: _____

Identify which category you will cover: _____

Speech Title: Give your speech a clever title: _____

Specific Purpose: Write a full sentence to show the purpose of your speech.

_____

Introduction:

Attention Step: Consider how you will get your audience's attention. Write all you plan to say using full sentences.

_____

Establish Need/Relevance: Explain why this topic should interest the listener. Write all you plan to say using full sentences.

_____

Establish Credibility: Explain why YOU are credible to speak about this topic. Write all you plan to say using full sentences.

_____

Thesis (Preview) Statement: Write a full sentence and clearly state the three points you will cover:

Point 1: _____

Point 2: _____

Point 3: _____

Body:

Transition Sentence: Write a full sentence to transition from the introduction step to the first main point.

_____

    I. **First Main Point:**
        A. **Sub-Point.**
        B. **Sub-Point.**

Transition Sentence: Write a full sentence to transition from the first main point to the second.

_____

    II. **Second Main Point**
        A. **Sub-Point.**
        B. **Sub-Point.**

Transition Sentence: Write a full sentence to transition from the second point to the third point.

_____

    III. **Second Main Point**
        A. **Sub-Point.**
        B. **Sub-Point.**

Transition Sentence: Write a full sentence to transition from the third main point to the conclusion.

_____

Conclusion:

Summary: Write a full sentence to summarize your three main points.

_____

Point 1: _____

Point 2: _____

Point 3: _____

Toast: Plan a toast to leave with your audience as you conclude the speech. Toasts can be original or you may use one that has been passed down for years and years. If you use a toast that has a copyright, be sure to cite the source and include a Works Cited page.

(NOTE: Place the Works Cited Page on a page separate from the outline).

Works Cited

Note: If you use visual aids, please include a Visual Aid Explanation Page
as a separate page following the Works Cited page.

Visual Aid Explanation Page

Outline Template

First Name/Last Name
Special Occasion Speech
Day Month Year

Speech Category: Special Occasion Speech
Title:
Purpose:

Introduction:
Attention Step:
Establish Need/Relevance:
Establish Speaker Credibility:

Thesis: Today, I want to share three points about (Topic): (1) _____,

(2) _____, and (3) _____.

Body:
Transition/Link: First, I will start at the beginning by sharing a little about (Point 1).
    I. First Main Point
        A. Sub-point
        B. Sub-point

Transition/Link: I've shared (Point 1) with you, now I'd like to tell you about (Point 2).
    II. Second Main Point
        A. Sub-point
        B. Sub-point

Transition/Link: You've heard about (Point 1 and Point 2), now I'll cover (Point 3).
    III. Third Main Point
        A. Sub-point
        B. Sub-point

Transition/Link: My purpose today was to (insert purpose and add a statement about the topic).
Conclusion:

Summary: Today, I shared with you three points: (1) Point 1 _____,

(2) Point 2 _____, and (3) Point 3 _____.

Appeal to Action: As I conclude this speech, (End with a BANG).

(NOTE: Place the Works Cited Page on a page separate from the outline).

Works Cited

*Note: If you use visual aids, please include a Visual Aid Explanation Page
as a separate page following the Works Cited page.*

Visual Aid Explanation Page

Example Outline

Penny J. Waddell
Roast and Toast
15 May 2017

Speech Category: Special Occasion Speech
Title: Out of the Frying Pan and Into the Fire: An Opportunity to ROAST my Students!
Purpose: The purpose of this speech is to roast and toast my speech students on the last day of class.

Introduction:
Attention Step: Have you ever opened the oven while you have potatoes roasting and felt the heat that comes from the oven? Well, that is nothing compared to the heat all of you might feel today as I take you out of the frying pan and throw you into the fire of an authentic speech roast and toast!
Establish Need/Relevance: We have spent 16 weeks together in the speech class and today will be our last class of the semester. This will be a perfect time for us to have fun with each other before we part ways.
Establish Speaker Credibility: Since I have had the pleasure of being your instructor this semester and I have graded every homework assignment, every speech, every outline, and every Chapter Quiz, I find myself completely qualified to roast and toast all of you today!
Thesis: There are three main points I would like to cover during this good-natured roast, (1) E-mails and frantic phone calls, (2) Outlines and visual aids, and (3) Speech day attire.

Body:
Transition/Link: Let's begin with the first point, e-mails and frantic phone calls the morning of speech assignments.
    I. E-mails and Frantic Phone Calls
        A. Yes, Students, due dates are due dates!
        B. All assignments are given to students the first day of class.
        C. Heartburn and Antacids are in your future, if you don't work ahead!

Transition/Link: I've shared stories of e-mails and frantic phone calls the morning of speech assignments, now I'd like to tell you about the Outlines and Visual Aids.
    II. Outlines and Visual Aids
        A. Outlines – Did you see the example I left for you in the textbook?
        B. Visual Aids – Are you going for "Hall of Fame" and "Hall of Shame"!

Transition/Link: You've heard about the e-mails and frantic phone calls the morning of speech assignments, the outlines and visual aids that I saw this semester, now, I would like to talk to you about the way you dressed for speeches.
    III. Speech Day Attire
        A. Yes, I would hire you, if you dress as if you are going to an interview.
        B. Oops, you are fired, if you show up in blue jeans, T-shirt that says, "Bite Me," and flip-flops!

Transition/Link: My purpose today was to Roast all of my speech students who gave speeches this semester that can only be defined as, "The Good, The Bad, and The Ugly"—No, Really, I would call them, "The Best Speeches I've Ever Heard!"

Conclusion:
Summary: Today, I shared with you three points: (1) E-mails and frantic phone calls, (2) Outlines and visual aids, and (3) Speech day attire.
Appeal to Action: I would like to propose a toast to all the SpeechSharks in this class! To those of you who said you would never give a speech and to those of you who are great at sharing your thoughts and feelings with others, I invite ALL of you to raise your glasses high as I wish you oceans of success. May you be as stealthy and goal driven as a shark and may all of your speeches be delivered with ease and finesse. Cheers!

(Note: Research was not used for this speech, so a Works Cited page was not necessary. The Visual Aids Explanation page is a separate page from the Outline).

Visual Aids Explanation Page

PowerPoint Presentation:
Slide 1:   Title of Speech—Out of the Frying Pan and Into the Fire
              Picture of the Class (Group)
Slide 2:   (Point 1): E-mails and Frantic Phone Calls
              Picture of Teacher at a Computer (hair frazzled and talking on the phone)
Slide 3:   (Point 2): Outlines and Visual Aids
              Picture of the Textbook
Slide 4:   (Point 3): Speech Day Attire
              Picture of Professionally Dressed Student/Picture of a Student in Jeans and Flip-Flops
Slide 5:   Picture—Champagne Glasses Raised in a TOAST with the word—CHEERS!

SPECIAL OCCASION SPEECH EVALUATION WORKSHEET
Instructor's Copy for Grading the Speech

Speaker's Name: _____   Title of Speech: _____

Time of Speech: _____   Date: _____

Grade: _____

Speech Performance 100 possible points	Excellent 5 points	Good 4 points	Average 3 points	Fair 2 points	Poor 1 point	N/A 0 points
Introduction Step Attention Step						
Establish Need/Relevance Establish Credibility						
Thesis (Preview 3 Points)						
Body Point 1 Direct Support of Point						
Point 2 Direct Support of Point						
Point 3 Direct Support of Point						
Transitions (4) To First Point To Second Point To Third Point To Conclusion						
Conclusion Summary (Review 3 Points)						
Closing Statements						
Language Skills Vocabulary Filler Words Sentence Structure Grammar Usage						
Vocal Delivery Skills Voice Volume Rate Vocal Variance						
Enthusiasm for Topic Passion/Energy						
Gestures						
Eye Contact						
Poise and Confidence						

Speech Performance 100 possible points	Excellent 5 points	Good 4 points	Average 3 points	Fair 2 points	Poor 1 point	N/A 0 points
Professional Appearance						
Movement Entrance to Stage Exit from Stage Movement on Stage						
Research (If Required) Source Verbally Cited and Supported Points ❑ ❑						
Time of Speech Meets Minimum Time Exceeds Maximum Time						
Handling of Notes/Note Cards						

Suggestions/Comments

Group Presentation

The task of presenting a group presentation is not always met with enthusiasm. That is because most of us have had the experience of working with a group and doing a majority of the group work on our own to make sure the project was completed on time and in good shape. We often think of group projects gone south when we think of group work in college. However, I can assure you that group work can also be a struggle in the corporate world. We wanted to cover group presentations in this book because you will be met with this task more often than you would like and it is a good idea to understand what is involved with a group presentation!

Everyone in a group is unique. That can be a bonus for your presentation, if you are able to use the strengths present within your group. As with any presentation, you should conduct an audience analysis, consider the purpose of the presentation and develop a topic that will enhance the knowledge of your audience members.

There are advantages for presenting a project as a group presentation. First, realize that you cannot possibly know everything. Working with a group will allow the opportunity to expand the knowledge base and will cause you to add to your own knowledge of the subject your group will be covering.

Avoid disagreements regarding the division of labor by verbally acknowledging the value brought to the group by your group members. This also builds a feeling of teamwork among group members and fosters collaboration for the project.

Brainstorming is always much more effective when you can include more brains! This will also cause more active discussions to erupt which in turn will spark more ideas for the topic. Since each group is unique and there are many diverse cultures and thoughts present in a group, this will allow the group to incorporate different speech styles during the presentation.

Finally, speakers who are a bit shy usually feel more confident when they realize they are not alone on the stage making a presentation, but surrounded by their peers who are working together for a positive result.

Use this checklist when planning a Group Presentation:

Things to Consider	Explanation
Know Group Members	☐ Introduce yourself to the group. ☐ Exchange names and contact information. ☐ Discover strengths and weaknesses of group members. ☐ Determine a meeting schedule that works with everyone. ☐ Record information and distribute it to group members.
Discuss Group Expectations	☐ Ask questions. Answer questions. ☐ Divide tasks equally among group members. ☐ Be realistic with due dates and job responsibilities. ☐ Indicate group member responsibilities. ☐ Exercise accountability/responsibility duties. ☐ Establish consequences if a group member does not follow through.
Understand the Task	☐ Research the topic. ☐ Learn the time requirement for the presentation. ☐ Know what is expected. Do you need a visual aid? ☐ Do you need handouts? ☐ Create a timetable for responsibilities. ☐ What order will group members speak? ☐ Is there a Question/Answer segment during the presentation? ☐ Will you have a group moderator to introduce and conclude the speech? ☐ How will you be evaluated?
Respect Diversity	☐ Keep an open mind for other ideas. ☐ Encourage members to speak without reservation. ☐ Allow opportunities for members to interject opinions for the project.
Communicate Effectively	☐ Use effective listening skills. ☐ Speak clearly and make yourself heard. ☐ Ask for clarification, if you do not understand something. ☐ Use positive communication skills with group members.
Rehearsals	☐ Plan rehearsal dates. ☐ Rehearse together as a group. ☐ Assign a Tech Team member to manage the visual aids. ☐ Assign a Tech Team member to distribute handouts. ☐ Rehearse using visual aids for the presentation.

During the presentation, there is a protocol that should be followed. Here is the plan to follow for a group presentation:

1. **Moderator:** The moderator will open with an attention step, establish a need/relevance for the group presentation topic, establish speaker credibility for the group by introducing each speaker (first name and last name) and provide a clear thesis and list a brief description of each main point identifying the group member designated to cover. The moderator will then transition to the first speaker by again stating the speaker's first and last name along with the topic they will cover. *One thing to note: the moderator will be responsible to keep the presentation flowing. If at any time there is an awkward moment, the moderator has the responsibility of keeping the presentation advancing in a positive direction.*

2. **Speaker 1:** The first speaker will thank the moderator for the introduction and then will proceed to cover the main point. This will include an introduction, body, and conclusion of the point. Speaker 1 will then transition to the second speaker by stating the speaker's first and last name along with the topic the second speaker will cover.

3. **Speaker 2:** The second speaker will thank Speaker 1 for the introduction and then will proceed to cover the next main point. This will include an introduction, body, and conclusion of the point. Speaker 2 will then transition to the third speaker by stating the speaker's first and last name along with the topic the third speaker will cover.

4. **Speaker 3:** The third speaker will thank Speaker 2 for the introduction and then will proceed to cover the next main point. This will include an introduction, body, and conclusion of the point. Speaker 3 will then transition to the fourth speaker. If there is not a fourth speaker, then Speaker 3 will transition back to the Moderator using his or her first and last name.

5. **Moderator:** The Moderator will thank the last speaker and will proceed to summarize the three main points covered listing each Speaker's first and last name with the summary. Next, the Moderator will open the floor for a question and answer session. During the Q&A, the Moderator is responsible for keeping the conversation flowing, directing questions to different group members, and making sure that not one member monopolizes the conversation. If questions from the audience are all directed to one or two members, the Moderator can call for the audience that may have a question for the Speaker who has not been questioned. After a few questions and answers, the Moderator can then close the Q&A and thank the audience for their attention as they discussed the topic and participated in the Q&A session. Finally, the Moderator will again thank the group speakers, one at a time before closing the speech with a prepared appeal to action, which should be designed to keep the audience thinking about the group presentation topic.

NOTE: Research will be needed to support the individual points. The Moderator and each of the Group Speakers are responsible for conducting research to provide credible support of the points covered. Personal stories and personal experiences are also very helpful to support the points and to bring in a personal touch regarding the topic.

For a group presentation to be successful, the group needs to work together as a cohesive unit to make one presentation. They should choose a topic with the audience in mind, make a plan to achieve the purpose, decide on tasks and work divisions, create visual aids and handouts, set times for completion dates, individually work on identified tasks which includes research for the point to which the group member is assigned, evaluate progress, rehearse as a group and then of course, present the group presentation.

Group Presentations may not be the easiest presentations on the schedule, but they can be very effective because the group has different levels of knowledge about the topic and can also bring diverse thoughts and ideas to the table for discussion.

How does the Moderator Handle the Question and Answer Sessions?

The way the Moderator handles the Q&A session will have a direct impact on the success of the group presentation. First, ask the audience members who want to ask a question to stand, identify themselves by first and last name, and then direct the question to a specific group member. The audience member should remain standing while the question is answered. Following the delivery of the answer, the audience member should thank the group member and then take a seat.

Group members should make sure the audience member has finished asking the question before they begin to answer the question. A good rule of thumb is to thank the audience member for the question and then repeat the question as mental preparation before answering. This step is important because it will mean that the group member will be answering the question that was asked. It also gives the speaker a moment to formulate the answer that will be given. After the question is answered, the speaker should say to the audience member, "I hope this has answered your question." The audience member can give a verbal or nonverbal response prior to sitting down so that the next question can be asked. Depending upon the time allotted for the Group Presentation, the Moderator can choose to take three to five questions or more.

The Question and Answer (Q&A) Session takes on the model of an impromptu speech. As the group member responds to unrehearsed questions and attempts to further add knowledge regarding the point, it is great to use the PREP model that is reserved for impromptu speeches and interview type situations. Here is how you PREP to prepare for any question!

P.R.E.P.

P = Point. Restate the question asked because that is the POINT. As you restate the question, it helps you to hear the question again and formulate the answer in your mind. Before you answer the question, be sure to follow the next step!

R = Relevance. Thank the person who asked the question for asking the question. Then, explain why the question is important because that is the RELEVANCE. After you cover the importance, then it is time to answer the question.

E = Example. Give a clear EXAMPLE as a follow-up to the answer of your question to make sure the audience has an understanding of the POINT. There is only one thing left to do, now!

P = Point. All good speeches will offer a summary and an impromptu speech requires the same. As you conclude, be sure to restate the question because that is the POINT and ask if you completely answered their question. If you get a head-nod or an affirmation, then you are good to go!

Group presentations involve brainstorming and constructing an outline as a group. All group members should be involved with this process as you work together to determine the topic, the main points, and group member assignments. Consult with your instructor to confirm requirements regarding research, visual aids, and benchmark due dates.

A quick look at the outline template will reveal that this outline looks different from other speech outlines you have used. Typically, each group member should conduct research for their own section of the presentation. Setting due dates will ensure all group members have their part of the presentation outline completed in time to design and create visual aids for the presentation. Due dates also help group members to be prepared for rehearsals prior to the presentation. Now, let's get ready to brainstorm a winning group presentation!

Brainstorming Worksheet

Speech Category: Group Presentation

Identify Group Members:

Moderator: _____

Group Member 1: _____

Group Member 2: _____

Group Member 3: _____

Speech Title: Give your speech a clever title _____

Specific Purpose: Write a full sentence to show the purpose of your speech.

_____

Introduction—This will be covered by the Moderator: _____

Attention Step: Consider how you will get your audience's attention. Write all you plan to say using full sentences.

Establish Need/Relevance: Explain why this topic should interest the listener. Write all you plan to say using full sentences.

Establish Credibility: Explain why the group is credible to speak about this topic. Write all you plan to say using full sentences. Introduce each group member and establish their credentials.

Thesis (Preview) Statement: Write a full sentence that clearly states the three points you will cover:

_____

Point 1: Name of Group Member and The Point to be Covered: _____

Point 2: Name of Group Member and The Point to be Covered: _____

Point 3: Name of Group Member and The Point to be Covered: _____

Body:

Transition Sentence: Write a full sentence to transition from the introduction step to the first main point.

    I. **First Main Point (Covered by Name of Group Member):**
         A. Sub-Point.
         B. Sub-Point.

Transition Sentence: Write a full sentence to transition from the first main point to the second.

    II. **Second Main Point (Covered by Name of Group Member):**
         A. Sub-Point.
         B. Sub-Point.

Transition Sentence: Write a full sentence to transition from the second point to the third point.

    III. **Third Main Point (Covered by Name of Group Member):**
         A. Sub-Point.
         B. Sub-Point.

Transition Sentence: Write a full sentence to transition from the third main point to the conclusion.

Conclusion—This will be covered by the Moderator

Summary: Write in full sentence format a summary of your three main points. Identify the name of each Group Member covering each point.

Point 1: _____

Point 2: _____

Point 3: _____

Moderator: Opens the floor for the Question and Answer Session.

Moderator: Concludes the speech with appreciation and a wrap-up: _____

(NOTE: Place the Works Cited Page on a page separate from the outline).

Works Cited

*Note: If you use visual aids, please include a Visual Aid Explanation Page
as a separate page following the Works Cited page.*

Visual Aid Explanation Page

Outline Template

Group Name 1

List All Group Members' Names Alphabetically
First Name/Last Name
Group Presentation
Day Month Year

Speech Category: Group Presentation
Title:
Purpose:

Introduction:
Attention Step:
Establish Need/Relevance:
Establish Speaker Credibility: Introduce each group member by first and last name.

Thesis: Today, I want to share three points about (Topic): (1) _____,

(2) _____, and (3) _____.

Body:
Transition/Link: First, I will start at the beginning by sharing a little about (Point 1).
    I. First Main Point—Presented by _____
        A. Sub-point
        B. Sub-point

Transition/Link: I've shared (Point 1) with you, now I'd like to tell you about (Point 2).
    II. Second Main Point—Presented by _____
        A. Sub-point
        B. Sub-point

Transition/Link: You've heard about (Point 1 and Point 2), now I'll cover (Point 3).
    III. Third Main Point—Presented by _____
        A. Sub-point
        B. Sub-point

Transition/Link: My purpose today was to (insert purpose and add a statement about the topic).
Conclusion:
Summary: Today, I shared with you three points—include each group member's name:

(1) Point 1_____, (2) Point 2 _____, and

(3) Point 3 _____.
Appeal to Action: As I conclude this speech, (End with a BANG).

(NOTE: Place the Works Cited Page on a page separate from the outline).

Works Cited

*Note: If you use visual aids, please include a Visual Aid Explanation Page
as a separate page following the Works Cited page.*

Visual Aid Explanation Page

Example Outline

Group 5

Ruth Joyner, Charles Hardnett, Bonnie Smith, Penny Waddell, Cassandra West
Group Presentation
1 August 2019

Speech Category: Group Presentation
Title: Preparing Students for Success
Purpose: The purpose of this group presentation is to provide the audience with useful tips to prepare students for the workplace.

Introduction: (Presented by the Moderator: Ruth Joyner)
Attention Step: Would you like to take your students from stress to success? How about from scared to prepared?
Establish Need/Relevance: Student success is a relevant topic as we all work to prepare students for the workforce. It is important, as educators, that you hear this presentation and learn tips for student success.
Establish Speaker Credibility: Realizing that experience is the best teacher, we have compiled a group of instructors with practical and experiential knowledge from elementary, middle, high school, and college settings.
Thesis: Today, I want to share four points about preparing students for success: (1) Charles Hardnett will share information about Time Management Skills, (2) Bonnie Smith will talk about Teamwork, (3) Penny Waddell will be covering Effective Communication Skills, and (4) Cassandra West will explore Cooperation.

Body: (Each point will be covered by an assigned group member)

Transition/Link: First, Charles Hardnett will share tips for Time Management Skills.
  I. **(Presented by Charles Hardnett) Time Management Skills**
     A. Managing Time
     B. Setting Priorities

Transition/Link: I've shared tips to encourage Time Management, now Bonnie Smith will tell how to foster Teamwork.
  II. **(Presented by Bonnie Smith) Teamwork**
     A. T.E.A.M. Acronym
     B. Tips for Teams

Transition/Link: You've heard about Teamwork, now Penny Waddell will cover effective Communication Skills.
  III. **(Presented by Penny Waddell) Communication Skills**
     A. Verbal Communication Skills
     B. Nonverbal Communication Skills

Transition/Link: Verbal and Nonverbal Communication Skills are essential for success, now Cassandra West will cover tips to encourage Cooperation.
  IV. **(Presented by Cassandra West) Cooperation**
     A. Respect Peers and Management
     B. Develop a "Do Whatever It Takes" Attitude

Transition/Link: Our purpose today was to share information with you to help you prepare students for success. At this time, I will relinquish the stage back to our Moderator, Ruth Joyner.
Conclusion: (Presented by the Moderator: Ruth Joyner)

Summary: Today, we shared with you four important work ethic skills to help your students find success: (1) Charles Hardnett shared information about Time Management Skills, (2) Bonnie Smith talked about Teamwork, (3) Penny Waddell covered Effective Communication Skills, and (4) Cassandra West helped us explore Cooperation.

Question and Answer Session: At this time, we would like to invite the audience to participate in a Question and Answer Session. Please stand to be recognized, provide your full name, address the group member by name and ask your question. (The Moderator will call on audience members one at a time and will conclude the session according to an established time by saying...) That is all the time we have for questions tonight. Thank you for attending. If you have further questions, please contact any of our group members by using the contact information supplied in your program. We challenge you to take your students from scared to prepared and from stress to success by encouraging strong work ethic skills in the classroom and in the workforce!

> **NOTE: For this outline example, research was not used; therefore, a Works Cited page is not included. However, if you do use research for your own group presentation, please add parenthetical citations in the outline and a Works Cited page following the outline on a separate page.**

The same is true if you use visual aids for a group presentation. Add a separate page that details the visual aids you plan to use and a description of each.

GROUP PRESENTATION EVALUATION WORKSHEET
Instructor's Copy for Grading the Speech

Speaker's Name: _____   Title of Speech: _____

Time of Speech: _____   Date: _____

Grade: _____

Speech Performance 100 possible points	Excellent 5 points	Good 4 points	Average 3 points	Fair 2 points	Poor 1 point	N/A 0 points
Introduction Step Attention Step Establish Need/Relevance Establish Credibility						
Thesis (Preview 3 Points)						
Body Point 1 Direct Support of Point						
Point 2 Direct Support of Point						
Point 3 Direct Support of Point						
Transitions (4) To First Point To Second Point To Third Point To Conclusion						
Conclusion Summary (Review 3 Points)						
Closing Statements						
Language Skills Vocabulary Filler Words Sentence Structure Grammar Usage						
Vocal Delivery Skills Voice Volume Rate Vocal Variance						
Enthusiasm for Topic Passion/Energy						
Gestures						
Eye Contact						
Poise and Confidence						
Professional Appearance						

Speech Performance 100 possible points	Excellent 5 points	Good 4 points	Average 3 points	Fair 2 points	Poor 1 point	N/A 0 points
Movement Entrance to Stage Exit from Stage Movement on Stage						
Research (If Required) Source Verbally Cited and Supported Points ❑ ❑						
Visual Aids (If Required) Types Used: _____ Setting up Visual Aids Handling Visual Aids Design of Visual Aids Visibility of Visual Aids Management of Tech Team						
Time of Speech Meets Minimum Time Exceeds Maximum Time						
Handling of Notes/Note Cards *Note: If research and visual aids are not required by the instructor, add the following point(s)* **Presentation** Cohesive Teamwork Audience Engagement						
Q&A Session Moderator Managed Session Questions Divided between Members Audience Participation Encouraged						

Suggestions/Comments

Sales Presentation

Sales Presentations follow much of the same strategies as persuasion speeches; therefore, we suggest that you review the persuasion speech section in this book. Pay close attention to the section about motivation. The purpose of your sales pitch is to motivate the audience to purchase an item or service that you are selling! To do this you will need to motivate and influence **values, beliefs, attitudes, or behaviors**.

Consumers today are quite different from consumers in the past and the sales force has changed from strictly face-to-face interactions to include Internet, telephone, videos, photographs, and social media. If you truly want to be a great salesperson, you will soon realize the importance of walking a fine line to create a balance between being persuasive, but not too pushy. This takes planning and practice. Once you can establish a solid strategy that works for your personality, then you will begin to close more deals.

Here are proven strategies to help you find success in sales:

1. **Identify the decision maker:** Whether you are making a sales pitch to a company or to a couple, you must first know the person that will ultimately make the decision to buy. Once you identify the decision maker, you can customize your sales presentation to the person. This is where it is important to use good listening skills. Listen carefully to understand the needs of the individual or the corporation so that you can provide what the customer needs.

2. **Care for the best interest of the customer:** Instead of working hard to sell the one product your boss is pushing, try to provide the product or service that your customer truly needs. Let the customer know that you care about their business and that your first priority is to help them solve the problem they are having by providing the product or service they need. The "deal" should not be more important to you than their satisfaction with the product or service. This is the way to foster repeat customers.

3. **Identify the deadline:** Again, you need to be a good listener. When do they need this product or service? Does your organization have a special price deal that is or will be available for the product or service they need? Can you help them make the right choice at the right time to save money or time?

4. **Overcome obstacles:** This is the time to focus on the problem which is motivating customers to make this purchase. Do they need to purchase the car you are selling by a certain date to meet a deadline? Is this a seasonal purchase? What potential objections might slow down the decision-making process? What questions or concerns may the customer have? If you can think ahead to prepare for problems or obstacles that could slow down or stop the sale, then you will have time to find a solution and close the sale!

5. **Know your competitors:** Depending upon the product or service you will be selling, you should understand that competition can be tough! Why is your product superior, less expensive, or more effective than the competition? If you want to make the sale, you need to conduct research on any competitors that might waltz in and take your business. Take time to prepare your sales presentation, conduct research to learn about any and all markets that may stand in your way, and make sure that you are providing something that your competitor will not, such as customer service and care for your customer. It has been proven time and again that customers return to the same salesperson if they feel like the salesperson has their best interest at heart.

6. **Create a positive reputation:** Say what you mean and mean what you say! If you tell your customer you will do something, make sure you do it. Even if it is a simple phone call to provide additional information. Make sure your conversations stay on the product or service that the customer wants. Customers don't want to hear about your problems, your bad cold, or your car that will not start. The customer is there because they are in the market for a product or service that your organization may be able to provide. They are not there to visit. Keep conversations professional and to the point. Create a reputation of caring for your customers, having their best interest at heart, and making the sales transaction a fast and enjoyable experience.

7. **Close the Sale:** Do you remember the Kenny Rogers song with the lyrics, "You've got to know when to hold 'em, know when to fold 'em, know when to walk away, know when to run!"? I wouldn't advise singing this song out loud around your customers, but it is good advice. If you are an effective listener, then you will know your customer's deadline for purchasing the product or service you represent and you should know when to make the pitch, when to back off and let the customer consider what you have shared, and then know when to provide a sense of urgency to purchase the product or service. Many salespeople are not successful because they simply do not know how to close the sale. A good salesperson will tell you that closing the sale is a matter of knowing when to encourage the customer to make the decision. The customer has a problem to solve. You can solve the problem with the product or service your organization provides. It is your job to convince the customer that the money charged is a deal and the time to purchase is now.

Here are some good phrases to use as a closer:

- If our company can provide a solution to your problem, would you make this purchase?
- When would you like to get started?
- Is there anything I can do to help you with this decision?
- It looks like we have two options for what you need. Would you prefer to choose A or B?
- It is against our policy to push an item on a customer that they really do not need; however, it appears that this (product or service) has exactly what you are looking for and the price is competitive with all others on the market. Are you ready to complete the paperwork?
- During our first meeting, you mentioned that you needed this product or service by July 1st. If you make this decision by Friday of this week, we will be able to meet your deadline and help solve your problem. Does this date sound like something to which you can commit?
- Are you ready to get started? I'll be happy to start the paperwork.
- We have a special price on this product or service that will begin next Monday. Do you want me to save that price for you?

Closing strategies are important, but there are no magic words or phrases that will work every time. That is why you must begin by listening to your potential customer and help the customer identify needs, wants, budget, and deadline to purchase the product or service.

Be a SpeechShark and not a sales shark! There are differences. No one enjoys a slicked-up salesperson whose only concern is the commission they will put in their own pocket. When it is time to make a purchase, customers want an honest salesperson who has their best interest in mind and will help them search to find the right product at the right price and available at the right time. If the buyer agrees to the purchase, congratulate the customer for making the right decision and wish them well as they begin using the new product or service. If the buyer does not make a purchase, kindly thank them for their time and offer to meet again to further explain your company's products or services. The goal is to be courteous, not pushy! Now, that is a sales strategy that will win every time and you will enjoy the benefits of having repeat customers!

Use the Sales Presentation Brainstorming Worksheet to help create your best sales pitch.

Brainstorming Worksheet

Speech Category: Sales Presentation

Speech Title: Give your speech a clever title _____

Specific Purpose: Write a full sentence to show the purpose of your presentation—what are you trying to sell?

Introduction:

Attention Step: Consider how you will get your customer's attention. Write all you plan to say using full sentences.

Establish Need/Relevance: Explain why this product or service should interest the customer. Write all you plan to say using full sentences.

Establish Credibility: Explain why YOU are credible to sell this product or service. Write all you plan to say using full sentences.

Thesis (Preview) Statement: Write a complete sentence that clearly states the three points you will cover:

_____

Point 1: Describe the problem with the product or service the customer has now:

_____

Point 2: Identify the new product or service that will solve the customer's problem:

_____

Point 3: Visualization of the results of solving the problem or the consequences if the problem is NOT solved:

_____

Body:

Transition Sentence: Write a full sentence to transition from the introduction step to the first main point.

    I. **The Problem:**
       A. **Discuss the problem they are having.**
         1. **Support the problem with research.**
         2. **Support the problem with examples.**
       B. **Explore the need for purchasing the new product or service.**
         1. **Identify who or what is negatively affected by this problem.**
         2. **Use logical and emotional Appeals.**

Transition Sentence: Write a full sentence to transition from the first main point to the second.

    II. **Solution to the Problem—the product or service you plan to sell:**
       A. **Offer a realistic, detailed explanation of the product or service as a solution to the problem.**
         1. **Explain how the customer can help to solve the problem.**
         2. **Provide examples and research to support your solution.**
       B. **Does your solution solve the problem?**
         1. **Does your solution affect values, beliefs, attitudes, and behaviors?**
         2. **Use logical and emotional Appeals.**

Transition Sentence: Write a full sentence to transition from the second point to the third point.

    III. **Visualization of Results**
       A. **Describe the benefits of using the new product or service.**
         1. **Does it answer questions of value?**
         2. **Use descriptions to help audience members visualize benefits.**
       B. **Consequences if the product or service is not purchased**
         1. **Use imagery to show the consequences of not purchasing the product or service.**
         2. **Use examples and descriptions.**

Transition Sentence: Write a full sentence to transition from the third main point to the conclusion.

Conclusion:

Summary: Write in full sentence format a summary of your three main points.

Point 1: The Problem _____

Point 2: The Solution to the Problem _____

Point 3: Visualization of Results _____

Appeal to Action: Leave your customer challenged to purchase the product or service and CLOSE THE SALE!

(NOTE: Place the Works Cited Page on a page separate from the outline).

Works Cited

Note: If you use visual aids, please include a Visual Aid Explanation Page as a separate page following the Works Cited page.

Visual Aid Explanation Page

Outline Template

First Name/Last Name
Group Presentation
Day Month Year

Speech Category: Sales Presentation
Title:
Purpose:

Introduction:
Attention Step:
Establish Need/Relevance:
Establish Credibility:

Thesis: Today, As you consider making this purpose, first consider these points: (1) _____,

(2) _____, and (3) _____.

Body:

Transition/Link: First, let's begin with (Point 1).
   I. **First Main Point**—The problem with the existing product or service.
      A. Sub-point—examples/research
      B. Sub-point—examples/research

Transition/Link: I've shared (Point 1) with you, now I'd like to tell you about (Point 2).
   II. **Second Main Point**—Identify the new product or service that will solve the customer's problem.
      A. Sub-point—values, beliefs, attitudes, behaviors
      B. Sub-point—logical and emotional appeals

Transition/Link: You've heard about (Point 1 and Point 2), now I'll cover (Point 3).
   III. **Third Main Point**—Visualization of results
      A. Sub-point—benefits of using the new product or services
      B. Sub-point—consequences of not using the new product or services

Transition/Link: My purpose today is to give you information about (Topic).
Conclusion:
Summary: Today, I shared with you three important points about (Topic):

(1) Point 1_____, (2) Point 2 _____, and

(3) Point 3 _____.

Closing the Sale: End with a strong appeal/closing statement.

(NOTE: Place the Works Cited Page on a page separate from the outline).

Works Cited

*Note: If you use visual aids, please include a Visual Aid Explanation Page
as a separate page following the Works Cited page.*

Visual Aid Explanation Page

SALES PRESENTATION EVALUATION WORKSHEET
Instructor's Copy for Grading the Speech

Speaker's Name: _____ Title of Speech: _____

Time of Speech: _____ Date: _____

Grade: _____

Speech Performance 100 possible points	Excellent 5 points	Good 4 points	Average 3 points	Fair 2 points	Poor 1 point	N/A 0 points
Introduction Step Attention Step						
Establish Need/Relevance Establish Credibility						
Thesis (Preview 3 Points)						
Body Point 1—Problem with existing product or service Direct Support of Point						
Point 2—New product or service that will solve the problem Direct Support of Point						
Point 3—Benefits of using new product or service Direct Support of Point						
Transitions (4) To First Point To Second Point To Third Point To Conclusion						
Conclusion Summary (Review 3 Points)						
Closing Statements						
Language Skills Vocabulary Filler Words Sentence Structure Grammar Usage						
Vocal Delivery Skills Voice Volume Rate Vocal Variance						
Enthusiasm for Topic Passion/Energy						
Gestures						

Speech Performance 100 possible points	Excellent 5 points	Good 4 points	Average 3 points	Fair 2 points	Poor 1 point	N/A 0 points
Eye Contact						
Poise						
Confidence						
Professional Appearance						
Movement 　Entrance to Stage 　Exit from Stage 　Movement on Stage						
Time of Speech 　Meets Minimum Time 　Exceeds Maximum Time						
Handling of Notes/Note Cards						

Suggestions/Comments

Types of Speeches

After reading this chapter, you will be able to answer the following questions:

1. What are the three basic purposes/types of speeches? _____

   _____

   _____

2. What are informative speeches? _____

   _____

   _____

3. What are entertaining speeches? _____

   _____

   _____

4. What are motivational speeches? _____

   _____

   _____

5. What is a good organizational strategy for introducing yourself? _____

   _____

   _____

6. What is an informative speech often called? _____

   _____

   _____

7. When would you choose to present a demonstration speech? _____

_____

_____

8. What three points should be covered in a demonstration speech? _____

_____

_____

9. What are the four areas you might consider influencing during a persuasion speech? _____

_____

_____

10. Explain values: _____

_____

_____

11. Explain beliefs: _____

_____

_____

12. Explain attitudes: _____

_____

_____

13. Explain behaviors: _____

_____

_____

14. Explain pathos: _____

_____

_____

15. Explain ethos: _____

_____

_____

16. Explain logos: _____

_____

_____

17. Who developed the Motivated Sequence Theory? _____

_____

_____

18. What three main points should be covered when using the Motivated Sequence Theory?

_____

_____

19. List the types of work-related speeches: _____

_____

_____

20. List the types of ceremonial speeches: _____

_____

_____

21. List the types of social occasion speeches: _____

_____

_____

22. What are six things to consider when involved with planning a group presentation?

_____

_____

23. Who conducts the question and answer session of a group presentation? _____

_____

_____

24. What strategy works best for a sales presentation? _____

_____

_____

25. List seven strategies important for making the sale: _____

_____

_____

26. What special occasion speech would you most enjoy presenting? _____

_____

_____

27. What special occasion speech would you least enjoy presenting? _____

_____

_____

28. What is a one-point outline and when would you use this? _____

_____

_____

Shark Bites

BRAINSTORMING A TOPIC

Let's work on a Clustering and Webbing strategy to help you brainstorm your next speech. Start with the speech topic. What three points will you cover? How will you begin the speech? How will you close the speech? Brainstorm the speech organization by filling in each bubble or use your new SpeechShark app to do this for you!

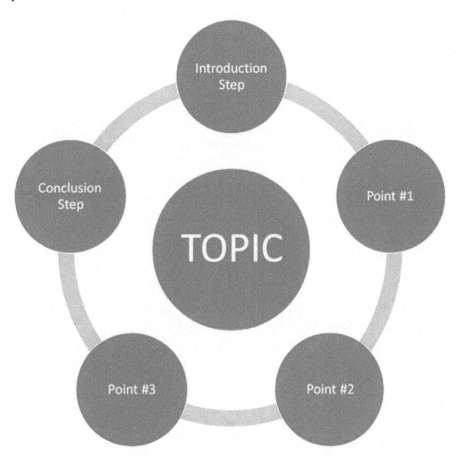

Chapter Four
Specialty Speeches

In this chapter:

What are TED Talks?

What are PechaKucha Presentations?

What do I need to know about Competitive Speaking?

How do I present a Humorous Speech?

Specialty Speeches are in a league of their own and involve situations that may require unique preparation strategies and varied delivery skills. This chapter will highlight several types of speaking opportunities that do not fit the descriptions of other speech types traditionally covered; however, these are presentations commonly found and enjoyed. There are as many different types of specialty speeches as there are different types of sharks in the ocean, but we will attempt to highlight just a few that many of you enjoy on a regular basis. The purpose of most specialty speeches is to provide the audience with something they may not be expecting, yet will produce the end result of reaching your speaking goals.

TED Talks

You've all heard about TED Talks. You watch them on your phone while waiting for an appointment to begin. You share them with your friends when you see a topic you think they will find interesting. You dream that one

day YOU will give your very own TED Talk. But, what do you really know about it? It is my belief that Speech-Sharks should know everything there is to know about speaking and speaking opportunities, so I would be remiss if I didn't include a segment here about TED Talks.

TED is an acronym that stands for **T**echnology, **E**ntertainment, and **D**esign. This organization first began as a method for delivering brief speeches (talks) about great ideas in a conference setting. Since that time, it has grown so that annual conferences are now held throughout the world. These days the topics are unlimited and include a way to share research, ideas, and stories to bring home a point. Speakers may include names that you would recognize along with Nobel Prize winners and speakers that you may never have heard of before the moment that you watch their TED Talk. Thousands of TED Talks are available to view online and many have been watched hundreds or thousands of times by viewers all over the world. Each TED Talk can last up to eighteen minutes and the speakers are challenged to share their ideas in the most engaging way possible. Many choose to use storytelling as their method.

TEDx conferences are like TED Talk conferences, but they can be organized by folks who obtain a free license from TED and agree to follow the TED basic principles. Since both groups are non-profit, they rely upon admission fees or conference fees to cover the costs of renting the venues, staging, lights, sound, tech crews, and all of the other expenses that go into operating a conference. There is also a division called TED-MED which focuses on the medical field, but it doesn't stop there. We can purchase TED Books, join TEDEd Clubs, attend conferences for TEDWomen, and participate in smaller events called TED Salon or listen to podcasts from the TED Radio Hour. If that isn't enough, you can also listen to TED Talks for Kids! To look through the different talks that have happened recently and in the past, please check out their website at https://www.ted.com/talks.

Yesterday I watched Richard J. Berry's "A practical way to help the homeless find work and safety" at: https://www.ted.com/talk/richard_j_berry_a_practical_way_to_help_the_homeless_find_work_and_safety/up-next. This is a short talk that could very well change your community! Think for a moment about this. If Mr. Berry gave this speech for his senior citizens monthly meeting in Albuquerque, New Mexico, only fifty people might have heard his message. But since he gave this speech as a TED Talk, thousands and thousands have heard this story about his idea to help the homeless and there is no telling how many lives his story might have changed. We already know that several other states are implementing the same experiment that Mr. Berry tried in his town.

Mr. Berry asks at the end of his speech, "Who is next?" (Berry). He is talking, of course, about his idea of helping the homeless, but I am going to ask YOU, "Who is next?" Could YOU be the next person to share your own ideas or thoughts through a TED Talk?

If that isn't enough, try watching Becky Blanton's "The year I was homeless," TED talk with over a million views at: https://www.ted.com/talks/becky_blanton_the_year_i_was_homeless/up-next.

Ms. Blanton is simply telling her story, but as she tells her story to millions of people during a TED Talk on the Internet, Ms. Blanton is able to deliver the moral of her story—her message—"People are not where they live. People are not where they sleep. People are not where their life situation is at any time . . . Hope always finds a way!" (Blanton).

As a speech instructor and speech coach, I've watched many, many TED Talks throughout the years and I've enjoyed them all. I may not have always agreed with the speaker's point of view, but I always learned something from each one. Often, I will refer various TED Talks to my students or co-workers. I'm sure you have done the same thing. If you've never watched a TED Talk and never heard about this amazing platform for sharing ideas, I would like to invite you to watch just one. Choose the one you would like to watch.

PechaKucha Presentations

OK, SpeechSharks, get ready for a little fun as we dive into the world of PechaKucha. Here are things you need to know about this type of presentation that has become quite popular in and out of the speech classroom!

According to the PechaKucha website at www.pechakucha.org, "The presentation format was devised by Astrid Klein and Mark Dytham of Klein Dytham Architects . . . PechaKucha Nights are informal and fun gatherings where creative people get together and share ideas, works, thought, holiday snaps—just about anything, really—in the PechaKucha 20×20 format" ("Frequently Asked Questions"). The architects who developed this were inspired because they were tired of presentations that went on and on forever. It was also developed as an anecdote to the dreaded "Death by PowerPoint" where a speaker reads PowerPoint slides to his audience. You've all been there, right? I'm sure you also would prefer a system to get the information in a more interesting format.

PechaKucha is synonymous with 20×20. If you've never heard of this type of presentation, then you are in for a wonderful Shark-o-licious treat. My first PechaKucha experience was at a National Communication Association Conference for communication and speech professionals. The speaker took the stage and began to describe this strategy which involved showing twenty slides that were timed for twenty seconds per slide. Each slide would advance automatically at the twenty-second mark while the speaker talked using images that were designed to define, demonstrate, and inform us about PechaKucha presentations.

One of the slides included the interesting ways in which people pronounced the term. We were all laughing before that twenty-second segment was over. SpeechSharks, do you want to know the correct way to pronounce PechaKucha?

- It should be pronounced as it is spelled, Pe-cha-ku-cha with equal time spent on each of the four syllables.
- It should NOT be pronounced as Pet-cha Koot-cha.
- Nor should you pronounce it as Pek-chak-u-cha.

Are you trying it out as you read this? Are you laughing? For some reason, it can be quite funny to sit around with your friends planning the next PechaKucha night and try to see the many different ways people pronounce this. It really doesn't matter how you pronounce it, the event is fun and can be a great way to share your sharky ideas or creative projects.

PechaKucha Nights are events held in public places that are equipped for showing PowerPoint, Prezi, or Haiku Deck slides. The events can center around a particular theme or various topics and include just a few speakers or many speakers. The purpose is to inform the audience about a topic in a fast-paced environment. I can already see your mental calculators working as you are trying to figure exactly how long this type of speech should last. The answer is that in four hundred seconds or six minutes and forty seconds, the speaker will cover a topic.

Would you like to see a PechaKucha presentation? Just go to YouTube in your Internet search and type in PechaKucha Presentations. There are hundreds to see and some are better than others, but they are all quite entertaining. You can also visit the PechaKucha website at www.pechakucha.org/watch and choose presentations posted there.

Here are tips to help you plan a PechaKucha presentation:

- Watch a PechaKucha presentation before you plan to present one.
- Each presentation needs to cover one really big idea.
- Organize your ideas so that they are interesting, but use the slides so they offer details which support the big idea.
- Plan your speech first before you create the slides.
- Use an outline and not a manuscript.
- As you plan slides, realize that twenty seconds may not be long enough to cover some points and may be too long to cover other points. Be open to adjusting the content so that it stays within the twenty-second goal.
- Use conversational language instead of a memorized script.
- Since a PechaKucha presentation uses lots of images, make sure the images are clear and make sense to the presentation.
- Set the timing in PowerPoint to have twenty seconds for each slide.
- Rehearse with a stopwatch to make sure you are keeping to the twenty seconds for each slide. Speakers should only speak about the slide/image that is being shown. Timing for this speech is crucial to the success of the speech.
- Avoid looking at the slides while you make the presentation. Establish good eye contact with the members of your audience.
- Use gestures and connect with your audience.
- Appoint a Tech Team person to start the slide show as you begin talking and will take it down after the speech concludes. You will not use a remote or Tech Team member to progress the slides because each slide will be timed within the PowerPoint presentation.

Does this sound like fun to you? If so, give it a try!

Competitive speaking is a lot of fun and getting involved in this arena will help you to hone your communication skills to a level beyond basic public speaking. In this section we will be sharing details about debates, storytelling, oral interpretation, and improvisational speaking.

When speaking of **debates**, most of us automatically conjure up the image of high school or collegiate debate leagues while others immediately move toward political debates. While the two can be quite different, they also have similarities and share basic features and formats. Debates are more competitive than other types of specialty speeches because they usually involve a judge that will determine a winner between two debaters or two teams. The very term—debate—brings to mind definitions of formal discussions which often become quite heated. They may sound like organized arguing or quarreling in order to voice a view regarding a controversial topic.

Although the first recorded political debate for the United States was in the 1800s, political debates are now commonplace to allow candidates a platform for speaking to voters about their positions on various issues. During the last presidential election, we were all glued to the television watching the initial lineup of candidates as they squared off to face each other in an organized game of "he said, she said." The result noted a winner, but most of us noted frustrations realizing it was time spent that truly did not yield more information than we already knew. In other words, we enjoy debates that cover the issues.

Debates involve appealing to the audience's logic using credible research to document facts interlaced with an emotional appeal to sway the audience's opinion of the topic. It takes a competent speaker to be able to mix so many different elements and effectively deliver a message which demands a resolution.

Debates can be formal or informal and involve two sides: the affirmative side which supports the status quo, or current view, and the negative side which supports an opposing view. Each side will be given the same amount of time to define, support, and defend their view of the topic which will be divided into two sections. During the first section, the speaker or team will lay the foundation for the debate in what is often called the constructive phase. The last section is called the rebuttal and is an opportunity for the affirmative and the negative sides to offer rebuttals for points brought up by the opposing team. Both sides alternate turns delivering their portion of the debate and end the debate by stating a resolution. It then becomes the task of the judge to decide which debater or team has achieved the purpose of refuting all points made by the opposition. Miss one point and the debate will be lost.

High schools and colleges are supporters of debates because this type of presentation involves the development of critical thinking and problem-solving skills as debaters or teams share different viewpoints of the same topic. Preparation for a debate requires that teams work together to research both sides of the topic. The affirmative team should know every point of reference that may be made by the negative team so they can establish a platform and be ready on-the-spot with points and research to refute points made. The same is true for the negative team. In high school and college debates, the team often does not know whether they will be debating the affirmative or negative side of the topic until they arrive at the debate and receive their orders. This further solidifies the importance of researching and understanding both sides of the topic.

As social networking and online access has evolved through the years, so has the online debating formats. This allows debaters to contribute in short "mini" debates using instant messaging, Twitter, or video conferencing. This method of debating is becoming quite popular and is a great way to hone communication skills, especially when you have to figure out how to deliver a message and achieve a purpose with a limited number of characters! As technology improves, we may see more online debating opportunities surface.

Different types of team debates include the following and are listed alphabetically:

- American Parliamentary Debates
- Australasia Debates
- British Parliamentary Debates
- Canadian Parliamentary Debates
- Cross Examination Debates
- European Square Debates
- International Public Debates
- Karl-Popper Debates
- Legislative Debates
- Lincoln-Douglas Debates
- Mace Debates
- Mock Trial Debates
- National Debate Tournaments
- Oxford-Style Debates
- Policy Debates
- Public Forum Debates
- Team Policy Debates
- World Universities Debate Championships

Have you ever tried to use **storytelling** to get your message across to an audience? Whether you are telling your story or someone else's story, a good storyteller will always include the moral of the story and will weave a tapestry of events together in order to bring the story to life. Storytelling is the process of sharing stories to educate, inform, and entertain. We all love a good story, especially when the story is used to illustrate something more. Good stories have the power to engage audiences and instill lessons that connect the past with the future. Storytelling can also be used as a way to share values and teach ethics in an environment that is warm and inviting.

I grew up sitting captivated at the feet of my parents and grandparents hanging on to each detail of stories they would tell. Whether the stories were told around a campfire in the dark as we huddled beneath warm blankets or at church in a Sunday School classroom, my happiest memories as a child involved listening to stories being told by my elders. As a grandparent, I find myself telling tall tales to my own grandchildren and hoping that the moral of the story is clear and will strike a chord with these little ones. We've all heard stories told in the form of fables, legends, folklore, and fairy-tales. Often stories reveal the same plot but with different characters and different strategies for sharing the story.

As a speaker, it is a great idea to incorporate stories in order to support points that you wish to make. Personal stories sharing real events that you have experienced will often make a stronger impact than supporting points with mounds of research, data, and statistics.

Here are tips to remember about storytelling:

- All stories do not have to begin with . . . "Once upon a time, a long, long time ago, there was a . . ."
- Good stories are designed with three parts as the foundational structure. The story begins, an event (confrontation, problem, or misunderstanding) occurs, and the story ends with a resolution.
- First, the speaker needs to set up the story. This part of the story will help to bring the listener up to speed by giving a bit of the history behind the story and a brief preview of what is to come. Describe the characters in your story so that your listener will recognize them as they make their appearance.
- Secondly, the speaker will need to detail the confrontation or the problem. After all, there should always be a little action or intrigue and a bit of excitement for each story you tell.
- Finally, the speaker will need to artfully move the confrontation to a desired resolution. Yes, we all still enjoy happy endings, but the main idea of the resolution is to make the moral of the story absolutely clear.
- Tell stories so they can be re-told. You'll soon find that people will remember the stories you tell before they remember the points in a speech. Weeks after your speech, it will be the stories they remember!
- Involve your listeners in the story by painting vivid pictures with your words, using their senses to hear sounds described, see images unfold, and feel movements or passions involved.

We hear this termed as the "Art of Storytelling" and indeed it is an art, one that is developed through years of practice and rehearsals. Good storytellers often tell the story a bit differently with each audience and they do this to make the stories fit to various occasions. Young and old alike enjoy a good story and are eager to hear them.

Did you know there is actually a World Storytelling Day? It happens every year in March and is a celebration of the art of storytelling. Another interesting fact about this event is that it follows a different theme for each year. Do a little research and you will soon find out the date for this year's World Storytelling Day. Perhaps you can volunteer at your local library or school to share your story!

Oral Interpretation involves making careful material selections and using interpretive or dramatic readings of prose, poetry, drama, plays, or oratorical speeches. Oral interpretations may be presented as a solo or as a duo interpretation and may involve a competition element also found in debates.

While reading the selection, the speaker will express meaning through vocal variety, gestures, and carefully planned movements. Oral interpretation is a basic part of all performance art as the speaker/dancer works to interpret the author's meaning using their vocal skills and movement. This is another form of storytelling because it is the speaker's job to bring stories to life; however, the speaker is interpreting the author's words and meanings instead of sharing his own words.

When presenting an oral interpretation, the speaker is charged with honoring the true meaning or integrity of the written word and delivering the message as the author intended. While this may be a hard task to do, it is often made clearer once the speaker researches the work being interpreted, the author's intention for the work, and also his viewpoint regarding the work at the time it was written. This will involve analyzing the various dimensions of the characters used in the texts. The reader should understand their emotional, social, and physical descriptions in order to adequately portray the character intended by the author and to give the illusion that the speaker is reading from the script.

Care must be taken to understand the pronunciations and meanings of each word and know the setting for the selection. Gestures and movement are a big part of oral interpretation by using shifts in posture, head nods, and hand gestures to correlate with the script being read. Vocal variance in the form of varying pitch, volume, rate, and effective pauses will help the speaker to bring the document to life.

Here are tips for presenting an oral interpretation:

- To present an oral interpretation of selected materials, be sure to start with a short preview from the materials that will get the audience's attention.
- Mention something of value about the material and the author.
- Establish a need/relevance for the audience to hear the interpretive reading and relate it back to an experience they may have had.
- Set the scene so that the audience will know the background of the scene and will be ready to hear a brief description of the characters included and the theme of the selection.
- Clearly state the title of the document and also state the name of the author before beginning.
- Rehearse, Rehearse, Rehearse.
- To conclude, restate the author's message with the document and thank your audience for their attention as you worked to entertain, educate, or enlighten your audience.
- Oral Interpretations are another type of specialty speech that speakers will enjoy using at different times and for different purposes.

For material selection, remember there is a difference between prose and poetry. Prose expresses thought through language presented in sentences and paragraphs, whereas poetry expresses thought through a creative writing of words according to their sound, rhythm, and meaning.

If making the presentation as a team, please make sure you rehearse as a team and use enough team members to cover all characters involved within the document. Don't be afraid to channel your inner drama queen when working to present an oral interpretation. The most important thing is to have fun!

Team up with other SpeechSharks to give this type of competition speaking a try and you will find that **Improvisational Speaking** combines several elements which include movement, technology, imagination, and discussion on a stage or in a classroom setting. This type of speaking will allow speakers the opportunity to think on their feet with no prior preparation and will help develop problem-solving and critical thinking skills. A keen awareness of self and location is important for improvisational speaking.

Are you ready to give it a try? This usually begins with an instructor or a group leader giving the group a challenge. The group can be as few as six people or as many as twenty people. The challenge can be designed according to who is in the group and the nature of the gathering. For example, if you choose to do this in a business setting, the challenge may deal with something going on within the department or a project that the group may be working on together as a unit.

Whatever the setting, once the challenge has been offered, each person in the group will pair up with one or two others and then quickly share their response to the challenge. Once they agree on a response to the challenge, they move over to join another group to see if their idea is better or if the other group's idea is better. They settle on one idea and then move to combine with yet another group. In the beginning stages, it will feel like a brainstorming session, but with movement. Everyone should have an opportunity to speak and in doing so, it helps the group members to move a bit outside of their comfort zone, but to become more comfortable with those within their group. Quickly it will become obvious which group members are more vocal than others and they may be tempted to run with the challenge and ignore the quieter ones; however, care should be taken to include ALL group members.

The goal or purpose of this type of speaking is to use each member's natural impromptu speaking skills and as they move from one group to join with another, they should become more comfortable presenting their joint ideas with confidence. The goal is also to help the quieter ones in the group to have opportunities to improve their speaking performance through normal interactions with others in their group.

If you choose to give this specialty speech a try, you may find that in the beginning many of the group members will tend to stand back and not join in 100%. They are doing this to see how the other members are reacting. This will be a bit awkward sometimes, but keep the challenge moving forward. Watch how the quieter ones will begin to become more vocal and to play a bigger part in the resolution of the challenge.

If you ever attended a meeting and wanted to stand up to share your thoughts or feelings about a subject, but didn't have the confidence to speak up, **Improvisational Speaking** may give you the practice you need to improve your speaking confidence.

Have you ever watched the television show, *Whose Line Is It Anyway?* The actors on the show are placed in a particular scene and sometimes assigned to play a certain character and they would have to act out the scene or play that character with no prior warning or rehearsal. Their performance would be hilarious and the entire cast along with people watching the television show would burst into uncontrolled laughter. This is one of those situations where we learn by playing, but you have to be open and vulnerable enough to play without thinking of the final outcome so that you can truly be creative. Too much thought about what you may say, how you may move, and what your actions may look like, will cause you not to be creative and to hold back.

You are SpeechSharks, so I already know you are brave! Would you like to give it a try? Check out the examples for Improvisational Speaking in the "Shark Bites" section of this chapter and think of one type that you might like to try at your next gathering with friends or family. Try these at your upcoming Toastmasters International meeting. Just choose one, take a deep breath, and jump in! The results will be unforgettable and you may discover this is your favorite specialty speech of all times!

Humorous Speeches

The purpose of a **humorous speech** is to warm up the audience, make them laugh, and keep them laughing! We saved this specialty speech for last because it is so entertaining. After you have given it a try, it may be one of your favorites, too!

Now, I can already hear you saying, "I am not funny! When I try to be funny, it falls flat before I can get to the punch line." That may be true, but with careful planning and a little practice you will be able to create a humorous speech and will have your audiences laughing in no time at all!

Before you can plan your first humorous speech, consider the idea you would like to use for the subject. Remember that the subject doesn't have to be funny.

It is what you say and how you say it that can get the laughs from your audience. Did I say, audience? Yes, I did and that means that as with all speeches, we need to consider who is in the audience before we decide the subject or topic of the speech. Here are questions to ask before you plan the speech:

- What is a common denominator with the audience members?
- Is there a particular type of subject to which they can relate?
- What type of humor will tickle their funny bones (make the audience laugh)?
- Do you want the topic to be informative or just funny?
- Is your primary purpose to make them laugh?
- Is there a topic that might lend itself to your personal sense of humor?
- What topics will be funny to your audience?

As we began the chapter, we mentioned that some of the specialty speeches do not follow the organizational plans that we follow for other types of speeches. Normally, you are accustomed to planning introduction steps for all of your speeches. The introduction step includes an attention getter, establishes need for the topic, your credibility for speaking about the topic, and a clear thesis to detail the three main points. We have to throw all of that out of the window as we plan a humorous speech. The most effective way to start a story is to go directly into the story. Begin with the "hook" that will get your audience laughing and will keep them interested. You can do this by including a personal story, providing "WOW" examples that will surprise or entertain your audience. You can even ask direct questions to give the audience a chance to laugh at themselves.

After you start the story, disclose the main points you are covering during the speech. Outlines are the way to go when planning a speech. Write first your three main ideas about the main point. Then go back and add sub-points to each of the three main ideas. The important tip here is to write simply and clearly. Write down the main points and sub-points, but avoid writing long, complicated sentences. Plan your speech by using vivid adjectives to paint a clear picture for your audience.

Repetition is a good strategy for this type of speech. As you repeat a sentence two or three times in succession, your repetition helps to escalate your audience to the punch line that you choose to use.

Self-deprecating in a humorous speech can be effective, but don't go too far into the other direction or you will turn into a "Rodney Dangerfield." If you are not old enough to remember this comedian, Google him to see a video of his self-deprecating humor. He was constantly saying things like, "I get no respect! When I was a kid, nobody would play with me. My mom would tie a bone around my neck just to get the family dog to play with me and the dog would still rather play with the cat. Yea (long pause), I get no respect!" Some people enjoy this type of humor, but it really has to be crafted just right in order to be effective and appreciated.

Don't lose sight of the main purpose of your speech—to speak about the topic you choose. Work humor into the text after you have completed the foundation for your speech. Read the points you have established and brainstorm ways to relate this information with specific things that will make your audience laugh. If it makes YOU laugh, it will probably make your audience laugh, too. Avoid jokes or humor that are not culturally sensitive and keep the humor you do use relevant for the topic.

Now that the speech is written, rehearse and make note of areas where you will need to edit the outline and revise the speech. As you rehearse, check to make sure your punch line punches hard. This may mean that you will need to practice in front of family or classmates to have them offer an evaluation of your humor!

Specialty Speeches, as you can see, are not a one-size-fits-all presentation. Be creative, follow our tips, and enjoy diving into clear waters to once again move toward your goal!

Types of Specialty Speeches

After reading this chapter, you will be able to answer the following questions:

1. What is the acronym used to named TED Talks?

_____

_____

2. How many slides are used in PechaKucha presentations?

_____

_____

3. What are the two sides that are represented in a debate?

_____

_____

4. Describe the process of storytelling:

_____

_____

5. Fill in the blanks: Oral interpretation involves making careful _____ selections

and using _____ or _____ readings of _____ ,

_____ , _____ , _____ , or

_____ . Oral interpretations may be presented as a _____ or as a

_____ interpretation and may involve a _____ element.

6. Improvisational speaking combines several elements which include _____ ,

_____ , _____ , and _____ on a stage or in a class-

room setting.

7. What is the purpose of a humorous speech?

_____

_____

Shark Bites

GETTING TO KNOW TED

Go to https://www.ted.com/talks to look at the different topics posted in TED Talks. Choose one topic that interests you and complete the questions below:

1. Which TED Talk did you choose?

2. What is the URL address for the TED Talk you chose?

3. What is the title of the TED Talk?

4. Who delivered the TED Talk?

5. Did you enjoy hearing about the topic? If so, what did you learn? If not, what was the problem?

Shark Bites

CHECKING OUT PECHAKUCHA

Go to www.pechakucha.org/watch to look at the different PechaKucha presentations. Choose one topic that interests you and complete the questions:

1. Which PechaKucha did you choose?

2. What is the URL address for the PechaKucha you chose?

3. What is the title of the PechaKucha?

4. Compare this PechaKucha presentation to the TED Talk that you watched.

5. What did you think about the images shown by the speaker?

Shark Bites

Try one of the following options for completing an improvisational presentation:

1. **Imaginary Object:** Pick up an imaginary object from the table and begin to interact with it. Pass it on to the person next to you. They will also interact with it, and continue to pass it around to others. For this to work well, the first person will need to make it very clear the subject of the object so that others will know how to interact.

   - Example: Pick up an imaginary apple, hold it up, and brush it against your sleeve to wipe away dirt or germs before taking a nice large imaginary bite. Pass the imaginary apple to the next person and watch how they also interact.

2. **Narration Station:** Two or more people will play this game. One or more of the people will be an actor who will act out the story and the other person is the narrator. If using more than one actor, be sure to identify the character for each actor. As the narrator tells the story, the actor acts out the story and the narrator responds by describing what the actor is doing.

   - Example: Poem—"The Old Woman Who Lived in a Shoe." One person will be the old woman. Other actors will be the children. As the narrator recites the poem, the actors will act out the story.

3. **Q&A:** This will involve two people. One person asks a question. Instead of an answer, the other person will ask a question that expands on the other person's question. No answers are ever given, just more questions.

   - Here is what this might look like:
     - Person 1: Do you like sweets?
     - Person 2: What type of sweets?
     - Person 1: What about cakes?
     - Person 2: Chocolate or vanilla?
     - Person 1: What about caramel?
     - Person 2: Does caramel interest you?
     - Person 1: Do you have pecans that can go on the cake?
     - Person 2: Do you want the pecans toasted or not?
     - Person 1: Could you also add birthday candles?
     - Person 2: Is it your birthday today?
     - And the story goes on and on until they run out of questions.

Chapter Five
Methods of Delivery

For the basic fundamentals of speech course, only extemporaneous and impromptu type speeches are covered; however, it is a good idea to understand the four methods of delivery so that you have a good idea of times when it might be appropriate to use one of the other methods. Planning the type of delivery to choose is just as important as planning the topic. Speakers will need to determine the purpose for the speech presentation and will make the method decision based upon the purpose.

The most effective way for a speaker to reach his audience is to present the speech using elements of formal speaking skills combined with aspects of conversational delivery. In other words, speakers should combine skills along with personality. Audiences want the experience of hearing a great speaker, but they LOVE speakers that are authentic and immerse themselves into the presentation. A true SpeechShark knows that it is not simply the information delivered that impacts the delivery of the speech. Decide which of the methods of delivery are the most effective for your purpose: extemporaneous, impromptu, manuscript, or memorized. Then you can begin planning a speech that will deliver!

EXTEMPORANEOUS SPEAKING

Most speeches required in a speech course will use the extemporaneous speaking model. We use this type for introduction, informative, persuasive, group presentations, demonstration, and special occasion speeches. You'll also notice that extemporaneous speaking models are used with all of the TED Talks you've heard. Extemporaneous speaking is audience-centered speaking and is presented using an outline instead of a fully written speech. It almost feels impromptu since it is not a manuscript or memorized speech, yet the speaker has had time to choose a topic, research the topic, write an outline, create visual aids and handouts, and rehearse the speech.

The benefit of presenting extemporaneously is that it gives the audience the impression that you are presenting the speech as it is created. In drama classes, we call this the "illusion of the first time." In other words, you have time to plan what you will do, but will make it sound as if it is the first time you have spoken about it. That's not to say that speakers can't memorize certain portions of their extemporaneous speeches. In fact, we suggest that speakers memorize their attention step and concluding statements so they are assured the beginning and ending of their speech presentations will go according to plan.

Extemporaneous speeches are conversational in nature and that is the key reason audiences prefer this type of speech over any others they hear. Speakers spend less time looking at notes and more time connecting directly with their audience members through direct eye contact and a more relaxed stage presence.

SpeechSharks are especially good with extemporaneous speeches when they use the SpeechShark notes feature in the app because it provides the brief notes needed, but allows the speaker the flexibility to speak conversationally without reading a speech.

Tips for Extemporaneous Speaking

1. Enthusiasm is contagious. Choose a topic you love and your audience will also enjoy the topic.

2. Use the SpeechShark app to plan the speech with your audience in mind. Think about areas of a topic the audience would like to know.

3. Include personal stories and research to support the topic. When using research, verbally cite the sources you use and explain how the research connects with the topic.

4. Create useful notes or use the app notes on your phone for the lectern. Keep them simple and easy to use. You might not need them, but it is always comforting to know they are there.

5. Rehearse the speech a minimum of three times so that you are familiar with the content. Time each rehearsal and get an average time for the three rehearsals in order to have a good idea of the amount of time your presentation will take. If your speech is too long, remove some of the sub-points. If it is too short, add sub-points. It is important to stay within the time frame expected.

6. Prepare effective visual aids. Choose a Tech Team member to help with the visual aids and rehearse with your Tech Team member using the visual aids.

7. Pack everything you need for your speech the day before the presentation.

8. Choose a professional outfit to wear the day of your speech and make sure it is comfortable. This is not the day to wear uncomfortable shoes!

9. Arrive early so that you can become familiar with the room, upload a copy of the PowerPoint, and set up a table display.

10. Greet others as they arrive so that you can establish a connection with audience members prior to giving the speech.

IMPROMPTU SPEAKING

During the first day of class and several times throughout the semester, your instructor may ask you to present an impromptu speech. This type of speech is used in college-level courses, at work, and in social gatherings. You'll start to recognize this as speaking without prior preparation, otherwise known as thinking on your feet. It is an informal way of communicating without having time to think of a clever answer or rehearsing what you might plan to say. Impromptu speaking requires you to give a quick answer or response at a moment's notice.

In the public speaking course, we lovingly call impromptu speeches **ZAPs**. If you have ever been asked to give a speech without notice and discover that you feel like you've had a surge of electricity running through your body, then you will understand why we call these ZAPs. For the sake of understanding, we've created the ZAP acronym to explain how impromptu speaking works.

Z stands for zero time to prepare for a speech.

A represents the attention to detail required during an impromptu speech.

P reminds us that points need to be clear and complete.

Of all the speeches learned during a public speaking course, students will say that this one is the most valuable because it has a practical application. People who learn this skill will find they are much more effective answering interview questions, responding to questions from customers and fellow employees, as well as being able to speak intelligently at any work or social function.

In Chapter Three as we learned about responding during Question and Answer sessions that follow Group Presentations, you were introduced to the **P.R.E.P. model** of answering questions without prior **prepa**ration. This works for any opportunity in which an impromptu speech or answer needs to be presented. Here is a quick reminder of this model and yes, it is another acronym:

Acronym	Stands for...	Description
P	Point	Restate the question asked and then clarify the point of the question.
R	Relevance	Thank the person who asked the question, explain why the question is relevant, and provide a brief answer to the question.
E	Example	Provide a clear example as a follow-up to your answer and to make sure the audience has an understanding of the answer.
P	Point	Summarize the impromptu speech by re-stating the point and affirm that you answered the speaker's question.

Tips for Impromptu Speaking

1. Anticipate impromptu speaking opportunities and be **PREP**ared.
2. Memorize the **PREP** model and be ready for anything.
3. Listen, so that you don't have to ask for the question to be repeated.
4. Don't rush! Take a moment to process the question before you begin to answer it. Restating the question before you answer the point of the question will help give you a little extra time to decide how to answer the question. Your audience members will just think you are establishing good eye contact with them, when in reality you are thinking of a clever answer. People who get in too big of a hurry are the very same people who forget the question and stumble over their answers. Take your time.
5. The **PREP** model calls for brevity. Answers that get directly to the point of the question, connect relevance of the question to the answer, and offer real-life examples will affirm your credibility as a speaker.

MANUSCRIPT SPEAKING

Manuscript speaking is a method that involves reading a speech word-for-word as it is written. Many politicians, executives, and broadcasters use this method of speech delivery when they have a message that must be delivered exactly the way it is planned. Speeches that include data, statistics, details, or critical information will need to be delivered from a written manuscript. This is not one of the best types of speech delivery simply because there is very little eye contact or connection with the audience; instead, it is simply an opportunity to present information.

Speechwriters understand the importance of opening and closing this type of speech with a personal note to break the monotony of having the entire speech read to the audience. Speakers who resort to manuscript speaking will often use teleprompters so that it does not fully appear the entire speech is being read.

Tips for Manuscript Speaking

1. Rehearse using a teleprompter prior to the speech.
2. Rehearse! Rehearse! Rehearse! While rehearsals are important for all types of speeches, it is especially important that the speaker be extremely familiar with the script. This allows more opportunity for eye contact and a connection with the audience. Pause often so that eye contact can be established.
3. Rehearse adding vocal variance to the speech. Avoid speaking using a reading cadence or a monotone quality. Adding variations to the pitch, volume, pace, and rate will create added interest in your voice.
4. Check pronunciations of names and places.
5. Use large gestures so they are evident as you stand behind a lectern. Gestures will add interest to a manuscript speech.

MEMORIZED SPEAKING

A manuscript speech that has been committed to memory is memorized speaking. Like the manuscript speech, this presentation involves presenting a speech word-for-word; however, it is memorized. Speakers will choose to memorize a speech when accuracy is of great importance along with a warm rapport with the audience that is not achieved when reading a speech.

Often during extemporaneous speech planning, students will try to write their entire speech and memorize it thinking a written speech will result in a stronger speech presentation. This is not always true because when memory fails, it is hard for the speaker to pick up where she left off and move forward. This is one reason why memorized speeches are usually short and to the point. The shorter the speech, the less opportunity the speaker has for forgetting parts of the speech.

Speakers will *not* use notes for memorized speaking because it is too difficult to glance down at a full written page of paper and immediately find the lost thoughts.

Another problem associated with memorized speaking is that the speaker will not be able to respond quickly to the audience if something unplanned happens. Flexibility is almost impossible with a memorized speech.

Tips for Memorized Speaking

1. Memorize the speech. Now you know why they call it memorized speaking!

2. Try memorizing the speech in the three sections they occur: Introduction, Body, and Conclusion. This will help in the event that you forget a portion of the speech and will need to move to the next area.

3. Rehearse, rehearse, rehearse! This is the best advice for preparing for a memorized speech. Knowing the speech from one end to the other will help with your confidence level.

4. Use "the illusion of the first time" and keep the material sounding fresh even though you might have rehearsed it hundreds of times.

5. Since it is memorized, you should establish eye contact with audience members.

6. Connect with your audience, respond to their nonverbal cues, and watch how the audience will also respond to you.

Methods of Delivery

After reading this chapter, you will be able to answer the following questions:

1. What are the four methods of delivery?

   _____

   _____

2. Which method involves using a written speech that is spoken word-for-word?

   _____

   _____

3. Which method involves a speech delivered with no preparation time at all?

   _____

   _____

4. Which method involves a speech plan that only includes a brief outline?

   _____

   _____

5. What does the acronym ZAP stand for?

   _____

   _____

6. Explain the PREP strategy.

   _____

   _____

7. What is "illusion of the first time"?

   _____

   _____

8. What type speech is most commonly used in a speech class?

   _____

   _____

9. When would a speaker use a teleprompter?

   _____

   _____

10. What type speech method should be used to deliver critical information?

   _____

   _____

Shark Bites

An excellent way to improve your delivery skills is to read out loud selections from works that require emphasis and feeling. You could select one of your favorite poems or plays that falls into this category.

1. Practice reading the selection out loud. As you read, utilize your voice to make the selection come alive. Vary your volume, rate, and pitch. Find the appropriate places for pauses. Underline the key words or phrases you think should be stressed. Modulate your tone of voice and use inflections for emphasis and meaning. Following these strategies will go a long way toward capturing and keeping the interest of your listeners. If possible, practice reading the selection and record it. Listen to the playback. If you are not satisfied with what you hear, practice the selection and record it again.

2. Listen to a presentation. You could also watch a speaker via TED Talk, or other channels to complete the assignment. Prepare a brief report on the speaker's delivery.

First, analyze the speaker's volume, pitch, rate, pauses, vocal variety, pronunciation, and articulation. Then evaluate the speaker's personal appearance, bodily action, gestures, and eye contact. Explain how the speaker's delivery added to or detracted from what the speaker said. Finally, note at least two techniques of delivery used by the speaker that you might want to try in your next speech.

SpeechSHARK™

Unit 3

Planning the Speech

Conducting an Audience Analysis

Defining the Purpose

Choosing a Topic

Conducting Research

Understanding Speech Outlines

Constructing the Outline

Key Terms to Know

Chapter 6—Conducting an Audience Analysis
- Ethos
- Logos
- Pathos

Chapter 7—Defining the Purpose
- General Purpose
- Opportunities
- Specific Purpose
- Strengths
- SWOT Analysis
- Threats
- Weaknesses

Chapter 8—Choosing a Topic
- Category
- Narrow
- Point
- Topic
- Type

Chapter 9—Conducting Research
- APA
- Blogs
- Citations
- Closed Question
- CMS
- CSE
- GALILEO
- Information Gathering Interview
- Internet
- Interview
- Job Interview
- Key Words
- MLA
- Open Question
- Paraphrasing
- Performance Review
- Plagiarism
- Probing Question

- Problem-Solving Interview
- Public Domain
- Research
- Wikis

Chapter 10—Understanding Speech Outlines
- Appeal to Action
- Attention Step
- Body
- Conclusion
- Establish Credibility
- Establish Need/Relevance
- Introduction Step
- Outline
- Preparation Outline
- Presentational Outline
- Speaking Outline
- Standard Outline Format
- Summary
- Thesis

Chapter 11—Constructing the Outline
- Attention Step
- Credibility
- Clustering and Webbing
- Cause-Effect Order
- Chronological Order
- Connectors
- Internal Preview
- Internal Review
- Links
- Main Points
- Problem-Solution Order
- Signals
- Signposts
- Spatial Order
- Thesis
- Topical Order
- Transitions

Chapter Six

Conducting an Audience Analysis

149

WILL YOU SINK OR SWIM?

Preparation is the key to success! It is the difference between success and failure and will make the difference in whether you will sink or swim! Never forget that the buck stops with YOU! When facing the task of making a speech presentation, it is your job to plan, prepare, and present the speech. These simple steps to SUCCESS will help you to swim with the sharks!

Even with a great tool, like the SpeechShark app, you still have to make time to work through the plan. The first thing that a speaker should do before planning a speech is to conduct an audience analysis and gain an understanding about the speaking environment.

Once you understand **WHO** is in your audience and **WHERE** you will be speaking, you will be able to make a better decision regarding **WHAT** content to include in the speech.

On the next page, you will find an **Audience Analysis Worksheet** that provides several key questions to ask yourself as you begin the planning process. Take time to answer each of the questions every time you plan for a speech. The questions will help you to know which topic is suitable for the audience and the speaking environment you will have.

Once you answer these questions, you have entered the planning stage. All that you have to do at this point is to take a deep breath and dive in. There will be no sinking here—you will swim and you will swim with ease!

All of these steps may seem time-consuming, but if you want to SWIM and not sink, these are details that cannot be overlooked or ignored.

Audience Analysis Worksheet

Questions to Consider:	Answers to Help Plan:
What is the purpose of the speech?	
When will the speech be presented? (Date/Time of Day)	
Do you have a time limit for the speech?	
Is this speech being directed to a particular type of audience? (Example: Senior Citizens, High School Glee Club, Community Volunteers, etc.)	
What is the occasion for this speech?	
Is there a stage?	
Will you have a lectern for notes?	
Will you need visual aids?	
Will you require a Tech Team for sound, lights, setup, breakdown?	
Will you need a microphone?	
Will someone introduce you or will you introduce yourself?	
How many people will attend the speech?	
How many women will attend?	
How many men will attend?	
Is there a large gender gap?	
What is the average age of audience members?	
Is there a large age gap?	
What is the cultural background of the audience?	
Is there a large cultural gap?	
Are there political and religious differences to consider? If so, explain.	
What is the educational status of the audience?	
Are there restrictions which might limit your topic?	
Will the audience enjoy your topic?	
Will the audience be receptive to you as the speaker?	
What does your audience expect from you?	
What kind of information should you share with your audience?	
What type of clothing should you wear for this audience? Are there certain types of clothing and/or jewelry items that would distract your audience?	
Is this audience formal or casual?	
Are there other factors to consider?	

Here is a diagram to help you understand the planning process better:

Planning the Speech

1. Conduct an Audience Analysis

2. Determine the Purpose

3. Select and Narrow the Topic

4. Research and Gather Materials

5. Develop Three Main Points

6. Develop the Introduction Step

7. Develop the Conclusion

8. Rehearse and Deliver the Speech

RESPECT DIVERSITY

Since all of us are unique in our own way, it is important that your presentation should be designed to respect everyone in your audience. Most likely, there will be diversity in religious and political beliefs, cultures, genders, age, educational levels, and a multitude of other pre-conceived notions held by each audience member. The larger your audience, the more diversity plays into the way you plan a speech.

Make no assumptions about the beliefs of your audience members and remain ethical by keeping this in mind as you plan presentations. Ethical issues should be considered as you speak and as you listen to the speeches of others. Establish positive ethos by being the kind of person the audience thinks you are based upon what you say and how you project yourself as a speaker.

You've heard the terms ethos, pathos, and logos. These are defined as follows:

Ethos is an appeal to ethics. This is answered as you establish credibility in the introduction section of your speech.

Pathos is an appeal to emotion. This happens as you appeal to the audience's passions or emotions and as you create an emotional response through story telling or argument.

Logos is an appeal to logic. We do this as we reason with our audience and provide logical uses of examples and research to support points we are making in the speech.

The combination of all three (ethos, pathos, and logos) are incorporated as we show respect to our diverse audience members. Know your audience so that you are sure to accomplish these appeals and exhibit respect. Avoid stereotyping and consider situations which might surface. As a speaker, seek to maintain the highest standards of ethics because you are responsible for the content you share with others. As you do this, you will show respect for your audience and they in turn will respect you.

Be aware of the nonverbal cues that are being sent your way during the speech and be flexible enough to change your plan if you notice that audience members are uncomfortable with your topic. A good speaker should never push his/her own agenda on the audience. Show respect for your audience by considering their views and incorporate them into your speech. This will show your audience that you are striving to meet them where they are.

Every person in your audience will have different perspectives, backgrounds, and experiences. We each see, hear, and respond to the world in our own way. It is because of this that we need to learn ways to embrace differences that we have and find common ground to connect with each person in our audience. Your primary responsibility as a speaker is to understand that differences between your audience members will exist. Therefore, you will need to consider every aspect in planning the speech so that your speech will be well received by the majority of people in your audience. In other words, for speaking situations you may need to adapt to others who are different than you and overcome barriers which tend to spotlight our differences.

Before I end this section about diversity, I would like to ask you to go to the Internet and in your search engine bar, type in: TED Talks: Chimamanda Ngozi Adichie: *The Danger of a Single Story.* For your convenience, I will post the URL address and a link:

https://www.ted.com/talks/chimamanda_adichie_the_danger _of_a_single_story

You've all heard of TED Talks and I'm sure you have spent time watching great speeches through this venue. All of the topics offered in TED Talks are fascinating to me, but this one struck a different chord because of the honesty shared. In less than twenty minutes, this amazing young woman tells a story of the dangers of knowing only one story and not seeing the whole picture.

As I watched this speech, I realized just how guilty **all** of us are. For the most part, we understand our own cultures and we think we understand the cultures of others, but often we do not. It is our own assumptions and perceptions that dictate our innermost thoughts about others from different cultures. Whether we are talking about a culture of gender, age, race, ethnicities, locations, political or religious beliefs, or any number of other categories that we seem to box ourselves and others into, we need to be aware that we may only view that culture as a single story. And, that is wrong. To reach a diverse audience population means that we must look further than the box or category that we perceive as the only story to realize there are always more stories to uncover and more perceptions to understand. Please watch this video and let me know if it also helps you to think in a broader term when planning for your diverse audience members!

What are the most common mistakes beginning speakers make?

The speaker may be confident, have a beautiful voice, and great delivery skills; however, the speech will fall flat if the speech does not contain usable and credible content that will add value to the audience's current knowledge of the topic. Know what your audience needs to know, but also know their current level of understanding about your topic. Choose a topic in which you are the expert and then add to the audience's knowledge base.

How can we avoid these mistakes?

Three simple steps can help avoid mistakes: Plan, Prepare, and Persevere! Plan what you want to say by keeping the audience in mind and understanding the purpose of your speech. Prepare by conducting credible research and including examples that will paint a picture for your audience. Persevere by rehearsing several times until you know your content is being delivered in a manner that is clear, concise, and to the point. The common denominator here is to make sure you conduct an audience analysis. Know your audience and make your plans with them in mind. If you do this, you will be successful!

Conducting an Audience Analysis

After reading this chapter, you will be able to answer the following questions:

1. Why should a speaker conduct an audience analysis? _____
_____
_____

2. What are the eight steps for planning a speech? _____
_____
_____

3. What is the definition of ethos? _____
_____
_____

4. What is the definition of pathos? _____
_____
_____

5. What is the definition of logos? _____
_____
_____

6. What does the combination of ethos, pathos, and logos do? _____

_____

_____

7. What are the most common mistakes beginning speakers make? _____

_____

_____

8. What are three simple steps to help avoid speaking mistakes?_____

_____

_____

9. What should you consider first when planning a speech? _____

_____

_____

10. What should you do before developing the three main points? _____

_____

_____

Shark Bites

CONDUCTING AN AUDIENCE ANALYSIS

Challenge: Learn who is in your audience and find out what they want/need to know.

Task: If you have been asked to speak for an event, contact the event manager and ask questions about the audience. If possible, get an e-mail or telephone contact list. Send a short message to welcome the potential attendees to the event and to briefly introduce yourself. Invite them to answer the following questions:

1. What is your purpose for attending this event?

2. What is it that you would like to learn?

3. How much do you already know about the subject?

4. Are there any pressing questions that you have about the advertised topic? If so, please list the questions.

Challenge Accepted: Craft your speech by including your audience in every aspect. Give your audience what they want or need to know. Answer the following questions:

1. Does your content address positive ethos, pathos, and logos?

2. Does your topic respect the diversity of audience members?

3. Did you seek to understand the audience's perspectives, backgrounds, and experiences?

4. Did you consider all aspects of the speaking event and choose a topic to add to the audience's knowledge base?

Chapter Seven
Defining the Purpose

In this chapter:

How do I define the purpose of my speech?

How do I set goals for my speech presentation?

What strategies are most effective?

What is the expected length of time for my speech?

DEFINING THE PURPOSE

Strategic planning is needed for speeches. Once you understand who will be in your audience, your next step is to define the purpose of the speech. Size up the situation and use this information to make choices to help you reach your goal. Strategic planning includes knowing when to speak, what topics to cover, how to phrase your points, how to explain, how to demonstrate a process or procedure, how to defend a point or motivate your audience to solve a problem, how to organize the message and relate the message to the audience. Making choices are important for strategic planning!

Your speech will have two purposes: a general purpose and a specific purpose. The **general purpose** is the type speech you will present. Are you speaking to inform, entertain, motivate, or perhaps all three? This is your general purpose. The **specific purpose** is more detailed. As you determine the purpose for a speech presentation, you are actually creating a plan to achieve a particular goal. Determining the purpose helps the speaker know what information to share in the body of the speech, how to introduce the topic, and how to conclude the speech.

Here is an example of how this might look on your speech outline:

General Purpose: Inform
Specific Purpose: The purpose of this speech is to inform my audience about the dangers of texting while driving.

General Purpose: Motivate
Specific Purpose: The purpose of this speech is to motivate my audience to give blood at the Red Cross Blood Drive at City Hall next week.

General Purpose: Entertain
Specific Purpose: The purpose of this speech is to entertain my audience as I roast and toast our volunteers at the annual end of the year celebration.

GOALS

Having a clear understanding of the purpose of your speech presentation will help you to achieve your speaking goals, develop strategies for a successful presentation, and stay within the time frame that has been offered.

Some use the SWOT strategy to define speaking goals: **S**trengths, **W**eaknesses, **O**pportunities, and **T**hreats. Work through each area analyzing the area and recording your responses. Consider each area as they pertain to the specific speech type that you will be presenting. Each speech is different. Each audience is different. With this in mind, you will want to revisit the SWOT strategy each time you plan a speech.

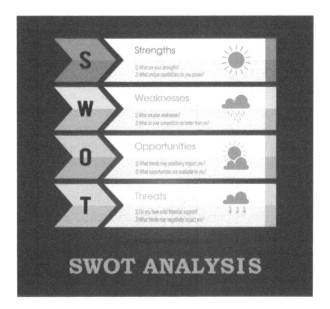

This table will help you understand the goal to achieve a general and specific purpose for each type of speech. Plan to use these suggestions for your general and specific purpose.

Type of Speech	General Purpose	Specific Purpose
Introduction Speech	Inform	The purpose of an introduction speech is to introduce yourself or someone else to the audience.
Informative Speech	Inform	The purpose of an informative speech is to inform the audience about a topic.
Demonstration Speech	Inform and Entertain	The purpose of a demonstration speech is to demonstrate a process or a product.
Persuasion Speech	Motivate	The purpose of a persuasion speech is to motivate the audience to solve a problem.
Special Occasion Speech	Inform and/or Entertain	The purpose of a special occasion speech is to inform or entertain an audience through work-related, social, and ceremonial occasions.
Group Presentation	Inform, Entertain, Motivate	The purpose of a group presentation is to present a topic as a group effort with each member taking equal responsibility to inform, entertain, or motivate the audience according to the topic.
Sales Presentation	Motivate	The purpose of the sales presentation is to motivate a buyer to purchase a product or service.

STRATEGIES

Develop a timeline for creating and presenting the speech. Start with the date for the speech and work backward from there. Allow time to conduct the audience analysis, determine the purpose, and select the topic. Critical thinking skills are used during this stage as you plan the topic with the audience and purpose in mind.

Once your topic has been selected, narrow the topic and begin conducting research to develop and support your points. Add personal stories and experiences along with research to appear more credible to your audience. Create the presentation outline by starting with the three main points of the body, build the introduction step, and finally, draft the conclusion.

Once the outline has been completed, it is time to create a visual aid and handout to support the speech and make presentation notes. The final part of the task is to *rehearse, rehearse, rehearse* to prepare for a successful presentation. Don't forget to pack supplies for your speech and meet with your Tech Team to make sure all is ready for your presentation! This is the easiest part, Sharks! This is where you are confident because you have taken the time to plan and prepare!

TIME

When asked to speak, make sure you meet with the organizer of the event and find out exactly how much time the organizer needs for you to speak. Plan your speech according to the time frame allotted. Many times, your speech will not be the only point of interest for the event. The organizer will appreciate knowing that you will stay on time because that will mean that her event will also end on time.

Time each rehearsal and take an average of each rehearsal time to get a good idea of the length of time for your speech. If you find that you are going "over time" you will need to cut some of your sub-points. If you find that you are going "under time" you will need to add sub-points. Now, you are almost ready! These details will not "just happen" and it is up to you to make sure that they do happen and at the time that you choose.

The SpeechShark app has a handy timer built in. Simply choose the amount of time you will need to complete your speech and the app will remind you when you need to move from one point to the next. Just another way that you can swim with ease through murky waters!

Defining the Purpose

After reading this chapter, you will be able to answer the following questions:

1. What two purposes should be written for the speech? _____

_____

_____

2. Define the general purpose: _____

_____

_____

3. Define the specific purpose: _____

_____

_____

4. What is the SWOT strategy? _____

_____

_____

5. What is the goal of the introduction speech? _____

_____

_____

6. What is the goal of the informative speech? _____

_____

_____

7. What is the goal of the demonstration speech? _____

_____

_____

8. What is the goal of the persuasion speech? How is the persuasion speech and sales presentation

similar? _____

_____

_____

9. What is the goal of the special occasion speech? _____

_____

_____

10. What is the goal of the group presentation? _____

_____

_____

Shark Bites

PRACTICE WRITING PURPOSE STATEMENTS

Challenge: You will need to introduce yourself to the board members of a new organization that you have recently joined. Please complete the following purpose statements for this situation:

General Purpose:

_____

_____

Specific Purpose:

_____

_____

Challenge: The topic of your informative speech is about organ donations. Please complete the following purpose statements for this situation:

General Purpose:

_____

_____

Specific Purpose:

_____

_____

Challenge: The topic of your persuasion speech is about texting and driving. Please complete the following purpose statements for this situation:

General Purpose:

_____

_____

Specific Purpose:

_____

_____

Chapter Eight
Choosing a Topic

SEARCHING FOR A TOPIC?

Now that you have conducted an audience analysis and determined the purpose of your upcoming presentation, you can begin to think of a topic that will interest your audience and a topic for which you have experience and prior knowledge! This can be an overwhelming task and you might feel like you are a shark circling the waters for just the right target. Truthfully, that is not too far from reality.

When asked to speak for a particular event, you may not have the luxury of choosing a topic because it may be assigned to you; however, you still have the freedom to plan, develop, and add your own personal touch to the topic. For this type situation, it is a good idea to meet with the organizer of the event and ask about their expectations. Some speakers have been known to make phone calls to random audience members to ask what topic they would like to hear and to pinpoint information that is relevant for their personal or professional situations.

If you are still having trouble settling on the topic for your presentation, look through books or magazines for inspiration. Meet with friends and colleagues to brainstorm possible topic choices. Listen to news stations or read news articles to pick up on trending topics. Dive into the Internet and search "Speech Topics" to see what you find. There are billions of topics. Choose the one that is right for your audience and the one that is right for you! Once you have your topic, you will be able to choose three main points, sub-points in the form of research, personal stories or examples, and create the message to make it memorable for your audience

NARROWING THE TOPIC

Narrowing the topic is one part of the process involved with choosing a topic. In a short ten-minute speech, you will not be able to cover everything there is to say about the topic. With this in mind, it becomes necessary to narrow the topic to a manageable size.

Here is an example: You LOVE sports, so you are thinking about giving a speech about sports. But, sports is a huge topic and can't be covered in less than ten minutes. Choose one type of sport. Do you want to talk about baseball, basketball, tennis, soccer, racquetball, swimming, skydiving, biking, golf, running, boating, parasailing, skydiving, zip lining, or—Oh My Goodness! Do you see the problem with this? There are so many sports and I love them, ALL! How do I choose? Well, it is obvious you can't speak about all of them in less than ten minutes.

Settle on one **type** of sport and then from that category, narrow the large topic down to a smaller manageable **category**. You are still not finished. Break that down again into a **point** about that sport that is interesting. Almost done . . . Narrow that point into three clear **points**! Aha, now you are swimming and thinking like a SpeechShark!

Here is a way to narrow a topic:

TOPIC
- Topic - **SPORTS**

TYPE
- Narrow this broad topic to a type of sport that is interesting for the audience and for you.
- **Tennis**

Category
- Narrow the topic of tennis to one category.
- **Professional Tennis**

Point
- Narrow the category to a more specific point
- **Types of Tennis Courts**

Points
- Narrow the point into three support points
- **(1) Clay , (2) Hard, (3) Grass**

Does this help you understand the process? Often people try to make speeches without really thinking about the points they will cover. It's time to get to the point. Think of specific and clear points that will add information to your audience's existing knowledge.

Why not give this a try with your own topic for the next speech? Write your answers here:

Topic
- Topic

Type
- Narrow the broad topic to a type

Category
- Narrow the type to a category

Point
- Narrow the category to a point

Points
- Narrow this into three points
- 1.
- 2.
- 3.

If you are using the SpeechShark app, there is a section early in the development stage where you will be prompted to share the topic of your speech. Before you begin that process, make sure you know the answer!

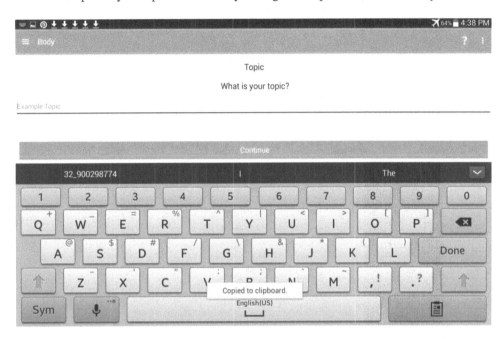

Whether you have been given a topic or if you can choose a topic, you will want to answer important questions to create a strategic plan.

Here is a guide to help choose the topic for your next speech.

General Topic Proposal

Write Your Topic Choice Here: _____ **Answer These Questions:**	YES	NO
Does your topic satisfy the general purpose for the presentation?		
Is your topic narrow enough to be completed within your allotted time?		
Will your audience relate to the topic?		
Will this topic be meaningful to the audience?		
Can you add information about the topic that your audience may not already know?		
Is this topic appropriate for your audience? Consult your audience analysis again and examine the topic as it will appeal to diverse audiences.		
Is the topic you have chosen controversial?		
Will your audience be receptive to a controversial topic?		
Are you passionate about this topic?		
Are you excited about sharing this topic with others? Remember, enthusiasm is contagious. If you are excited and enthusiastic about the topic, there is a good chance that your audience will "catch" your enthusiasm.		
Can you choose three points to develop for this topic? List the three points here: 1. 2. 3.		
Do you need to conduct research to support your topic?		
What type of research do you need?		
Do you have personal stories and experience about this topic to share?		
Can you provide simple examples of your main points that are clear and easily understood?		
Will you need to supply your audience with a handout after the speech?		
Will you need to create a PowerPoint or Prezi Presentation as a visual aid?		
Will you have a Tech Team to handle your visual aids?		
Can you think of a creative way to introduce this topic to your audience?		
Is the setting for the speech conducive to this topic?		

Complete the topic proposal for the next speech you are planning and present it to your instructor for approval.

Informative Speech Topic Proposal:
Student's Name:
Speech Date:
Topic:
Title of Speech:
Three Main Points: 1. 2. 3.

Persuasion Speech Topic Proposal:
Student's Name:
Speech Date:
Topic:
Title of Speech:
Three Main Points: 1. What is the problem you want to solve and why is this a problem? 2. What is a realistic solution to this problem? 3. How will solving this problem make things better? What will happen if we do not solve the problem?

Special Occasion Speech Topic Proposal:
Student's Name:
Speech Date:
Topic:
Title of Speech:
Three Main Points: 1.   2.   3.

Demonstration Speech Topic Proposal:
Student's Name:
Speech Date:
Topic:
Title of Speech:
Three Main Points: 1. What background or history needs to be shared?   2. What materials are needed for the demonstration?   3. How will you complete the demonstration?

Group Presentation Topic Proposal:

Moderator's Name:

Group Members' Names:

Speech Date:

Topic:	
Title of Speech:	

Three Main Points (Identify which group member will complete each point):

1.

2.

3.

Sales Presentation Speech Topic Proposal:

Student's Name:

Speech Date:

Topic:	
Title of Speech:	

Three Main Points:

1. What is the problem with the existing product or service?

2. What product or service will solve the problem?

3. How will replacing the faulty product or service solve the problem?

Topic Suggestions to Get You Thinking

Informative Speech Topics:	
Bargain Shopping	Learning Disabilities
Body Piercings	Learning How to Knit
Carpooling Tips	Meditation
Cloning	Privacy Rights
College Requirements	Recycling
Coping with Online Courses	Rescuing Pets
Dressing for Success	Smoking Policies
Facebook Security	Television Viewing Habits
Finding Balance	To Tweet or Not to Tweet?
Going Green	Volunteering in Homeless Shelters
Home-schooling	Wikis are Wonderful
Healthcare Options	Working from Home
Kid-Friendly Activities	Would you like to go Skydiving?
Labor Unions	Zip-Lining in Costa Rica
Learning a Foreign Language	Zoo Animals at Risk

Demonstration Speech Topics – Notice They All Begin with "How to . . ."	
How to Arrange Flowers	How to Light a Fire
How to Ask for a Date	How to Make Ice Cream
How to Bake a Cake	How to Make a Mojito
How to Belly Dance	How to Pack a Suitcase
How to Change a Tire	How to Plan a Party
How to Clean Shoes	How to Rearrange Your Closet
How to Fold a Flag	How to Sew on a Button
How to Grate Carrots	How to Sing a Lullaby
How to Hang Christmas Lights	How to Tune a Guitar
How to Juggle Three Balls	How to Write a Speech

Persuasion Speech Topics – Notice the Topics All Begin with an Action Word	
Adopt a Grandparent	Go Back to School
Avoid Artificial Sweeteners	Grow a Vegetable Garden
Apply for Scholarships	Invest in Your Future
Ban Beauty Pageants	Join a Club
Be a Mentor	Join a Community Theater
Become a Vegetarian	Learn to Cook
Buy Organic	Learn to Play
Care for Your Elders	Lose Weight
Donate Blood	Lower the Drinking Age
Don't Text and Drive	Make a "Bucket" List
Dress for Success	Practice Safe Sex
Eat Healthy	Prayer in Schools
Exercise	Register to Vote
Keep Prayer in Schools	Save Money
Search Your Family History	Support the Arts
Make a Bucket List	Teach Children to Save Money
Freedom of Speech	Train Your Dog

Group Presentation Topics:
Choosing a College (report on different aspects: history, courses, sports, campus life, cost)
Creating a Bucket List (travel, adventure, learning a new skill, volunteering)
Health Benefits of Exercising (heart, lungs, muscles, mental)
Making Money (time involved, benefits, getting started, mentor/mentee)
Movies to Remember (categories, story lines, themes, genres)
Plan a Meal (include recipes: appetizers, soup, salad, main course, desserts, beverages)
Plan a Trip (who, when, where, how)
Report on a Country (culture, foods, government, sports, traditions)
Sales Presentation (product, demonstration, costs, benefits)
Volunteer Opportunities (time, money, benefits, getting started)

Choosing a Topic

After reading this chapter, you will be able to answer the following questions:

1. If given the chance to choose a topic for a speech presentation, what strategies might help with this

   task? _____

   _____

   _____

2. Why is it important to narrow your topic? _____

   _____

   _____

3. What is a good strategy for narrowing your topic? _____

   _____

   _____

4. What are five steps for narrowing your topic? _____

   _____

   _____

5. What questions should you answer when considering a topic for your next speech? _____

   _____

   _____

6. What is an informative speech topic that interests you? _____

_____

_____

7. What is a demonstration speech topic that interests you? _____

_____

_____

8. What is a persuasion speech topic that interests you? _____

_____

_____

9. Why is the title of the speech important? _____

_____

_____

10. What is a good informative speech title for a speech about volunteering in your community? _____

_____

_____

Shark Bites

LET'S CHOOSE A TOPIC

To choose a topic, you first need to understand the culture of your audience and choose a topic that will interest them and add to their knowledge base. Choose a topic with which you have experience.

Make a list of possible topics and indicate reasons this topic may work well for your audience. Use this list to help make the right choice! If you can't think of a good reason why the topic may work for your audience, cross it out and go back to the drawing board!

Possible Topics	Reasons This Topic May Work Well
Example: Packing for a Trip to Italy	The audience is made of adult members who belong to a travel club.

Chapter Nine

Conducting Research

In this chapter:

What do I need to know about conducting research?

What is plagiarism?

What guidelines and methods should I consider when conducting research?

How do I include a personal interview in my research plan?

What are citation guidelines?

CONDUCTING RESEARCH

Now that you have chosen a topic for your speech, it is time to develop your understanding of the topic by conducting research. During the research process, speakers will often refine three main points or use research they have gathered to craft sub-points. Information found during research can be used as the attention step, the conclusion, or as support for main points within your speech.

Research can come in the form of data, statistics, opinions, or ideas, but can also be as simple as someone's experience or a story that supports your topic. It is up to you to decide what type of research will be most effective for your particular topic. Speakers also use videos, music, art, photography, and other mediums to support points or create visual aids to support the speech topic. In all cases, if it does not belong to you, it is necessary to cite the source.

Research is defined as the process for finding support materials and credible information. This information will be added to your already vast knowledge of the topic you have chosen to cover. One mistake people often make is to use a base search engine on the Internet to find support material. While this is a simple way to conduct research, it does not always promise credible results.

Read the research guidelines and methods in this chapter to learn the best way to use online resources to support your topic. Credible research will help you appear more credible as a speaker. On the other hand, weak research choices can undermine your speaker credibility and may create confusion, especially if sources are not vetted and reviewed.

As you begin to conduct research, please follow these simple checkpoints:

- ✔ Use research that is current: preferably less than five years old.
- ✔ Use research that is credible. Avoid using Wikis, blogs, advertisements, or web pages.
- ✔ Use research that will support the topic and your view of the topic.
- ✔ Use research that will clarify the topic.
- ✔ Use research that will expand your knowledge of the topic.
- ✔ Use research that has been written or published by recognizable credible sources.

In years past, the only way that someone could conduct research was to visit a brick-and-mortar library and spend hours looking through books and reference materials. Once the desired article or data was found, the research would need to be photocopied or typed into a document. Thankfully, finding credible research now is simply a click away as most of us conduct research using the Internet. If you do choose to visit a library to conduct research, you will be pleasantly surprised by the amount of online materials available through the library and also by the helpfulness of local librarians to help narrow down sources to find the most useful and productive sources for your topic.

Whether you conduct research online or at the library, you may find it helpful to create a speech materials file to store articles which may prove helpful as you plan your speech. Online articles can be e-mailed to yourself and digital files can be created to store quotes, data, brainstorming ideas, anecdotes, or stories to support your topic. This will be helpful as you sift through possible sources searching for the two or three best sources to serve your needs.

Plagiarism

We can't talk about research without including tips to avoid plagiarism. The interesting thing about plagiarism is that it can occur verbally as well as in writing, so make sure you cite everything you use that is not your own. **Plagiarism** is the act of using someone else's ideas or work as if they are your own. In essence, this is stealing and in the educational and professional arena, plagiarism is an act which may lead to immediate dismissal. Copyright laws are in place to protect authors of written works.

The best way to avoid plagiarism charges is to verbally or in writing cite everything that belongs to someone else. Turnitin.com is a website that checks for plagiarism. Many colleges and universities use this site regularly to check students' work for plagiarism. In the corporate world, a plagiarism charge can harm your reputation and career. Just to be safe, always verbally and in writing cite the source of research and give proper credit. Citation guidelines are noted toward the end of this chapter.

Guidelines

How do you know if a source of research is credible? Blogs on the Internet can appear to be quite credible. They can be written and posted by someone with a Ph.D., but even that will not determine if the source is credible. Often blogs or Wikis will provide interesting or amusing information, but that also does not determine if the source is credible. Interesting or amusing does not equal credible. With this in mind, I always warn the speech students that I coach to never use a blog, Wiki, or advertisement link—no matter how legitimate it may sound. The point is to evaluate the research and make decisions regarding whether or not the source is credible and offers information you can use to support your speech.

Use credible research owned, reviewed, and monitored by reputable organizations, government sources, newspapers, journals, books, and magazine sources. Stay away from blogs, Wikis, and advertisements which might link to credible sources, but are not credible in their own rights.

Use the following checklist to determine if the source is credible:

- ☐ Would my audience recognize the source?
- ☐ Does the source list an author?
- ☐ Does the author have credentials to verify his/her credibility?
- ☐ Does the source list copyright information?
- ☐ Was this source published within the past five years?
- ☐ Is the content clear and helpful? Is the content accurate and unbiased?
- ☐ Does the content offer opposing viewpoints?
- ☐ Does the content support my topic?

Research Methods

Gathering materials online has never been easier than it is right now. Through the Internet, online research has become the primary source for gathering information for college students and professionals. The Internet can be an incredible source for locating great information, but it is also a source for spreading misinformation! Take care to choose sources of research from credible sources and confirm that the information you share with your audiences is something that will clarify the topic and not confuse your audience.

The **Internet** is one of the most popular go-to sources for people who want to conduct research for any topic in the world. Online search engines like Google, Bing, Yahoo, and Google Scholar have become quite popular. Do not rely solely upon Google; however, if you search Google Scholar, it is possible to find credible research for your speech. Print materials from periodicals, newspapers, encyclopedias, dictionaries, journals, and books are also available through the Internet in digital formats.

Many states offer credible online search engines for a small fee. A student in any of the state of Georgia high schools, technical colleges, community colleges, and university systems are able to use the well-known virtual library called GALILEO (Georgia, Library of Learning Online). Everything in GALILEO is credible. Students are able to search, save, e-mail sources, and get citation help through this easy to navigate system. Many of the sites found in GALILEO offer audio versions of articles, as well as translations into many other languages. Other states have programs similar to GALILEO to help with student research.

Through various search engines, we are able to use key words in a search window to limit the search and to make the research process simpler. The downside is that search engines usually provide a broad expanse of materials, all of which are not credible or relevant for the topic you have chosen. Directories, on the other hand, allow people to link with key words or matches regarding the topic and are manned by a librarian who chooses the prospective sites based upon the quality of that site.

Here are other options:

- **Government and survey sites** such as the Gallup Polls offer reliable information that can be used as support materials.

- **Libraries** often have resources that cannot be found online; therefore, you may want to visit your local library as you conduct research for your speech.

- **Magazines and journals** are the most common forms of research and are readily available in hard copy and online.

- **Television and radio programs** provide transcripts of trending stories that can be used as support for speeches.

- **Newspapers**, available in hard copy and online, offer current and trending information about topics of interest.

- **Books** are an excellent source of information, but readers should understand that it takes months for books to be published and the information contained in a book may not be the very latest information released to the public. Be sure to check the copyright date before using a book.

- **Interviews** are a perfect way to get stories and personal experience about your topic. Just make sure your interviewee is a credible source for your topic.

When using **key words** to initiate a search, take care to spell the key words correctly, use nouns and avoid using more than six words per search. If your search is not successful, try using different key words. As you type in key words into the search box, you will notice that other popular searches will pop up. Sometimes following the pop-up trails will lead to sources that are useful, but other times they will not.

Research is a way to find the answers you need to support points and explore facts that will make you appear more credible to your audience.

Just remember that conducting research is a process. It's like fishing. You have to bait a lot of hooks before you catch the prize fish. With research, you have to review a lot of sources before you find the right data, anecdote, or information to support the point you want to make!

Interviews

Interviews are often used as a source of experiential research to support speech topics. For example, you may choose to integrate an interview with credible print or electronic research to support your topic. We often associate interviews as part of a job-search process and that is true; however, interviews can provide information to help further your knowledge about a subject. An **interview** is defined as the asking of specific questions with the intent to gather information from the person being interviewed. All interview types follow the same basic formula. Prepared questions are chosen depending upon the purpose. Questions are asked and answers are provided. Here are the different types of interviews:

- **Information gathering interviews** are often conducted with many people responding to a question asked.

- **Job interviews** are structured conversations with a goal to discover if a person is suitable for an open position within a company.

- **Problem-solving interviews** are designed to bring peace or solve grievances between two parties. A mediator is usually present in the event of a problem-solving interview.

- **Performance reviews** are considered interviews and are initiated by management authorities in a company to review the performance of employees.

There are three parts to every interview: opening, body, and closing.

The **opening** sets the stage for the type of interview and is usually a time where the interviewer creates a rapport with the interviewee to establish open communication lines in the hope of having a positive interaction between the two.

The **body** of the interview includes questions that are asked. There are different types of questions used for interviews. The most appropriate question to use during the interview is the **open question**. These are broad questions that cannot be answered with a simple "yes" or "no" answer. These questions open the interviewee to answer in-depth thereby adding knowledge for your topic.

Probing questions are good questions to use during an interview because these questions encourage the interviewee to elaborate about the topic.

Avoid asking **closed questions**, as this limits the responses you might receive and will also limit the amount of information you are able to gather about the topic. Closed questions are usually answered by a "yes" or "no."

The **closing** of the interview is an opportunity to summarize the interview and to close on a positive note. Each person, the interviewer and the interviewee, has a responsibility to the other.

Audio or video recording an interview is a good idea, especially when you will be writing and presenting a transcript of the interview. After the introductions and before beginning the interview, ask your interviewee if they would mind if you record the interview. You can decide if you want to audio or video record the session. Most electronic devices, whether it is your phone, tablet, or iPad, have the audio and video recording feature, making this an easier task. If the interviewee agrees to the interview, place your electronic device in full view of the interviewee and pointed toward the speaker so that it will pick up both of your voices. If by chance the interviewee does not allow the recording, then it will be your responsibility to repeat back the interviewee's answers to make sure that your note-taking skills are accurate and that you are able to fully understand the interviewee's response.

During 2020, COVID changed how our world conducted business, held classes, and visited with each other. We had to quickly move to virtual meeting platforms in our home offices instead of driving to see clients, co-workers, students, friends, or family. Students in public speaking classes across the world adapted to speaking through virtual meeting platforms instead of standing on a stage. In person meetings required social distancing and wearing masks often interfered with communication. While it was different and often difficult to navigate these strange waters, we also learned that we are resilient, and we made every effort to chart a path that would help us meet our goals. After all, we are SpeechSharks, and we swam confidently ahead.

Interviews were another part of our day-to-day interactions that suddenly involved the Internet and a computer screen. As a director, I was interviewing potential employees using WebEx or Microsoft Teams. As an instructor, I was teaching classes using the college's Learning Management System and holding virtual office hours instead of on-campus office hours. As a wife, I was helping my husband conduct online meetings when he didn't feel confident using technology that was suddenly new to him. As a mom, sister, and daughter, I was arranging for virtual Zoom visits with our family. As a grandparent, I was helping grandbabies navigate schoolwork online. Our family began to conduct personal business and shopping online. Yes, things changed quickly, but we all adapted and were pleasantly surprised by our sharky thick-skinned attitudes and willingness to keep our eyes on the bigger goal. Business had to continue. Education had to continue. Relationships had to continue. Now that we appear to be making progress toward recovery from the pandemic, we find that online work is becoming a norm rather than the exception. More employees are seeking online work opportunities from home and more students opt for online classes than before COVID.

As you consider conducting virtual personal interviews to use as research for speech support and consider involving virtual interviews as you seek job positions, please refer back to the information posted in Chapter One of this textbook, ***What should I know about public speaking through a virtual platform?*** You'll find this information helpful as you navigate virtual meetings of any type.

The advantages and disadvantages of various types of interviews:

Advantages:	Disadvantages:
E-mail, telephone, and virtual meeting platform interviews take less time than a personal visit.	You cannot be sure who is replying to your e-mail or phone questions.
E-mail questions are efficient and provide a paper trail.	A breakdown in communication can happen with phone conversations.
E-mail questions allow the interviewee time to formulate a response.	Virtual meeting platform interactions rely on Internet connections and contact could be disrupted.
E-mail responses are useful if the interviewee lives in another time zone.	E-mail restricts your ability to question the response.
E-mail, telephone, and virtual meeting platforms are more convenient for both parties.	E-mail and telephone interviews cannot communicate nonverbal cues.

To include experiential research as support for your upcoming speech, here is a convenient checklist to make sure you are prepared:

BEFORE the Interview	DURING the Interview	AFTER the Interview
Decide WHO you will interview.	Behave professionally.	Thank the receptionist as you leave the office area.
Prepare interview questions.	Shake hands with the interviewee.	Write a thank you note or e-mail as soon as you return from the interview.
Craft open-ended questions.	Smile and make eye contact.	Include an invitation to hear the speech.
Contact the interviewee.	Wait to sit until you are invited by the interviewee.	Use the audio recording to write the transcript.
Request an appointment.	Ask permission to audio record the interview. Ask permission before taking a photo with the interviewee.	Include the entire conversation in the transcript.
Pack a recording device.	Ask questions clearly and one at a time.	Using the transcript, include the interview as a source of research in your outline and speech.
Arrive ten minutes early.	Wait patiently for answers.	Correctly cite the interview source in the outline.
Dress professionally.	Clarify answers.	Include the interview on the Works Cited page.
Have note-taking materials.	When through, stand and extend your hand for a handshake.	If the interviewee attends the speech, be sure to acknowledge this during the speech.
Introduce yourself to the receptionist.	Thank the interviewee for his time.	Correctly cite the interview verbally during your speech.
Wait to enter until you are invited into the office.	Invite him to hear your speech. Provide the day/time/location.	During the speech, be sure to offer the interviewee's credentials for the audience.
Enter the room with a smile!	Do not overstay.	If using the audio or video, preface the content and then offer a recap during the speech.

A thank you note following the interview should follow standard letter-writing guidelines.

Example of Thank You Letter:

Name
Address, City, State, Zip Code
Phone Number
E-mail Address

Date of the Interview

Interviewee's Name
Interviewee's Address

Dear Mr./Ms./Dr. Last Name:

Thank you for taking time to meet with me and answer questions I had about (enter the topic of your speech). I appreciate your time. The information you supplied will be used as research to support my speech.

I would like to invite you to attend the speech that will be given at (time) on (date) and held at (location). It would be an honor to have you as a guest.

Thank you again!

Sincerely,
(Add your signature)
Type Your Full Name

Type the interview transcript using this template:

Interview Transcript Template

Interviewer:
Name
Address, City, State, Zip Code
Phone Number
E-mail Address

Interviewee:
Name
Address, City, State, Zip Code
Phone Number
E-mail Address

Interviewee's Credentials: Provide details regarding why you chose to interview this person as a source of research for your speech topic. What experience have they had with this topic that would prove credibility for the topic?

Interview Date/Time:
Interview Location:

Question 1:

Interviewee's Response:

_____

Question 2:

Interviewee's Response:

_____

Question 3:

Interviewee's Response:

_____

Question 4:

Interviewee's Response:

_____

Question 5:

Interviewee's Response:

_____

WRITTEN CITATIONS OF RESEARCH

Let's talk about citation of sources, since this is a big responsibility for the speaker! First, you should know that there are different ways to cite research. The most frequently used citation styles are APA, MLA, CSE, and CMS. With each style, you will notice a specific set of rules and guidelines established to indicate the author, title, publishing source, date of publication, and page numbers of the source.

Additionally, you will notice there are different ways to cite each type of source, whether it is a book, e-book, dissertations, websites, radio or television episodes, videos or film clips, magazines, journals, or newspaper articles, music, art, or pictures.

How do you know which style to use and what makes each style unique? Each style is formulated for a particular discipline. If you are not tasked with using one specific guideline, then please follow the notations below to make sure you are using the style most suited for the topic you are covering. We have also included the links to their websites so that you can go directly to the source to see clear instructions regarding how to cite the source of research in your outline or document.

Here is a breakdown of styles, a notation of when they should be used, and the link to their websites:

APA is known as the American Psychological Association style of citing research. Disciplines that cover psychology, sociology, social work, criminology, education, business, and economics may use the APA style of citing research. For APA Guidelines, please visit their website at http://www.apastyle.org/.

MLA is known as the Modern Language Association style of citing research. Documents using research for literature and language will use this style of citing research. Since you are learning about public speaking and crafting speeches to inform, persuade, and entertain, you will need to cite your sources of research using the MLA Guidelines for source citations. We'll provide examples of MLA citations in this book. For MLA Guidelines, please visit their website at https://www.mla.org/MLA-Style.

CSE citations follow the guidelines established by the Council of Science Editors and are used primarily when the writer or speaker is citing research in the applied sciences areas. These will include biology, chemistry, physics, astronomy, and earth science. For CSE Guidelines, please visit their website at https://www.councilscienceeditors.org/publications/scientific-style-and-format/.

CMS is known as the Chicago Manual of Style. These guidelines are used to cite research that involve the arts and humanities. For CMS Guidelines, please visit their website at http://www.chicagomanualofstyle.org/home.html.

Example of a written citation for a book following MLA Guidelines:

Waddell, Penny. SpeechShark: A Public Speaking Guide. Kendall Hunt, 2022.

Example of a written citation for an electronic source following MLA Guidelines:

Cox, Lindsey. "Six Secrets to Urban Gardening with No Yard." *OffTheGridNews: Better Ideas for Off the Grid Living,* Off the Grid News. 2019. https://www.offthegridnews.com/survival-gardening. Accessed 15 April 2019.

The example shown above is demonstrating the documentation of two different types of sources using MLA Guidelines for a Works Cited page. The Works Cited page should be introduced as a separate page from the outline and only include sources used for the speech. Center the words, Works Cited, on the page and follow MLA Guidelines for all citations. Entries should be double-spaced and shown in alphabetical order according to the authors' last names. If no author is listed, the writer should alphabetize the articles. Titles beginning with A, An, or The should be alphabetized by the title's second word and the A, An, or The is moved to be the final word of the title.

A simple formula to follow for MLA entries in Works Cited is as follows:

1. Author (Last name, First Name).
2. Title of source.
3. Title of container,
4. Other contributors (editors),
5. Version,
6. Number,
7. Publisher,
8. Publication date,
9. Page numbers.
10. Website.
11. Accessed day month year (access date is optional).

Notice that each of the ten areas above include punctuation following the notation. Many of the notations end with a period, but others end with a comma. Also, if the source does not contain the notation listed, the writer can eliminate that part of the citation.

For example, for the book citation, there isn't a container, other contributors, version, or number. Therefore, those areas are eliminated.

For the electronic citation, there are no other contributors, version, or number. Therefore, those areas are eliminated.

Sources with more than three authors should be listed as showing the first author as last name, first name and any subsequent authors as first name then last name. If the source has three or more authors, the writer should name all of the others or simply use the first author's name and add the term et al., which is a Latin term for "and others."

If the full written citation takes up more than one typed line, the writer should use **hanging indentions** for additional lines. Notice how the electronic citation in the example uses hanging indentions. The first line goes to the far left of the margin while the additional lines are indented.

In-text citations are required for the speech outline. Writers will need to place the primary source information in parenthesis within the area where the source will be used. We call this a **parenthetical citation** and it involves having the author's last name and the page number of the work surrounded by parenthesis.

If citing the title of the book mentioned above, the written citation would be shown as (Waddell 168). If the speaker mentioned the author's name in the preceding statement along with the title of the book, the writer could then simply include the page number as (168). Notice how there is no punctuation between the author's last name and the page number. Also, notice how the period goes outside of the parenthetical citation.

Quotes that are longer than four typed lines should be included in the written document and there should be a parenthetical citation following the **block indented margin**. It is obvious to see the block indented margins because they are one inch or ten spaces from the left margin. Quotation marks are not used for block indented quotes.

VERBAL CITATIONS OF RESEARCH

Whether in writing or verbally, any source of research used must be cited. To avoid plagiarism charges during your speech, cite every source you use. In recent news, we learned of a case where one prominent politician plagiarized the words and ideas of another. The words used were so identical that the news reporters and commentators had a field day reporting how this one person blatantly used the very same words as the other. It was quite embarrassing for the politician, who then made a formal statement apologizing for the error. Make sure that you do not find yourself in the same situation.

When you are speaking to an audience and you want to support your point with a credible source of research, it is important to give a verbal indication that you are using someone else's work, ideas, or opinions. The best way to do this is to lead into the research and then indicate whether you are offering a direct quote of the research or paraphrasing the information. Audience members cannot see when the research begins or ends as they do when reading your written document and having the benefit of a parenthetical citation. For this reason, it is the speaker's responsibility to clearly detail the research verbally.

Transition into the research using a signal word which offers a cue for your audience that you are going to cite a source. Vary the signal words you use as the transition and use words that move nicely into the information you are sharing. Here is a short list of signal words that you might use: said, claims, asserts, denies, disputes, expresses, generalizes, implies, lists, maintains, offers, states, suggests, responds, replies, reveals, acknowledges, advises, or believes. Here is an example of how you might use these words:

> **Example of a verbal citation of a direct quote:** In his 2013 New York Times Bestseller book titled *Cooked*, Michael Pollan said this about bread, and I quote, "One way to think about bread—and there are so many . . . is simply this: as an ingenious technology for improving the flavor, digestibility, and nutritional value of grass." End quote.

This process will involve indicating the author's name, the title of the article or the title of the book, and the publication date—not necessarily in that order. If it is a direct quote, you will add the words, ". . . and I quote." Following the direct quote, you will end with the words, ". . . end quote."

PARAPHRASING

If paraphrasing, you will indicate the author's name, the title of the article or the title of the book and the publication date, just as you would for a direct quote. Then you will announce that you are paraphrasing the content. This allows your listener to know where your research begins and where it ends. The listener will know which words belong to the author of the source and which words belong to you. This can be a bit tricky, but with a little practice, you will find that inserting this information as you use a source of research will also help you to appear more credible for your audience. It is easier to paraphrase thoughts, opinions, or ideas, such as the following:

> **Example of a verbal citation of a paraphrased quote:** I would like to paraphrase a unique perception held by Michael Pollan in his 2013 New York Times Bestseller book titled *Cooked*. As the author was talking about bread, he explained how a great recipe can produce something extremely delicious, even though it is nothing more than grass.

Notice in the paraphrase example, the speaker still needed to transition to the research material, supply the author's name, the title of the book, and then paraphrase the idea of the information read in the book.

Some research can NOT be paraphrased. This would include information that includes numbers, dates, proper names, and places. For example, you cannot paraphrase the number 12,643,279. That number is too precise to be paraphrased. For the same reason, you cannot paraphrase June 30, 1935. To paraphrase these, you will need to generalize the information. You can do that by saying "over twelve million" or for the date you could say toward the middle of 1935. The same is true for a person's name or the name of a place. For example, you cannot paraphrase Savannah, Georgia. What do you think you would say, if you needed to paraphrase a person's name? How you would paraphrase the name of a city and state? When do you think paraphrasing would be appropriate?

CITING PRESENTATION AIDS

Citations also need to be included in your visual aids. The only time you will not need to cite visual aids will be if the visual aid belongs to you or if it is considered **public domain**. Merriam-Webster's Online Dictionary defines public domain as "the realm embracing property rights that belong to the community at large, are unprotected by copyright or patent, and are subject to appropriation by anyone" *("Public Domain")*. Here is an example of a PowerPoint slide with a picture that belongs to me and therefore does not need to be cited:

Here is an example of using a picture that does not belong to me and is <u>not</u> public domain. In this case, I included a full citation on the PowerPoint slide where the picture is shown. It is not good to have a Works Cited slide at the end of your PowerPoint Presentation because the audience will not know which citation goes with which picture. Cite the picture in the footer area of the slide where the picture is shown.

ADDING PERSONAL STORIES

Storytelling, personal stories, anecdotes, even hypothetical examples are ways to add interest to your speeches. While it is good to have credible sources to support points, don't forget to always add the human element by including stories. Whether they are your own personal stories or stories from some of your friends or family, including this into your speech will make your topics so much more interesting for the audience.

This is a good time to use material discovered while conducting a personal interview with an interviewee who has experience with your topic. Asking questions and receiving personal stories and information from the interviewee will provide strong material to support points during your speech. Don't forget to also verbally cite the sources for your stories!

> **Example of a verbal citation of an interview:** Last week I was able to interview Mr. Thaddeus Nifong, who is a public speaking instructor and advises a college Toastmasters International Club. During the personal interview, I asked Mr. Nifong what is one of the biggest challenges of advising a college club? Mr. Nifong revealed, and I quote, "The biggest challenge of advising a college Toastmasters International Club is to continually recruit officers and members. College members are going to graduate, transfer to other colleges, and sometimes life just gets in the way. It is because of this that our club officers and members are continuously recruiting and spreading the word about this great club on our campus! With that said, yes, there are challenges, but the rewards far outweigh the challenges when you can become involved as a college club advisor." End quote.

As you can see, when verbally citing a personal interview, it is important to use a transition to lead into the quote, include the interviewee's name, tell your audience why you chose to interview this person based upon his experience, and set the stage for the response. Here is another way to think about it:

1. Transition to citation
2. State the interviewee's full name
3. State the interviewee's credentials
4. Share the question asked
5. Share the response

If you are including a direct quote, preface the quote with . . . "and I quote" before sharing the quote. Following the quote, it is important to conclude with . . . "End quote." In doing this, the audience will clearly differentiate between the words said by the interviewee and your own words. When paraphrasing content within the interview, include all of the information shown above, but indicate that you are paraphrasing instead of using a direct quote.

Conducting Research

After reading this chapter, you will be able to answer the following questions:

1. Define the process of research. _____

   _____

   _____

2. Why should you use credible research? _____

   _____

   _____

3. What are the preferred research checkpoints? _____

   _____

   _____

4. What is plagiarism? _____

   _____

   _____

5. How can you avoid being charged with plagiarism? _____

   _____

   _____

6. Are blogs considered credible research sources? _____

_____

_____

7. How can you determine if the source is credible? _____

_____

_____

8. What does the acronym GALILEO stand for? Do you have something like this in your state? What is it

called? _____

_____

_____

9. What is the purpose of conducting an interview as a source of research? _____

_____

_____

10. What are the different types of interviews? _____

_____

_____

11. What are the three parts to every interview? Explain each part. _____

_____

_____

12. What is the difference between open questions and closed questions? _____

_____

_____

13. What are the advantages and disadvantages of e-mail interviews? _____

_____

_____

14. What should you do to prepare yourself before the interview? _____

_____

_____

15. What is expected from the interviewer during the interview? _____

_____

_____

16. What is expected from the interviewer following the interview? _____

_____

_____

17. What are the four most frequently used citation styles? _____

_____

_____

18. How do you know which of the four styles of citations to use? _____

_____

_____

19. What is an example of using a signal word when verbally citing research? _____

_____

_____

20. How do you paraphrase research? _____

_____

_____

21. What research cannot be paraphrased? _____

_____

_____

22. Where do you cite pictures/photographs on PowerPoint or Prezi slides? _____

_____

_____

23. Do personal interviews need to be verbally cited in the speech? _____

_____

_____

24. What are the steps involved with citing a personal interview? _____

_____

_____

25. Let's practice! Hypothetically, how would you verbally cite a personal interview between you and a mechanic at a local auto shop about the informative speech topic of properly maintaining your car?

_____

_____

_____

Shark Bites

CITING RESEARCH SOURCES

Find one source of research about your topic from the following sources: newspaper, book, journal, interview. Cite the source below using MLA Guidelines for citations.

Written Citation of a Newspaper Article:

Verbal Citation of the Newspaper Article:

Written Citation of a Book:

Verbal Citation of Book:

Written Citation of a Journal Article:

Verbal Citation of a Journal Article:

Written Citation of a Personal Interview:

Verbal Citation of a Personal Interview:

Chapter Ten

Understanding Speech Outlines

In this chapter:

How do I write a speech outline?

What are the types of speech outlines?

How do I create useful notes?

Have you ever planned a trip to a place you've never been before? I'll bet you began by dreaming of visiting the place before you decided how you were going to get there. Having the end goal in mind will give you the motivation to plan the trip.

It's the same type of thing SpeechSharks do when planning a speech. First, imagine yourself standing onstage, delivering a show-stopping speech, and hearing the thunderous applause affirming that you have done a great job. That is the end result, but you'll never get there without proper planning and that includes understanding why we use speech outlines. You've heard the saying, "If you don't aim for something, you'll hit nothing every time."

CREATE A STRATEGY

This means that you need to have a strategy to help achieve your goals. Think of the outline as a roadmap to help reach your desired destination. With a roadmap, you will pinpoint where you are now, the stops you need to make along the way, and then the location of where you want to be. From there, you can see several different ways of achieving your goal. There may be a way that would involve less traffic and better roads as compared to a way that may involve back roads, but with more beautiful scenery. At this point, think about your priorities, the amount of time you have, and how many stops you plan to make. Knowing this information is important for planning the route that suits you best.

The speech outline will help you sequence your information and include all main points to present a speech that is clear and coherent. Like a roadmap, the **outline** *is a tool that will help place related items together and will ensure that your ideas flow from one main point to another supported by sub-points.* As with a roadmap, the outline helps create a plan or structure for the speech. Just as you have to take time to plan a trip, you will also need to allow time to plan for a great speech presentation. It doesn't happen in just a few minutes, but the results are well worth your time.

In previous chapters, we explored the types of speeches, methods of delivery, the importance of conducting an audience analysis, defining the purpose of the speech, and narrowing the topic you plan to cover. We also looked at ways to add research to support your topic and to add to your audience's knowledge of the topic. Depending upon the amount of time given for the speech, the speaker will usually choose three carefully designed main points. Additional main points can be covered if additional time is provided. Now, it is time to learn about the speech outlines and what is involved with writing a great outline.

TWO TYPES OF SPEECH OUTLINES

There are two types of speech outlines to consider. First, we create a ***preparation outline*** and from that we create a ***presentation outline*** and useful notes for the presentation.

The Preparation Outline

Preparation outlines begin with a header, which includes your name, course name, and date of the speech. If using MLA Guidelines, show the last name and page number in the top right corner of your page. The date should be written as day month year without any commas. Double-space between the date and the next section as shown in the diagram below. Following this, you will complete the header by including the speech category, title, and general and specific purpose of the speech. The general purpose will state whether you plan to inform, entertain, demonstrate, or motivate your audience. It is the specific purpose that breaks down your speech plan in one sentence to show how you will achieve the primary focus of the speech. If you want to review this process, please go back to Chapter Six: Defining the Purpose.

Porter 1

Katie Porter

Public Speaking 1101

4 September 2022

Speech Category: Informative Speech

Title of Speech: How to Improve Time Management Skills

General Purpose: Inform

Specific Purpose: The specific purpose of this speech is to inform the audience how to improve time management skills in order to make time for priorities in life, use time effectively, and save time for themselves.

The next part of your preparation will include the **Introduction, Body, and Conclusion**. Each one of these three areas will include basic speechwriting details as follows:

The Introduction Step will include the Attention Step, Establish Need/Relevance, Establish Credibility, and Thesis. Also, the introduction step will include a transition/link to the body of the speech. For more information on how to plan the areas included in the introduction step, please see Chapter Ten of this workbook.

To follow the standard outline format for the **Body** of the speech, you will need to be systematic and logically structure the speech by using a consistent pattern of symbols. We accomplish this purpose by using Roman Numerals for the three main points in your outline and follow that with capital **ABCs** for the subpoints and numbers **123s** for the sub-sub-points. Add a **Transition/Link** sentence between each of the three main points and one leading into the conclusion. The body of the outline should look like this:

Transition/Link to the Body and First Main Point:

Body

    I. First Main Point

       A. First Sub-Point

          1. First Sub-Sub Point

          2. Second Sub-Sub Point

       B. Second Sub-Point

Transition/Link to the Second Main Point:

    II. Second Main Point

       A. First Sub-Point

       B. Second Sub-Point

Transition/Link to the Third Main Point:

    III. Third Main Point

       A. First Sub-Point

       B. Second Sub-Point

Transition/Link to the Conclusion:

Notice how the **Roman Numerals** are offset from the left margin and the sub-points are indented and line up directly under the main points. This type of outlining creates the structure needed to offset important main ideas from the supporting sub-points.

During a short 5–7-minute speech, you may not need to include sub-sub-points; however, during a longer speech, this second set of sub-points may become necessary as demonstrated above in the first main point. In the case that you use sub-sub-points, these should be noted with numbers.

The **Standard Outline Format** is used in speech writing and is expected as you plan the speech. If you have an A) Sub-Point, you must also include a B) Sub-Point. The standard outline format can include as many sub-points as needed to cover the main points. The same type pattern is expected if you use sub-sub points. For example, if you have a 1) Sub-Sub-Point, you must also include a 2) Sub-Sub-Point. As with sub-points, you can use additional sub-sub-points as needed, but they do not have to match the sub-points used in other main points.

The **Conclusion** of the speech will include a summary of main points and closing statements which are usually noted as an appeal to action.

Use the following Preparation Outline Checklist to make sure you have everything you need for your outline. More details of what to include in your outline will be found in Chapter Ten: Constructing the Outline.

Preparation Outline Checklist

Completed	Standard Preparation Outline, Works Cited Page, and Visual Aid Explanation
❑	Header includes Name, Course, and Date
❑	Speech Category (Introduction, Informative, Demonstration, Persuasion, Special Occasion, Group, Sales Presentation)
❑	Speech Title
❑	General Purpose (Inform, Demonstrate, Entertain, Motivate)
❑	Specific Purpose
❑	Introduction: • Attention Step • Establish Need/Relevance • Establish Credibility • Thesis (Preview of Three Main Points)
❑	Body: • Transition to the Body of the Speech • Roman Numerals to Indicate the Three Main Points • ABCs to Indicate Sub-Points • 123s to Indicate Sub-Sub-Points • Transition/Link between each Main Point and to the Conclusion
❑	Conclusion: • Summary • Appeal to Action
❑	Works Cited or Bibliography Page—*separate page from outline* • Did you check with your instructor to determine which citation style is expected? Are you using MLA or APA? • Did you parenthetically cite all research in the outline (in-text citation)? • Did you include a full citation for each source of research used?
❑	Visual Aid Explanation Page—separate page from outline • List and describe all visual aids you plan to use during the speech

The Presentation Outline

Now that you have completed the **Preparation Outline**, it is time to begin work on the **Presentation** or **Speaking Outline** that is used during the delivery of the speech. This outline will look different from the preparation outline because it is designed to help the speaker remember what to say by providing a scaled down version of data or statistics, key words, phrases, quotes, or cues. Speakers should rehearse using the presentation outline so that when needed, they will remember where to look for the information.

If you are using the SpeechShark app, this has already been done for you. Just place your phone, iPad, or tablet on the lectern while speaking. A quick swipe of the screen will take you to the next on-screen note card.

If you prefer a paper copy of notes instead of using the notes feature in the app, simply e-mail the speech to yourself. Copy and paste the e-mail into a Word document. This will automatically format your speech using MLA Guidelines and will give you a paper document to use for notes.

CREATING USEFUL NOTES

For those not using the app, you will want to create a *very* brief outline to be used as notes during the delivery of your speech. The more streamlined your notes, the less chance you will read notes to the audience. Audiences do not want speakers reading to them and they will enjoy your speech so much more if you talk to them

in a conversational tone instead of a reading cadence. My tool of choice for transporting notes to the stage is a simple black folder. Attach only one or two note cards or attach a streamlined one-page outline inside the folder. Tuck the black folder under your arm on the side of your body that does not face the audience. This allows you to take notes to the stage without being obvious that you have notes. As you approach the lectern, place the folder on the lectern in an open position and begin your speech.

Avoid holding notes in your hand while speaking, as shown in the picture, because this will prevent you from gesturing and will also cause problems with eye contact. Speakers who hold notes are more inclined to read or fidget with their notes during the speech. As you might imagine, this will be distracting to the audience and will make the speaker look less confident.

Create Presentation Notes

First, save the presentation notes as a separate file. Create presentation/speaker notes and a script for the tech team by a quick "copy and paste" of the preparation outline onto a blank document. Then, begin deleting information. Take out all of the header information, category, title, and purpose. Leave the attention step and keep the notation of establish need/relevance and establish credibility, but it is not necessary to include the entire credibility content because this is information you know. For the thesis, just write your three main points.

In the body of the speech, keep all of the main points and sub-points using your Roman Numerals, ABCs, and 123s. Remove most of the words in the main points and sub-points so that you only have one key word or a short phrase for each one. Keep the summary and closing statements.

If you are using research to support the introduction, body, or conclusion, keep the parenthetical citations to remind you of the research and the source. The key information is all that is needed in order to jog your memory and to keep you on track. Often, speakers will not use presentation/speaker notes, but just knowing you have them nearby may be all that is needed to boost confidence. I said it before, but it stands to be repeated. Rehearse using your presentation/speaker notes. By doing this, you will have a good idea of where on the paper you can quickly find the point, sub-point, or research that you have forgotten. As you move to look at notes, make the movements smooth so that it is not obvious you are moving back to the lectern to peek at notes. If you use one-word or short phrase main points, a quick glance down will allow you to see the words and then your eye contact is back with the audience as you continue the speech.

Presentation notes should be typed with a larger font size than used for the preparation outline. Small type and handwriting are hard to read at a quick glance. Highlight key words in different colors to remind you of places where you need to slow down, pause, breathe, or speak louder. Use one color for key words, one color for research, and another color for directions. You can also include a smiley face at the top of the page to remind you to smile at your audience.

On the following page is an example of brief presentation notes. Notice how the key thoughts are highlighted in yellow, the research and support items are in green, and directions are in blue. Some people choose to circle or **bold** key words instead of using highlighters. If all of these colors distract you, use a system that works for YOU. After all, you are the speaker and the presentation notes should be designed to help you. All you have to do is put this in a black folder, rehearse, and you are ready for your presentation.

Attention Step: Play video clip from Alice in Wonderland's "I'm Late"
Scene: 23 seconds: https://www.youtube.com/watch?v=zpiB0COTM_M

How many of you can identify with the White Rabbit because you are continuously late? Pause and wait for the audience to respond.

Establish Need, Credibility, and Thesis:
    I. Spend Time on Priorities
        A. Faith
        B. Family
        C. Fitness and Health
   II. Use Time Wisely
       Stephen Covey's *Seven Habits of Highly Effective People*
        A. Budget Time
        B. Avoid Procrastination
        C. Learn to say NO
 III. Save Time for Myself
        A. Focus on Personal Goals
        B. Focus on Relaxation

Summary: Three Points—Spend Time, Use Time, Save Time

Closing Statements: Play video clip from Alice in Wonderland's "Opening Three Doors"
Scene: 10 seconds: https://www.youtube.com/watch?v=di7dZwidXZU

Just as Alice opened three doors in a search to satisfy her curiosity, Pause and move toward the center of the stage. I hope that I've satisfied your curiosity about ways to manage time so that YOU are not continuously late. Pause and SMILE.

Manage your own time more effectively. Pause.

You'll find that you will enjoy the time you spend, use, and save!

Outline Organizing Basics

After reading this chapter, you should be able to answer the following questions:

1. Why is it important that speeches be organized clearly and coherently? _____

   _____

   _____

   _____

2. How many main points will your speeches usually contain? Why is it important to limit the number of

   main points in your speeches?_____

   _____

   _____

   _____

3. What are the two types of speech outlines? _____

   _____

   _____

   _____

4. How is a preparation outline different from a presentation outline? _____

   _____

   _____

   _____

5. What requirements does a standard outline format have for posting sub-points?_____

_____

_____

_____

6. Why is it important to outline your speeches? _____

_____

_____

_____

7. What is a preparation outline? _____

_____

_____

_____

8. What are the guidelines discussed for writing a preparation outline? _____

_____

_____

_____

9. What is a speaking outline? _____

_____

_____

_____

10. What is the best way to carry useful notes to the stage? _____

_____

_____

_____

Shark Bites

Scenario: You are crafting an informative speech titled "Caring for a Family Pet." Use standard outlining format to create a Preparation Outline in the area below.

- Your three main points are Diet, Exercise, and Training.
- Your sub-points are: Manners training for your pet, Knowing what to feed the pet, Potty training your pet, Walking your pet, Knowing when to feed the pet, Playing games with your pet, Kennel training your pet, and Knowing how much to feed the pet.
- Include the introduction, body, conclusion, and transition/links. Arrange sub-points to support main points.

Chapter Eleven
Constructing the Outline

WRITING STYLE

Style. You show it in the way you wear your hair, the clothes you choose, the car you drive, even the type of computer you use. Every one of us has style. You also show your style in the way you write and speak. Depending upon your audience, your writing style may vary. As you conducted the audience analysis, I'm sure you found out a great deal about your audience. What do they need to know about your topic? How will hearing this topic help your audience? Do you need to gather supporting materials to make your speech more credible? True, the public speaking class is a captive audience and they are asked to stay for your full speech even if the topic is not appealing to them. With this in mind, please try to consider what topics your audience may want to hear. Think of them as individuals and find out as much as you can about them prior to planning a presentation so the speech will be more appealing. Your ability to grasp and retain the attention of your audience will make you a more successful speaker. How do you do this?

1. Get organized
2. Get the audience's attention
3. Get to the point
4. Get the audience motivated.

As mentioned in Chapter Nine, you learned about the two different types of outlines that speechwriters use. But I'm sure you are wondering, "How do I come up with the material to go into the outline and where do I start?"

FIRST THINGS FIRST

The first step in creating style with your writing is to begin at the beginning. If you think I mean to start with the Introduction Step, then you are wrong. Speechwriters actually begin with the body of the speech. You can't possibly know how to begin or end a speech until you know how your speech will be developed. **Get organized** and decide how you will order the body of your speech. This step is not as hard as you might think when you use a simple brainstorming technique better known as **Clustering and Webbing**. There are as many ways to conduct clustering and webbing as there are sharks in the sea. I use this process all of the time and even used it when writing this guidebook. It works for writing a speech, but also works for other projects where organization is important such as planning a party, a vacation, or a shopping trip. I'll share my favorite way with you and, of course, you can adapt this method to make sure it fits your own way of thinking and your own writing style.

Clustering and Webbing is a visual way of organizing and mapping a plan. Consider the road map again that we discussed in Chapter Nine. Seeing the various roads and traveling options sometimes is the best way to determine the route you plan to take. The same is true with the Clustering and Webbing method. When you finish this, you will actually SEE potential ideas to use when designing a speech.

Begin with a blank sheet of paper. Somewhere near the center of the page, draw a circle and write the topic of your speech inside the circle. You might not know the title just yet, and that is OK. Just focus first on the topic.

Now, write any ideas that relate to the topic. You'll add lines and circles all around the topic that relate to the topic. As you brainstorm the ideas, you will begin to cluster or group ideas that seem to belong together.

Continue this planning session until you have no more ideas to add. Using several different colors to highlight clusters or groups that make sense together may help you to visualize the speech taking shape. Once completed, you can look at the paper and notice how the groups begin to take shape. Count the number of groups you have and those become main points. Extensions become sub-points. Draw lines through points you don't have time or don't want to cover. This process may look messy and that is fine because your outline will be neat and organized. The Clustering and Webbing page will highlight options as groups and clusters of ideas. It might also reveal if the topic is too broad or too narrow and needs to be adjusted.

Here is an example to show the possibilities when planning a speech using ecology as the topic. Notice there could be five possible main points to cover with this plan: climate change, water, soil, air, and energy. Also notice that you can easily see the sub-points developing.

If the speech will last for thirty to forty-five minutes, having five main points is not unreasonable, but if the speech will last only five to seven minutes, you could be in trouble with five hefty main points. In this case, it is a good idea to **get to the point** as you narrow the topic and shift to one of the main points that has ample sub-points. Notice how the Clustering and Webbing project will help visualize the direction needed for the speech topic.

Look at the three sub-points for Climate Change. Obviously, Climate Change has the potential to become the topic of a five- to seven-minute informative speech. Notice how one of the sub-points, sustainability, easily moves into three main points: Resource Management, Environmental Management, and Green Building. Here is how my next speech plan may look:

Climate Change Sustainability

If I go with this plan, I'll still need to consider the sub-points that will support the three main points. My next task will be to conduct research on the topic of Climate Change: Sustainability. As I do this, the research will reveal sub-points that will be a perfect fit for the speech. It might also help as I decide which of the three main points should come first in the speech. This brings us to our next subject: how do we order our main points?

ORDERING MAIN POINTS

After the general and specific purpose of the speech has been targeted and the topic has been chosen, the biggest question I get is, "How do I know which point to put first, second, and third?" There are strategic ways to organize main points for a speech. As the speechwriter, it is up to you to determine which way is more effective for your topic and for your audience.

Examine the various ways for ordering main points, but keep in mind the amount of time you have for the speech. Use that information to decide if you can cover the topic's main points in the time allotted. If not, you may need to choose different main points or choose to develop only one of the main points you are considering.

The following table will help you to understand the different options for ordering speech points:

Order	Description
Topical	Consider the topic of your speech and divide that one topic into three sub-topics. If the order is not critical as long as points are covered, you will choose to use the topical order.
Chronological	If you are crafting a speech that involves time, you will want to use the chronological order. The first point will show what needs to happen first, then subsequent main points will follow. This order is most often used when discussing the history of something or when demonstrating a process or the use of a product. Chronological order is also used when introducing yourself or someone else and you cover that person's past experiences, present or current events, and future plans.
Cause-Effect	Often referred to as a causal order, this type of order is used when the speaker needs to show a relationship between a cause and effect. The first point will expose a problem (cause) and the next point will cover the consequences that arise (effect) due to the problem. For a third point, the speaker will usually tell a story to describe the cause-effect of the topic. This type of order is used to explain why something may be happening.
Problem-Solution	This order is used with persuasion speeches as we work to motivate someone to do something or think differently about something. The problem-solution order is referred to as Monroe's Motivated Sequence. During this type of speech, the speaker will first discuss a problem. Second, the speaker will offer realistic solution(s) to the problem. Third, the speaker will help the audience to visualize the results if the problem is solved and consequences if the problem is not solved.
Spatial	When the topic involves location or direction such as up or down, left or right, top or bottom, north or south, the speaker will use spatial ordering. Using this type of ordering will help the audience to visualize the place the speaker is describing and helps the audience to experience the information shared. Consider a high-rise office building as the topic. The speaker may give a virtual tour starting with the bottom floor and moving to the top floor. If the zoo is a topic, the speaker may give a tour starting at the first gate and work through the exhibits to the last gate.

USING WORDS THAT MATTER

When creating the outline and showing the main points, it is advisable to make sure you keep the main points separate and clear. Begin each main point or sub-point using the same type of pattern. For example, you might begin each main point with a question, a verb, or with a noun. Look carefully at each main point and think of ways to develop each point equally. Instead of spending too much time on any one point, try to approach each one equally so there is a balance. This will help your outline to be consistent and clear.

As mentioned earlier in this guidebook, each speech has three main parts: Introduction, Body, and Conclusion. With the body of the speech taking shape, it is time to focus on how to **get the audience's attention** with the **Introduction.**

Introduction

This part of the outline will include the **Attention Step**, **Establish Need/Relevance**, **Establish Credibility**, and will preview the body of the speech with a clear **Thesis**. Use full sentences as you craft this step because it will force you to think in complete thoughts, help as you learn the speech, and will help gauge its length. The full introduction step will usually last about a minute to a minute and a half and certainly not more than 10% of your speech time. Once you have the content for the introduction step, you will move seamlessly from one part to the next without citing the headings, even though they are shown in the preparation outline. Let's look at each one of these steps so that you have a better understanding of how to craft different areas with the finesse of an accomplished speechwriter.

It has been said that you have between three to five seconds to get an audience's attention and for them to decide if what you have to say is worth their time and attention. The key word here is attention. What will you say or do to get the audience's attention? How will you plan to keep their attention once you have it?

Your speech begins from the moment you stand up to enter the stage. The audience watches as you enter the stage and as you move to the lectern. Make a conscious effort to walk with a purpose and avoid lingering at the lectern looking at notes before you begin speaking. Never begin your speech by saying, "Hello! How is everyone today? My name is _____ and I want to speak to you about _____." Do this and you will notice how their first glance at you will lead to the second glance as they check their phones, look at the program, begin making a grocery list, or speak to the person sitting next to them. You've lost them already and there is a good chance that your message will never reach them.

Instead, walk confidently to the stage, smiling and nodding to your audience as you approach the lectern. Quickly place your notes on the lectern and step to the side as you begin the first words you planned for the speech—the **Attention Step**.

Attention Step

Chapter One includes a few of my favorite ways to get an audience's attention, but I wanted to expand on these ways by giving you more details and, of course, adding a few extra strategies. With all of these options, remember that you must be able to relate the attention step back to the main idea or topic of your speech. It is not good enough to simply get the audience's attention; instead, your attention step should be a clear preview to the topic you have chosen. Try using one of these or a combination of these to get your audience's attention and keep it!

1. **Startling statement:** Winston Churchill, known for his powerful speeches, would often begin the speech with a powerful statement that would command the attention of his audience from the very first word. Some speakers choose a shocking statement that might have been featured as front-page news,

and will hold up the newspaper as the statement is spoken. Others start by boldly stating a problem that needs to be solved and then follows this with a question to ask "How can YOU help to solve this problem?"

2. **Refer to a historical event:** Gain the audience's attention by choosing a historical event that will introduce the topic of your speech and beginning by saying, "On this day in history, ___ years ago. . . ." The important thing to remember is that after you introduce the event, it is important to relate how that same type of event is prevalent today. Show the correlation between the historical and current events.

3. **Quote from a person:** Anyone can open a speech with a quote. They are a dime a dozen, but using a carefully chosen quote can be quite effective and will set the tone for the rest of your speech. Choose a quote that directly relates to the topic you are covering and be sure to tell your audience where you found the quote. Avoid using a quote by an unknown author because it packs less of a punch.

4. **Quote from recent research:** This can be an effective strategy as the speaker will begin the speech by quoting a recent research report or journal article. Be sure to lead into the quote with the source of the research by saying, "According to a story . . . recently published in . . ., I learned that . . ."

5. **Data or statistics:** Powerful or personalized data and statistics will speak clearly to your audience and will get to the point right away. Making data or statistics relevant to the audience by explaining how it impacts the audience will help the speaker to immediately grab attention in a show-stopping way.

6. **Question:** Whether you are asking a rhetorical or a literal question, this type of attention step will cause the audience to think of ways they would answer. If you want them to answer your question out loud, you will need to prompt the response. Also, let the audience know if you want them to respond by a show of hands. Be careful with this type of attention step and make sure your question is meaningful and leads to the main point of your topic. Correctly phrasing a question will determine whether it is rhetorical or literal.

7. **Refer to a recent conversation:** Start the speech by telling a story about a recent conversation with someone as it deals with your topic. This is a good place to use a personal interview. For example, you could say, "Two weeks ago, I was speaking to . . . about . . . and he told me that . . ."

8. **Imagery:** Invite the audience to be part of the attention step by using imagery to help the audience visualize or imagine an extraordinary thing. You might begin by saying, "Imagine you are . . ." Then follow up the imagery with a question. "How would this change your . . .?" Or "What would you think about . . .?"

9. **Scenario:** Ask the question, "What if . . .?" and your audience will immediately be drawn into the speech as it invites the audience to consider their own answer to the question. "What if" scenarios may also start with "What would happen if . . .?" or "How different would our lives be if . . .?"

10. **Story:** Everyone loves a good story, especially a personal story. For this to be effective, be sure to paint a picture using words so that the audience will feel as if they are part of the story. Just any story won't do. It needs to be a story that lends a dramatic effect to the topic of your speech using vocal variance and gestures to make the story come to life. Once, I heard a speaker begin a story by moving as close to the end of the stage as possible, leaned in toward his audience, and motioned to the audience as if he was pulling them closer to say, "Let me tell you a story." It was a powerful opening and he had us so involved with the story that we were sad when he didn't finish it during the attention step, but saved the ending of the story for the conclusion of his speech.

11. **Share information about a personal experience:** Allow the audience to identify with you as you share a personal experience as it relates to the topic of your speech. You might start by saying, "When I was eighteen years old, I never guessed that I would be standing here in front of you forty years later explaining . . ." Audience members will feel you are authentic and credible if you start with a personal experience.

12. **Begin with a music tag:** This could be music played as you enter the stage. The tag should last only until you reach the lectern and then should include a comment about the music. For example, if you are speaking to a group of students about a SkillsUSA competition, you could enter with the music from Queen playing, "We are the champions, my friends; and we'll keep on fighting 'til the end; we are the champions, we are the champions, no time for losers 'cause we are the champions—of the world." Your first words following this will need to refer back to the SkillsUSA champions that are being celebrated!

13. **Begin with a scene from a movie:** One of the best speeches I've heard this year was from a student who was giving an informative speech about professional sports management. The attention step from his speech was a brief ten-second clip from the Jerry Maguire movie starring Tom Cruise in which we heard Tom Cruise shouting, "Show me the money!" After the clip, and with the audience still smiling, the student began with a strong statement about sports management and the money players are paid.

14. **Humor:** Be careful with this one! Don't just tell a joke to get the audience's attention and don't tell just any joke! If you decide to use humor, make sure you are good with using humor and make sure what you are saying will be accepted by your audience. Avoid off-color humor or humor that may be offensive to a diverse population. Remember that your goal is to get the audience's attention in a positive way so that you can keep their attention throughout the speech. You'll also want to make sure the humor you use will point directly to the topic of your speech. If you get a good laugh from your audience, please wait until the laughter begins to settle down before adding your next lines that lead to your core idea of the speech.

Establish Need/Relevance

Now that you have the audience's attention and they have an idea of the topic you will be covering, it is your job to establish why the audience needs to hear your speech. In one or two brief sentences, explain the relevance of the topic to their lives.

During this step, you might say, "It is important that you are here today because I'm going to speak to you about (the topic). This affects everyone in this audience because . . ." You could also say, "The topic of ___ should be particularly interesting to you because . . ." The primary goal is to keep the audience's attention by letting them know the next few minutes will provide valuable information and the time they take to hear your speech will not be wasted.

Establish Credibility

What experience do you have with the topic? Why are you the person to speak to this audience and provide information about the topic? These are questions you need to answer as you establish your own credibility as the speaker. A brief statement regarding your personal experiences which led to your understanding of the topic is necessary. If possible, add the number of years you have had experience with the topic or if you have conducted research regarding the topic. The audience needs to know you are up for the task and that you are speaking from experience.

Thesis

The thesis is the point in the Introduction Step where the speaker can preview the topic and the main points that will cover the topic. It needs to be brief and clear. Here is a good example: "Today, I will explain the topic of _____ by covering three areas of importance: (1) First Main Point, (2) Second Main Point, and (3) Third Main Point."

The thesis is the last step in the Introduction Step and now you will be ready to connect the introduction to the body of the speech.

Connectors

Moving from the introduction to the body of the speech, to each of the main points, and then to the conclusion can be awkward unless the speaker uses effective connectors to accomplish the task. These will be accomplished by using ***transitions*** *also known as links, internal previews, signposts or signals, and internal reviews.* Audiences respond well to speakers who do this, because it is clear where the speaker has been and where she is planning to go.

Internal Previews are statements which will let the audience know what will be covered next in the speech. These are excellent to use for the transition that links the introduction step to the body of the speech. The thesis is also considered a preview of the full speech as you detail which three main points you will plan to cover during the speech.

Internal Reviews are areas where you summarize what you have covered in a previous area of the speech. Often speakers will include this in the transitions between main points as you summarize the point just covered and before you lead into the transition to the next point. You'll also provide a complete summary of the three main points in the conclusion step.

If you are using the SpeechShark app, the transitions are automatically built in; however, if you are manually building your speech, you will need to carefully place transitions in four areas of the speech. Creating these transitions ahead of time and placing them in the correct area of your outline will help you to remember to use them and you won't be struggling to find the right words during the delivery of the speech. This is when some speakers have that awkward moment of silence as they consider how to get from one point to the next. Nonverbal cues can emphasize your links. Pausing, gesturing, changing locations on the stage area, facial expressions, smiling, and changing the pitch of your voice or the rate in which you speak can help to signal to the audience that you are moving from one point to another.

Here are examples of how you might craft the four transition/links that should be found in your speech outline.

Transition/Link 1: This is placed after the introduction step and leads to the first point in the body of the speech. It can be as simple as saying, "Let's begin with the first point, (Add the point heading) . . ."

Transition/Link 2: This follows Point 1 and leads to Point 2. It will provide an internal summary that leads smoothly to the next main point. Here is an example: "Now that we have covered the first point, (Add the point heading) . . ., let's move to the second point, (Add the point heading) . . ."

Transition/Link 3: This follows Point 2 and leads to Point 3. Again, as an internal summary, it will lead to the final point. You might say, "Now that you understand Point 1 (Add the point heading) . . . and Point 2, (Add the point heading) . . ., allow me to share with you about Point 3, (Add the point heading) . . ."

Transition/Link 4: This follows Point 3 and leads to the conclusion step of the speech. This internal summary shouldn't summarize the entire speech since that is done in the conclusion step, but will wrap up Point 3 and lead seamlessly into the conclusion step. A signpost in conjunction with a transition/link is effective for this point in the speech. An example of this is, "It's been a privilege to speak to you about (the topic) and to hopefully add additional knowledge of this topic to the information you already have. Above all, you need to know (Add something about the topic's relevance) . . ."

From these examples you can tell that transitions are ways of signaling movement from one point to another as well as how the points relate to each other. There are four separate types of transitions to consider. Below is a table that will help you find the words you need to craft each type of transition:

Transition Types	Definition	Example
Time	Demonstrates the passing of time	Now that we have . . . We are now ready to . . . First . . . Next . . . Later . . .
Viewpoint	Demonstrates a situation shift	On the other hand . . . However . . . Although . . .
Connective	Unites related thoughts	In addition to . . . Also . . . Another . . . Not only . . . but also . . .
Concluding	Signals the end of the section	To summarize . . . In conclusion . . . As a result . . . Finally . . .

Conclusion

This is the very last step that you will take when planning your speech. Audiences appreciate a speaker who will use a **signpost or signal** at the end of the speech. This can be easily done as the speaker says, "To conclude . . .," "To summarize . . .," "As I conclude . . .," or "Above all, remember. . . . This signal will lead smoothly to the conclusion of the speech which includes a **Summary** or internal review of the three main points and a final statement, also known as the **Appeal to Action**.

Summary

The purpose of the summary is to offer a review of all that was covered in the speech. This is a brief sentence or two in which the speaker will review the topic and the main points covered during the speech. The clearer, the better! Here is an example: "To summarize, it's been a pleasure to meet with you today to discuss (the topic) and I've been able to share three areas of importance as they deal with (the topic): Point 1 . . ., Point 2 . . ., and Point 3 . . ." After you finish the summary of the speech and before moving to the closing statement, slow down the pace of your speech to add impact to the final words you will say.

Closing Statements

This is the point where the speaker can **get the audience motivated**! The final words of a speech should be carefully crafted word-for-word in order to keep the audience thinking about the topic and the main points shared. Double the number of pauses you used during the speech or in normal conversation in order to emphasize what you are saying. The audience will be able to tell from this that you are about to share something they really need to hear. Use dramatic pauses at the end of a sentence to allow time for the audience to process what you have said.

SpeechSharks never end a speech with, "That's all" or "That's all I've got." That may be humorous for Porky Pig's *Looney Tunes Cartoons*, but a weak conclusion may mean that the audience will not retain the main points covered. They will only remember the last words you say and you don't want them to think that's all you've got. It is for this reason that speakers must spend time constructing a closing statement that will be remembered and acted upon. There are different strategies to end a speech, but the strategy you choose should leave the audience begging for more. The ultimate goal is to motivate your audience to action and end the speech with a BANG!

While you can use many of the same strategies that are used to introduce a speech topic, here are some strategies for ending a speech so that you get a standing ovation.

1. **Appeal to action:** A strong appeal should leave the audience with a positive lasting impression of the topic and a desire to act upon the speaker's challenge. Sometimes labeled as a "call to action," this part of the speech should make the audience want to get out of their seats and DO something about the topic covered. You'll want to carefully craft this and say it as if it has ten exclamation points after it!!!!!!!!!!

2. **Story:** Just as you might open a speech with a personal story, it is also effective to end the speech with a personal story. Better yet, finish the story you begin in the attention step so that the audience is hanging on throughout the speech just to hear the end of the story. As a child, I would listen to Paul Harvey, a noted radio celebrity who perfected this in his show entitled, "The Rest of the Story." Speakers can follow his lead by presenting little known or forgotten facts in the introduction of the speech only to complete the rest of the story during the closing statements. Paul Harvey's ending tag

line was, "and now you know the rest of the story." As he would say this line, all of my family members who were gathered around to listen would all smile a knowing smile. Yes, we did know the rest of the story and it was worth listening to the full program just to learn the ending.

3. **Humor:** Again, be careful when using humor. It can be so effective, yet can fall flat if not delivered correctly. If choosing a joke, make sure it circles back to the topic and repeats the main points you are making with a story that will cause the audience to laugh. Smile or chuckle if the line you are saying is funny and be serious if the line is more thought-provoking. The audience will follow your lead. It is fun to end a speech with an audience full of people laughing at the last lines you say.

4. **Quote or inspirational poem:** There are many quotes and poems that contain messages which might summarize the main points of a speech. Selecting a quote or poem for the closing statement is effective, but will need to be moving or emotional. Leaving the audience with moving final lines will keep them thinking about your topic.

There are conflicting views of whether the speaker should end a speech with "thank you" or should simply leave the stage. As a member of Toastmasters International, our club members are taught to say the final words planned for their closing statements, pause, and then relinquish the stage back to the Toastmaster of the day by saying, "Mister or Madam Toastmaster," waiting until he comes to the lectern, shake his hand to signify giving the stage back to the Toastmaster, and then leave the stage area while members applaud.

While attending conferences, I notice that it is not unusual for conference speakers to thank the audience with a brief, "thank you" following the closing statements. Sometimes they end their speech with a closing "thank you" slide signaling that the speech has ended. I'm never offended by this because I believe they are being courteous and thanking the audience for their attention, just as the audience will show appreciation by applauding as the speaker leaves the stage.

In the classroom, I ask students to finish the prepared closing statements, pause and look at the audience, nod their heads, smile toward the audience, pick up notes from the lectern, and while the audience is applauding, confidently leave the stage area and move to a seat. Sometimes, it is difficult to know if a student has finished the speech or if he is still thinking about what he wants to say. This is especially true if he continues standing at the lectern for too long after saying the final words. That usually occurs because the closing statement is not effective.

For students who want to include a thank you following their speech, I suggest they add a thank you as part of the summary as it leads to the conclusion. Do this by saying, "It's been a privilege to speak to you about (the topic) and to cover (List all three points). Hopefully, this has added additional knowledge of this topic to the information you already have. Thank you for your time and for your attention. Above all, you need to know . . ." Then follow the sentence with the closing statement.

Bibliography or Works Cited Page

The outline is not complete until you've attached a separate page which includes a complete source citation of all research used during the speech presentation. This could be noted as a Bibliography or a Works Cited page depending upon whether you are following APA or MLA Guidelines for citing research. Be sure to ask your instructor which type of citation guidelines should be followed for your class.

For most public speaking situations, MLA Guidelines are used. On this page, the speaker will offer a full citation which will identify the author's name, the title of the source, title of the work, other contributors, version, volume number, publisher, publication date, page number, location, and accessed day month year. More information regarding the different types of guidelines and suggestions for citing research can be found in Chapter Nine: Conducting Research.

In Chapter Three of this textbook, as you read through the types of speeches, you will find that for each type of speech there is a brainstorming worksheet along with an outline template, and an example of a speech outline. Please use the brainstorming worksheet and the template when writing your next speech or use the SpeechShark app and you will be very pleased with the end results.

As this chapter comes to an end, remember that having a great preparation outline can be a confidence booster. Knowing your material is the best way to lower anxiety. The best way to learn material in your speech is to rehearse, rehearse, rehearse. Being meticulous, comprehensive, and systematic when creating the outline of your speech is just another form of rehearsal. Every semester, I realize that a great outline usually leads to a great student presentation and that, of course, leads to a higher end of course score. Spend extra time creating the outline and you will be pleased with the speech you present.

Constructing the Outline

After reading this chapter, you should be able to answer the following questions:

1. Define Clustering and Webbing.

    _____

    _____

2. What are some methods you can use in the introduction to get the attention and interest of your audience?

    _____

    _____

3. Why is it important to establish your credibility at the beginning of your speech?

    _____

    _____

4. What is the purpose of the thesis?

    _____

    _____

5. What are the major functions of a speech conclusion?

    _____

    _____

6. What are two ways you can signal the end of your speech?

_____

_____

7. How should I order a speech that involves steps of a process?

_____

_____

8. What are transitions and how are they used?

_____

_____

9. What is the purpose of the summary?

_____

_____

10. What are two strategies for writing the closing statements of a speech?

_____

_____

Shark Bites

Think of a speech topic (preferably one for your next speech in class). Create an introduction for a speech dealing with any aspect of the topic you wish. The beginning, or introduction, prepares audience members for what is to come. In your introduction, be sure to gain the attention of the audience, reveal the topic to the audience, establish your credibility, and preview the body of the speech.

_____

_____

_____

_____

Using the same topic as above, create a speech conclusion. The conclusion ties up the speech and alerts audience members that the speech is going to end. Be sure to let your audience know the speech is ending, recap the major points, and make the conclusion vivid and memorable.

_____

_____

_____

_____

SpeechSHARK™

Unit 4

Creating Visual Aids

Creating Effective Visual Aids

Working with a Tech Team

Key Terms to Know

Chapter 12—Creating Effective Visual Aids

- Bar Graph
- Chart
- Figure-Ground
- Font
- Gestalt
- Graph
- Handouts
- Hierarchy
- Line Graph
- Organizational Schemas
- Pie Chart
- Presentation Technology

Chapter 13—Working with a Tech Team

- Scripts
- Tech Team

Chapter Twelve

Creating Effective Visual Aids

In this chapter:

What is the purpose of a visual aid?

What are the different types of visual aids?

What design theories should I use to design my visual aids?

How should I incorporate a table display?

How do I create a handout that is appealing and usable?

What are some of my favorite and not-so-favorite examples of visual aids?

After the preparation and presentation outlines have been completed, it's time to complete the fun part of the speech—the visual aids. This isn't just one more assignment for you to do in a speech class. In fact, there is a very important reason behind the task. Why do speakers need visual aids during a speech? *A well-designed visual aid clarifies the topic, generates interest, and promotes retention of the material.*

CLARIFIES THE TOPIC

Visual aids can be powerful tools to help bring your topic to life. Words and images seen as the speaker covers a point will add structure and power to the spoken words. Keeping visual aids simple is key, but will help your audience to see the topic unfold as they visualize key points covered. Technical terms, often lost by many in the audience, will be better understood if they are seen as the speaker is discussing them. Images shown will lend clarity and an understanding of points which might be new knowledge for audience members. Charts and diagrams answer questions which will support the credibility of the speaker and add credence to the subject content.

GENERATES INTEREST

Audiences come in all sizes, shapes, and each one has a diverse knowledge base. Using visual aids helps keep the audience's attention, because they help the audience to become involved visually. Visual aids serve as a memory aid or learning support. Since we have so many different types of learners in an audience, a visual aid can expose the audience to information in a way that will help improve interest in the topic. Showing key words will keep the audience's interest as you move from one point to another. Interactive technology used during a speech will not only jazz up the presentation, but will help gain and keep the interest of audience members. Including music sound-bites or video clips will add interest and variety to presentations.

PROMOTES RETENTION

Attention spans vary for individuals. It is for this reason that many people in an audience have a difficult time remembering information they hear during a speech. When speaking one-on-one, it is easier to keep someone's attention; however, when speaking to a large audience, it is more of a challenge to retain each individual's attention. The larger the audience, the more challenging this becomes. It's even difficult to read and remember the information in a textbook unless that information is illustrated for you.

Speakers should plan speeches so they reach the intended audience and so the audience will retain the message. Take into consideration the many different types of learners that may be in your audience. Some people react better to information presented visually, while others react through using the other senses: hear, smell, taste, and touch. Visual learners make up the largest majority of learners in our population; therefore, it is important for speakers to consider ways to present material that can be processed and understood by the majority of audience members.

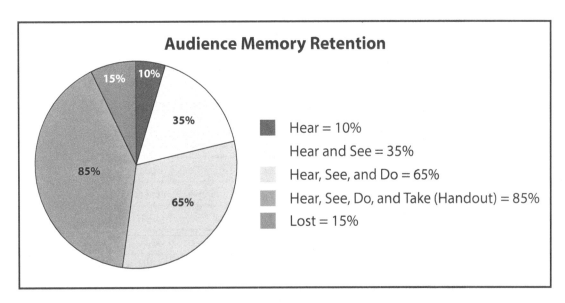

While earning a degree in instructional design, I learned that three days after a speech or class, my audience will remember only about **10%** of what they hear. If I add a visual aid to my presentation, their ability to recall the information will increase to somewhere around **35%**. Adding a visual aid and having the students do something during the presentation with the information I present, will improve their recall to somewhere around **65%**. Adding a physical handout for the students to take with them following the speech will further add recall to somewhere around **85%**. Ultimately, this means that there is about **15%** of a presentation that will be lost completely. Hopefully, my experiences will help you to realize the importance of using visual aids to promote retention.

Most of us can only retain a small percentage of what we read or hear. However, if we add a visual stimulus to the information read or heard, our brains are better able to interpret the information so the content is processed and understood. The more senses involved during the presentation, the longer your audience will remember the message delivered. A big part of this is because a good visual aid can make the information clearer and more appealing. It also helps to emphasize key ideas the speaker wants to share. The more data and statistics included in a speech, the more important it is for the visual aids to include charts, graphs, or tables. Pictures or diagrams will help audience members to visualize the items or processes that are discussed. Video clips and music add emotion to content and that will also aid in retention of content. We often use technology to deliver some of the different types of visual aids by creating PowerPoints or Prezi Presentations that can combine all types of visual aids making abstract ideas much more concrete and more retainable.

A visual aid can be any number of things that adds value to content presented. These may include yourself, objects, models, photos, maps, graphs, charts, diagrams, table displays, handouts, video clips, music, PowerPoint, Prezi, and technology. Here are some basic things to remember as you create your visual aids: Keep it Simple, Keep it LARGE, Keep it Interesting, Keep Visuals in the Background, and Keep It Going by following the basic DOs and DON'Ts.

BASIC DOs AND DON'Ts	
Do	**Don't**
KISS: Keep **I**t **S**imple **S**weetie!	Don't clutter posters or slides with too much
Limit each visual to ONE main idea	Don't use more than six lines
Use sans serif fonts—large enough to be visible by all audience members	Don't change font styles
Be consistent with fonts and colors	Don't use dark fonts with dark backgrounds
Bullet points, key words	Don't use complete sentences unless it is a quote
Use very little text	Don't use too many visual aids
Illustrate with pictures, graphs, charts	Don't add more visual aids than you can handle
Rehearse using the visual aids	Don't wait until the last minute to get a Tech Team
Cue video clips and music sound-bites to desired screen	Don't use more than thirty seconds of video for a five-minute speech
Check audio for desired levels	Don't show things that can't be seen by the entire audience
Explain purpose of video or music before playing it or summarize purpose directly after showing it	Don't turn your speech into a dull slide show
Show interest in video or music while playing it	Don't write on a dry-erase board or flip chart unless you are an amazing artist
Make sure visual aids support content	Don't read from a slide
Cover tables with a table cloth	Don't break eye contact as you show visual aids
Position table displays so all items are visible	Don't turn OFF all audience area lights while showing a video or PowerPoint
Pick up items on display table and show them as you speak about them	Don't ignore items on a table display
Use a Tech Team to set up visual aids	Don't use equipment or props you don't understand
Have a back-up plan if visual aids fail	Don't have items saved in just one way
Pack visual aids the day before the speech (USB drives, memory sticks, items for table displays)	Don't wait until the last minute to organize or rehearse with visual aids
Ignore the visual aid during presentations and talk to the audience	Don't talk to the visual aid

DESIGN THEORIES

Without taking you through a complete instructional design course, I'd like to share some of the highlights to help as you plan visual aids. There are three design theories that may be used separately or in conjunction with each other to create and manage visual aids for clearer understanding and retention. The three design theories are *Figure/Ground, Hierarchy, and Gestalt.*

Figure/Ground is a design theory that allows the audience to see information that is most or least important. Our brains will seek distinctions between the subject of the image and the background. The visual aid designer will demand attention for the figure (subject) by using fonts that are larger, smaller, bolder, brighter, or subdued on the screen. Spacing of fonts can be used in conjunction with size and color to achieve the desired effect.

As you design a visual aid using the Figure/Ground theory, you will be able to visually thrust the key information toward the audience or withdraw the information toward the background depending upon the purpose of your visual aid. As audiences see a larger, bolder presentation of material, they will perceive the information as being more important and worthy of consideration. Likewise, smaller, less obtrusive presentations of material (ground) will cause the audience to perceive the information as not as important. Since a picture is worth a thousand words, I'd like to show an example of how this might look:

Figure/Ground

Brings

IMPORTANT

Information to the Front

Three Design Theories:

- Figure/Ground
- **Hierarchy**
- Gestalt

Figure/Ground

Can Take

Less Important Information

To the Background

In the examples shown above, notice how the word, **I M P O R T A N T** jumps out from the slide? Simply using a bolder, larger font, and adding a space between each letter helps us to incorporate the Figure/Ground principle. In the same way we can make Less Important Information move into the background by using a smaller font and a lighter, less obtrusive color.

The Figure/Ground design is an arrangement of shapes, sizes, and space. Consider how proximity uses space to connect and separate the elements. Because of this, space also becomes a design element and performs visually by allowing design elements room to speak. I've heard it explained in relation to music. If every note on a piano was played at the same time, we would have noise instead of music. However, if you give space for the notes to be played with silence between keystrokes, then we get a pattern of sound which creates the rhythm that is beautiful music.

Hierarchy is an organizational tool which uses graphs, charts, tables, diagrams, directional arrows, outlines, lists, and maps to command the audience's attention. We use these types of visual aids often to show information in relation to other information. This design theory is based upon the way our brains organize and group things of importance together and can follow several different types of paths to accomplish the same type of thing.

Hierarchy can be demonstrated with our use of headings and bullet points in PowerPoint slides. The same slide is often duplicated and the separate bullet points are highlighted to show the information as it is discussed. Here is an example of a slide about the design theories and shows that we are focusing on Hierarchy.

Organizational schemas are another way of demonstrating the hierarchy design theory. Notice how the title of the theory is in the larger quadrant and the smaller quadrants detail support for the topic.

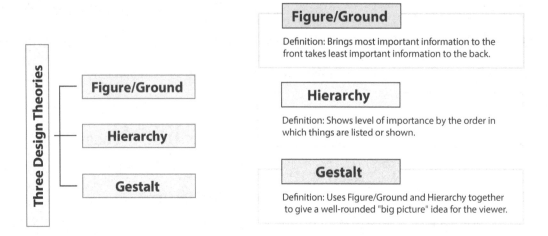

This type of hierarchy design is demonstrated as a list and is a good choice when you need to show several different areas and supply definitions.

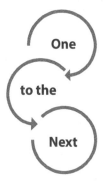

This type of hierarchy design indicates a cycle and will demonstrate the order in which the cycle progresses.

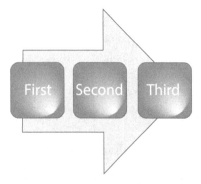

This example uses directional arrows to show a process. Arrows can be used in conjunction with text boxes or separately to show direction.

This example can show relationships of one type thing to another. Identifying PROs and CONs are a good way to illustrate relationships.

As you make choices regarding which types of hierarchy designs to use, just remember to choose the type that will produce the results you hope to see.

Line graphs, pie charts, bar charts, tree maps, tables, and combinations of these are other options that can be used to allow the audience a graphic which moves the eye from one bar of information to the next. This helps the instructional designer choose where the audience's eye will follow and that in turn leads to a point the speaker wants to make. Here are some examples:

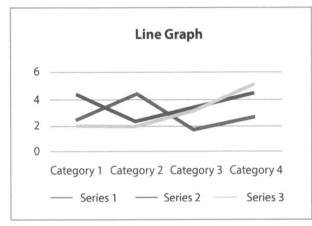

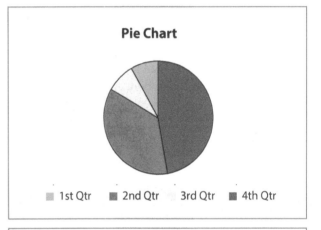

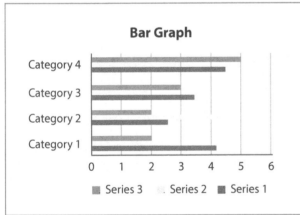

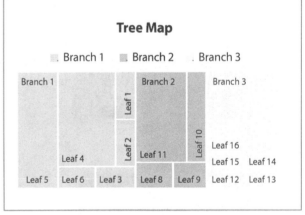

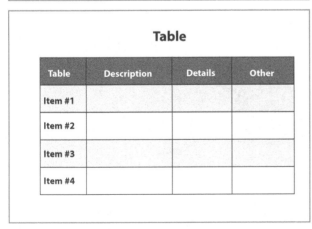

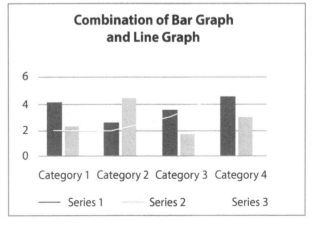

All of these graphics are easy to design and insert into your PowerPoint or Prezi slide using the features in Microsoft Word. I created all of the charts and tables found in this textbook to illustrate various concepts. Go to the top of your computer screen in Microsoft Word and choose the "Insert" tab. From there, you can choose to add SmartArt, Charts, or Tables. From there, you can customize any of the templates to fit your needs. If I can do it, you can do it too!

Gestalt is the last design theory that I would like to share with you. This one is actually my favorite because it incorporates figure/ground AND hierarchy. This type of design theory is based upon the big picture. Gestalt is not the name of a person, as you might suspect. Instead, it is *a German word which means the whole is greater than the sum of many parts* and was developed by a group of German psychologists who were developing theories of visual perception. Using a combination of design elements will help your audience to view your visual arrangements as connected.

One area to note is that audiences will pay attention to designs where there is a similarity between elements of color, size, shape, texture, or value. The new Amazon logo uses Gestalt continuation in the logo where the arrow entices the observer to see a curve or path as a continuous figure rather than separation. Also, the arrow can be seen as a smile indicating the customer will be happy. As the logo was designed, it was done so with the underlying theme for the customer to perceive continuous and happy service from the organization as it moves to the customer. This makes sense, doesn't it?

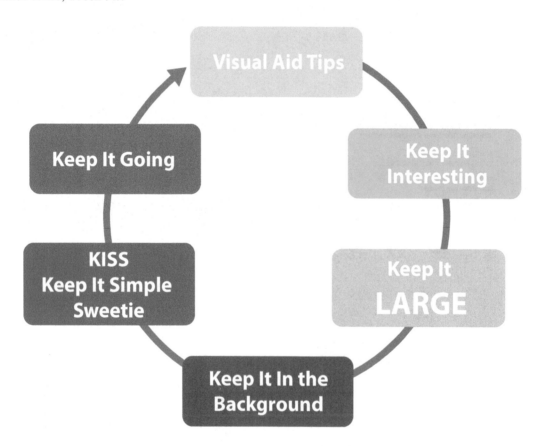

When you use Gestalt to design a visual aid, you are going to use words, colors, shapes, textures, and pictures to produce one primary thought. For example, when creating a PowerPoint presentation, you might choose to use a heading at the top of the slide and the picture to illustrate a point.

We're not through, yet! Here is another example of Gestalt design which will remind you of all the visual aid design principles in one visual aid.

PRESENTATION TECHNOLOGY

The most commonly used presentation technology used now are PowerPoint and Prezi. Both are excellent tools and create easy to see visual aids. Most speech instructors will require students to use presentation technology for the informative and persuasion speeches. Some will also require this for group and special occasion speeches. Please check with your instructor to make sure you are following their assignment requirements for speech presentations.

When creating a PowerPoint or Prezi as a visual aid, there are several things to keep in mind. As with any presentation, you will want to create the presentation outline first and then create the visual aid to follow the presentation plan.

Most speeches are better served with a simple PowerPoint that only includes five slides:

- Slide 1: Title Slide (Title of the speech and a supporting picture)
- Slide 2: Point 1 (Name of the point and a supporting picture or three bullet points)
- Slide 3: Point 2 (Name of the point and a supporting picture or three bullet points)
- Slide 4: Point 3 (Name of the point and a supporting picture or three bullet points)
- Slide 5: Conclusion Slide (Statement or quote and supporting picture)

Guidelines for Creating and Using Presentation Technology

Guidelines	Explanation
Advance Planning	Consider the topic, audience, and room where speech will be presented. Rehearse with the Tech Team prior to the speech. Make sure the Tech Team understands the presentation technology. Give the Tech Team a script so they will know when to advance slides.
KISS	Keep It Simple Sweetie. Make visual aids simple, clear, and concise. Do not overcrowd slides with words and pictures. Avoid animations and background music.
Visibility	Make sure visual aids can be seen. Use fonts that are easily seen and read by everyone. Check all seats in the room to make sure the screen is visible. Use color effectively. Use dark fonts on light backgrounds. Use light fonts on dark backgrounds. When adding pictures, make sure pictures are not stretched. Choose high-resolution images that will not blur. Show slide while speaking about that point.
Design	Use sans serif font types. Use consistent font sizes, colors, and types. Titles and headings should be 36–44-point type. Sub-titles and text should be no less than 24-point type. Use consistent background colors with consistent headings. Limit the amount of text used on slides. Avoid using all CAPS on slides—even for headings. Line up pictures and graphics so they are balanced on the slides. Balance pictures and text on slides by limiting content. Leave whitespace when placing graphics and bullet points. Have one-line bullet points—keep lines to words and simple phrases. Check spelling before showing the slides. Keep charts and graphs simple. Add a title or heading for each chart or graph. Edit video or music sound-bites to be the length allowed. Limit charts to show no more than eight items.
Cite Sources	Cite research used in the footer of each slide. This includes photographs, graphs, diagrams, data, statistics, and quotes.
Rehearse	Rehearse with Tech Team prior to speech presentation. Provide a script for Tech Team members so they know what to do. Play videos and music sound-bites before speech to check volume. Look at PowerPoint or Prezi design in the room where it will be used. Make adjustments as needed to make sure slides are visible and clear. Rehearse to make sure visual aids are displayed properly. Discuss visual aids only as they are being used.

TABLE DISPLAYS

Let's talk about table displays! Often speakers will use a table display to show off objects or to create interest for their speech topic. They can be very effective when designed well and are used to enhance the speech topic. Here are some things to remember:

- Use a clean, ironed tablecloth placed so the table is evenly covered.
- Design the display so that it is eye appealing and useful.
- Coordinate colors, textures, shapes, and sizes.
- Include items that will be used during the speech. Show it and use it, or don't include it in the display.
- Make sure all items can be seen by every member of the audience.
- Use picture stands or easels to lift up items and show contents standing. Avoid laying items flat on the table.
- Rehearse using the items on the table display.

Notice how the tablecloth is placed on this table. It is important to have the tablecloth draped neatly. If you have one side longer than the other, your audience will have a hard time focusing on your speech because they will want to straighten the cloth.

This SpeechShark is using the notes feature on his phone while giving a demonstration speech. Using the red cooking pot as the centerpiece, he has the vegetables to the right and mixing bowls to the left. All of these colors are a good contrast to the white chef's coat and hat he is wearing for the speech. Of course, he is also demonstrating that he is using the Speech-Shark app for speech notes and that is my favorite part!

HANDOUTS

As discussed earlier in the chapter, the purpose of a handout is to help the audience to retain information shared during the speech. Many of the same rules for designing a PowerPoint or Prezi presentation will apply to creating a handout, so you will want to KISS and *Keep It Simple Sweetie* when planning the handout for your speech. Please check with your instructor prior to creating a handout to make sure you are following his or her assignments created for you.

Most instructors prefer for students to create their own handout rather than using a handout that is created by a company. The reason for this is because if created by a company, it will usually advertise that company or the company's product. For example, if you are giving a speech about spaying or neutering family pets, you could go to your local veterinarian's office and get one of their beautiful handouts that covers all of the areas pet owners need to know about spaying and neutering pets. This handout will be filled with useful information to support the speech, but the flyer will also contain the name, phone number, and address of the veterinarian who owns the office. Since we are giving speeches for a closed or captive audience, speakers need to make sure they are not endorsing any one company or product unless, of course, they are making a sales presentation. As examples of items you should not use, please know that a copy of your PowerPoint is NOT a handout. It's a note-taking device. A printed copy of an article found on the Internet is also NOT a handout.

Handouts come in all shapes and sizes. I've seen everything from personally crafted items to items purchased in a store and then personalized. Handouts should support the speech. Speakers who are demonstrating a cooking activity will create a beautiful recipe card for the audience members. If the speech is to motivate the audience to drink water, a water bottle with a personally printed label printed with "Drink More Water" is appropriate. Refrigerator magnets are great reminders for audience members to "Choose Healthy Snacks" and posters created to detail "Items to Recycle" can later be placed on home recycling bins as a reminder of what can or cannot be recycled. A bookmark is a great handout idea when the speech topic is motivating the audience to read hardcover books instead of e-books.

The key purpose of the handout is to provide your audience members with something that will further explain the topic or will help audience members remember the message of the speech.

Please keep the following tips in mind when designing the handout for your speech:

- Plan to tell your audience about the handout while presenting the speech. It is best to do this in the part of your speech where it makes the most sense. For example, if the handout is supporting a particular point in the speech, that is when it should be introduced.
- SHOW the handout to the audience as you speak about it and tell them what you want them to do with the handout they receive.
- Ask your Tech Team members to distribute the handout.
- Design an appealing handout using quality paper, color, and usable content.
    - —Paper: Heavy cardstock is best for recipe cards, bookmarks, tri-fold brochures, and posters.
    - —Color: Use color fonts and pictures when printing on a white background. Use color paper if using black-and-white ink with no pictures.
    - —Content: Put the title of your speech on the handout along with any supporting information.
    - —Use consistent font styles, font sizes, and colors.
- Use a tri-fold brochure, twin-brochure, or book format when applicable.
- Use diagrams, charts, pictures, or graphs to illustrate a point.
- Design the handout to complement the speech presentation.
- Make one handout for each person in the class including the instructor.
- Use technical writing skills when designing a handout.
- Laminate handouts when needed to protect the content. Not all handouts need to be laminated. Speakers should laminate items that could be damaged after repeated use such as recipe cards, instructions, and book marks.

Distributing the Handouts

Knowing when and how to distribute the handout is just as important as designing the handout. Work with your Tech Team members before the day of your speech so that they will know you expect them to distribute the handout you have worked so hard to create. Consider the following suggestions:

1. **Enlist Tech Team Members to distribute handouts.** The speaker should not distribute their handouts personally. Having a Tech Team member distribute handouts will make the presentation appear more professional and will help ease the speaker's stress because it is one less thing to think about.
2. **Avoid distributing handouts to the audience during the middle of a speech.** Doing this will require the Tech Team member to walk through the audience and distribute handouts while the speaker is still talking. Audience members may even be asked to pass handouts to those around them. This is

disruptive and your audience will quit listening to the speaker to turn their attention to the person distributing the handouts.

3. **Distribute handouts BEFORE the speech** if the handout will be used as a note-taking aid, a fill-in-the-blank format, or if it is to be used as a visual during the speech. Be sure to relay any instructions from the speaker to the audience as you distribute the handout.

4. **Distribute the handout AFTER the speech** if the handout is offering additional information for your audience to read later.

I thought you might like to see a handout Kendall Hunt produced when promoting this book at a Georgia Communication Association Conference. They took bottles of water, created a new label for the water, and put the labels on the water bottles to give to attendees of the conference. While this wasn't for a speech, it served as an excellent handout for the conference attendees and it was another way for us to get the SpeechShark brand in front of people who teach speech in the state of Georgia.

WILL YOUR HANDOUT BELONG TO THE HALL OF FAME OR HALL OF SHAME?

As a speech instructor, I've seen all types of visual aids. Some visual aids shown in my classrooms have been very effective while others were not effective at all. In the area below, I'd like to share some of my favorite and not-so-favorite visual aids over the years.

Self

Favorite: A couple of years ago I had a wonderful student from Nigeria, who gave an informative speech about wedding ceremonies in Nigeria. She wore her own wedding dress as she explained the Nigerian marriage ceremony. This student had a PowerPoint presentation to accompany her speech, but we were so enthralled with her speech and her beautiful dress that most of us never paid attention to the PowerPoint slides. To this day, I couldn't tell you one thing about her PowerPoint presentation, but I can describe the beautiful aqua and white dress and headdress with great detail. She did a beautiful job of using herself as her own visual aid.

Not-so-favorite: Another student gave an informative speech about yoga. He decided not to dress professionally, as suggested, but wore a pair of much too tight sweat pants and an old T-shirt. I can't remember the details of his speech, but I'll never be able to forget a 45-year-old man wearing tight sweatpants and demonstrating yoga moves. It was not pretty!

Table Displays

Favorite: Table displays can be very effective. One of my favorite table displays was used by a student to demonstrate how to make brownies. The student used a plain red tablecloth for the table, but used several different heights of boxes and put an additional red tablecloth to cover the boxes. When setting up the display, she had beautiful white ceramic bowls higher on taller boxes, while the boxes of ingredients were lower on the table. By creating more dimension with the table, she was able to show all of the items she wanted to use and display. The design combined dimension with beautiful dishes and ingredients needed for the demonstration. This also allowed room for the demonstration.

Not-so-favorite: Every semester as we discuss handouts, I will cover a table with a tablecloth and will lay student handouts all over the table. I call this my "Hall of Fame" and "Hall of Shame" Handout Table. The purpose is to show a truly bad design for a table display even though many of the handouts are wonderful. We will talk about how hard it is for the audience to see twenty-five to thirty different handouts on the table and how the table display is not effective because the audience cannot see everything. Also, it is not effective because it looks messy. I use it as a teachable moment and my students usually understand this concept from the first moment because I've never had a really bad table display in all of the years I've taught public speaking.

Objects

Favorite: About four years ago, a particularly shy student was in my class and wasn't looking forward to speaking to a group of twenty-five students. The student said that she taught a motorcycle safety class to teenagers every week, but that speaking to her college class made her break out in hives. I asked how she taught the class and she said that she wore her motorcycle safety gear and actually straddled her own motorcycle while speaking to the teens about how to safely ride and operate a motorcycle. So, I suggested that she give her informative speech about motorcycle safety, wear her safety gear, and bring her motorcycle. She did this and aced her first speech! She came to class wearing her pink and black motorcycle jumpsuit, pink helmet, black boots, and brought her—you guessed it—pink motorcycle that was shining like a brand-new penny. Although she was still nervous, by the time she pushed the motorcycle to the front of the classroom and climbed on it to begin her speech, she was in her element and did the best job! This proves that sometimes working with an object can help the student to forget the nerves and focus on the object.

Not-so-favorite: While this example could have had potential, it really didn't turn out so great! One of my veterinarian students who was working toward a vet tech degree, brought in a small dog in a kennel to demonstrate how to trim a dog's nails when grooming a family pet. This is a good topic and one that students who have pets would enjoy hearing. Everything was going great for the speech. The student put down a plastic tablecloth, set up the equipment needed for the demonstration, and placed the kennel on the end of the table. The problem came when the student took the dog out of the kennel. Obviously, Fido was not accustomed to being around people and barked the entire time my poor student was trying to give a speech. Then right before the big conclusion, the puppy decided he had enough, lifted his leg and the rest is history. The audience had a huge chuckle that day, but the student was so embarrassed. Lesson learned! Well, I have to tell you that I felt so bad for the student that I asked if he wanted to re-do the speech the next week using a stuffed animal. I was relieved when he did and that speech ended beautifully.

Models

Favorite: The radiological students in my class will often show models of the human anatomy that are fascinating. Not too long ago, we had an informative speech given by a rad tech student who was able to talk to us about the chambers of the heart using one of the models from the classroom. Using a black cloth tablecloth and a stand to hold the model, the speaker moved from the lectern over to the table, picked up the model, and as she described the information, was able to point to each area of the heart to make the information clear. We were glad it wasn't an actual heart like they use in the classrooms, but enjoyed seeing the model and could understand the functions of the heart so much better after her speech.

Not-so-favorite: Models can be people, too. My not-so-favorite example was from a student who decided to use her tech team to model how not to dress for an interview. While the speaker was dressed appropriately for an interview and was the model of how to dress for an interview, the speaker did not rehearse with her team. They were awkwardly standing around not sure of where to go or what to do while they were on stage. Let me be clear. This was a good idea, but wasn't executed properly. If she had rehearsed the speech with her tech team, they would have known where to stand while she was speaking about their clothing choices and they would have known where to go after she had discussed their clothing choices. With six models, on a small stage, they stood awkwardly around and looked glazed and confused as the speaker finished her speech. While glazed works with donuts, it isn't a good look on a model who doesn't know what to do! It is the speaker's responsibility to make sure all details are covered.

Technology

Favorite: Have you heard of Kahoot-It? If not, you'll want to conduct a search and find out ways to use this! During a professional development session, one of our instructors used the Kahoot-It to get the audience to participate in a survey by using their cell phones. Everybody has a cell phone, so this was a great idea and one that every audience member loved. Check it out at https://kahoot.it/. The speaker gives the audience a game PIN (personal identification number). Everyone in the audience will go to the website using their phone and will enter their game PIN to begin participating. This activity turns phones into an opportunity for learning and is engaging for audience members. Every person in the room was involved and the speaker was able to use this form of technology as a way to make the discussion more interactive. Of course, you'll need WiFi to get the best from this type of activity.

Not-so-favorite: Any type of technology is a great idea, especially in our part of the world where we live, work, shop, learn, and play using technology. I'm a technology nut, but I've seen speeches that were ruined because of technology. One example was a student who was using dinosaur technology on an old computer at home to design a presentation that was going to be used in the classroom with our software and programs that were up to date. Have you heard of Murphy's Law? If something can go wrong, it will go wrong and during YOUR presentation. Our computers in the classroom could not read the floppy disk (do they really still use those?) that the student was using. When the student switched to use the attachment e-mailed to himself, the computer could not read the program which was not compatible with our classroom computer. Always rehearse with the equipment prior to standing in front of a group to speak. I'm sure his speech would have been good, but he was so rattled from not being able to use the plan he had, that he just couldn't pull out of the tailspin.

PowerPoint and Prezi

Favorite: Most recently, my favorite was a Prezi demonstration about being organized. The student used Prezi presentation software (free for students) to create an impactful and engaging presentation. First you sign up, choose a template, and work through story blocks to build a speech. The student had our attention from the beginning and a simple zoom from one place to another allowed the students to keep the momentum of the speech moving as the presentation moved. Check it out at: https://prezi.com/product/

Not-so-favorite: Death by PowerPoint is real! My least favorite PowerPoint presentation was by a student who truly read everything on every slide and never looked once at the audience. We all had checked out before the student ever got to slide 3 and I'm sure all of us were busy making a grocery list or planning what we were going to have for lunch that day. Don't read your PowerPoint presentation. Instead, PowerPoints should be used as a backdrop for your presentation. Allow the PowerPoint slides to be the pretty bow on the package, but the gift is your presentation.

Video Clips and Music

Favorite: In an earlier chapter, I shared my favorite speech using video clips. It's hard to top that one, but last semester I had a student who is a member of our area's symphonic orchestra. The title of her persuasion speech was "Learn to Play an Instrument." We were all motivated when she opened the violin case and played a beautiful short piece as the conclusion of her speech. Words were not necessary as we all listened, entranced at the beautiful music she shared. Yes, we were motivated. Yes, she achieved her purpose. Yes, her use of music as a conclusion made it to my "Hall of Fame" examples of how to keep your audience thinking about your presentation even after you've left the stage. Bravo!

 Not-so-favorite: I want to remind you that video clips or music sound-bites should be thirty seconds or less so that the video or the music doesn't overtake a short speech. The clips can last longer, if you have a longer speech. My least favorite speech using a video clip was from a student who simply introduced a sales video and for the next five minutes stood to the side as we all watched a salesperson try to convince us all to purchase a Rainbow vacuum cleaner. Needless to say, the student's five- to seven-minute speech was thirty seconds of the student speaking and five minutes of the salesman on the video. Really?

Photos

Favorite: Photos on a table display can be effective, if they are large photos, framed, and used during a speech. My favorite speech using photos was of a student who began with all three photos lying flat on the table. As she stood behind the table, she picked up one photo at a time and told us about the person in the photo. After each one, she would lay the photo back facedown on the table, pause, look at us, and say, "But that person isn't here anymore." She continued this until she went through all three photos and then went on to explain that all three people shown in the photos had been killed by a drunk driver. Her use of the photos was so effective and it touched us all. I don't think there was a single person in that audience who would ever think of drinking and driving after listening to her speech.

 Not-so-favorite: While photos can be very effective, it is how the speaker uses them that truly makes or breaks the speech. I've had students who would talk about someone or some event and then pass pictures around the classroom while continuing to talk about someone or something else. Lesson learned! This is so distracting because audience members will only pay attention to the one photo they are holding at that time and will completely miss the rest of the speaker's message.

Maps

Favorite: We live in a big world with lots of places that some of our audience members may never have visited or heard of. One of my favorite uses of maps was from an introduction speech where a student was introducing herself to the audience. She began with a large map of the world on a PowerPoint slide and used a laser pointer to show where she was born. As she continued with her introduction, she moved to show the several different places where she grew up, which was almost half a world away from where she was born. Then she showed us where she lives today. During each step, she would introduce each new location with the language of that place and then translate it to the English that we understood. It was a WOW moment, to realize she knew eight different languages from living in eight countries in a short twenty-five years. What a great way to use visual aids to introduce herself!

 Not-so-favorite: Another speaker used the same plan, but used a paper map of the world instead of a slide on a PowerPoint. Needless to say, the paper map was awkward and none of the audience members could really see the countries as the student introduced each one. Use a visual aid that can be seen by all members of the audience.

GRAPHS, CHARTS, AND DIAGRAMS

Favorite: If you want to illustrate something, show it to your audience in the form of graphs, charts, or diagrams. This helps to clarify the concept and supply the most important information at a quick glance. We have a diverse college population. One of my students gave a speech about diversity and used a graph to show the diversity of the population in our college. I've known this information for years, but it really made the point that we live and work in a wonderfully unique place that includes many different cultures. Needless to say, I truly loved knowing and seeing this information.

    Not-so-favorite: Showing information using a chart is a great idea, but it does nothing if you do not spend a few minutes talking about what you are showing. My not-so-favorite example of this was a student who was showing this very detailed chart while speaking about spaying and neutering pets. The information on the chart was written in a tiny font and was impossible to read. I was hoping the student was going to tell us about the chart we were seeing, but it became obvious that he was just using it as a backdrop and didn't share any of the important details verbally. What a pity, as they say on the Great British Baking Show. All of the ingredients for a great speech, but none of the substance we wanted. Having a visual aid without using the visual aid or referring to the visual aid is a true waste of time. It is a waste of time for the student creating it and a waste of time and a source of frustration for the audience members who are trying to figure out what they are seeing.

Handouts

Favorite: Over the years, I've seen some of the greatest handouts in my speech classes. It's really hard to think of one that was over the top, so I'll just tell you about the one that I have had for the longest time! About eighteen years ago, one of my students demonstrated how to break a board in half. He told us the history of board breaking, showed us the materials needed to break the board, and then demonstrated breaking the board. The student told us that it is a technique that if followed, can be completed by anyone—even his speech teacher. Well, I was not prepared to break a board that day, but as his conclusion step, he asked me to come to the stage and break a board for the students in the class to prove his point. The student had everything set up perfectly with the two concrete blocks and enough boards for each person in the room. He had us write a bad habit on the board we wanted to break! I wrote the habit that I wanted to break and stepped up to the board. Realizing I was almost fifty at the time, I was just afraid I would break my hand. Yet, I didn't want to let him down. I took a deep breath, lined my hand up with the board, and came down as hard as I possibly could. The board broke and my student snapped a Polaroid picture at that moment and gave a copy of the picture to me. That picture is still hanging in my office. I didn't break my hand, but I did break the board. The picture is a constant reminder of a speech that I will never forget! Favorite handout—EVER! And now for the rest of the story . . . We finished class early that day, but not one student left until they all had broken a board.

    Not-so-favorite: I've got too many of these. They are pages of handouts printed with worthless information and handed to students after a speech. I know they are worthless because the students will not even take them with them as they leave the classroom for the day. If you are going to make a handout, please make sure it is something that is done so well that the audience will not throw it away or leave it on the desk at the end of the speech.

Visual Aids

After reading this chapter, you should be able to answer the following questions:

1. What are the three reasons that speakers need visual aids during a speech?

2. What are three types of instructional design theories?

3. What is figure/ground design theory?

4. What is hierarchy design theory?

5. What is Gestalt design theory?

6. Which type of design theory uses arrows?

_____

_____

7. How many slides are best for a three- to seven-minute speech?

_____

_____

8. What is a handout?

_____

_____

9. When should you distribute a handout if it is being used during the speech?

_____

_____

10. What is an example of presentation technology?

_____

_____

Shark Bites

Watch a how-to television program (a cooking show, for example) or the weather portion of a local newscast. Notice how the presenter uses visual aids to help communicate the message. What kinds of visual aids are used? How do they enhance the clarity, interest, and retainability of the message? What would the presenter have to do to communicate the message effectively without visual aids?

_____

_____

_____

_____

Plan to use visual aids for your next speech. Be creative in devising your aids, and be sure to follow the guidelines discussed in the chapter for using them. After the speech, analyze how effectively you employed your visual aids, what you learned about the use of visual aids from your experience, and what changes you would make in using visual aids if you were to deliver the speech again.

_____

_____

_____

_____

Chapter Thirteen

Working with a Tech Team

ASSIGNING A TECH TEAM

As a speaker, you will notice there are many pieces to the speech puzzle and you will need help pulling it all together. To do this, you need a **tech team**. What is a tech team? This is a group of people qualified to help complete your speech presentation by setting up or breaking down, managing the PowerPoint/Prezi slides, managing lighting and sound requirements, and distributing handouts. Most speeches will require visual aids, handouts, lighting effects, sound, microphones, and backstage support. As with anything, the buck stops with you. The success of your speech depends upon you to cover every detail and that includes working with a tech team.

Never assume that your tech team will know what you want them to do. Consider yourself as a project manager and the speech is your project.

To accomplish the project, there are many strategies for getting the job done and according to expectations. Yet, these things do not just happen on their own. You have to plan for the success of your speech presentation.

First take a look at your speech plan. Answer the following questions:

1. What will you need to complete the speech project?

   _____

2. Who can help you reach your goals?

   _____

3. Is your tech team member qualified with the areas where you need help?

   _____

4. Did you supply a script for the tech team?

   _____

5. Can your tech team rehearse with you?

   _____

6. Do you have the materials and supplies needed for the tech team to do their jobs?

   _____

7. Can you count on your tech team member to be there and to be prepared?

   _____

Once you know what you need, you can begin assigning responsibilities for your tech team.

Ask questions! Make sure you KNOW that your tech team members understand how to run a simple PowerPoint or Prezi presentation. If they do not know, make plans to rehearse with them and show them how to do this. OR, fire that tech team member and appoint a new one!

Choose the number of tech team members you need for the speech. One or two tech team members may be enough, but if the presentation is complicated and involves multiple aspects, you will need to add tech team members.

Without a shadow of a doubt, you should be able to count on your tech team members to arrive on time and to be prepared. There is nothing in this world that can shake your speech-making resolve faster than to arrive for the speech and not see tech team members until five minutes before the speech begins! YIKES! That is when you will feel like a guppy navigating in murky waters and the results may not be pretty. Be a Speech-Shark and be prepared!

Use the following Tech Team Checklist to make sure you are prepared.

TECH TEAM CHECKLIST

Complete this form as you plan the use of visual aids so that you are prepared for the speech. Speakers who use visual aids will need to make use of a tech team. It is the speaker's responsibility to meet with the tech team ahead of time, provide a script, and rehearse with the tech team to make sure they understand what is needed. Visual aids are an important part of the speech and a direct reflection of your credibility as a speaker.

Date: _____ **Time of Speech:** _____

Type of Speech: _____

Description of Visual Aids:

_____

_____

_____

_____

Note: In the area below, please list each tech team member's name and assigned duties. Be sure to assign a member for the PowerPoint, sound, lights, setup, breakdown, and distribution of handouts. All duties may not be needed for all speeches.

Tech Team Member's Name: _____

Duties Assigned: _____

Tech Team Member's Name: _____

Duties Assigned: _____

Tech Team Member's Name: _____

Duties Assigned: _____

Tech Team Member's Name: _____

Duties Assigned: _____

_____

REHEARSING WITH A TECH TEAM

This part of your responsibility does not happen on its own. It is YOUR speech and it is YOUR responsibility to arrange the rehearsals with your tech team. Your speech will only be as good as your tech team! One slide out of place, one video that does not play as planned, one sound-bite or music segment that is not properly executed will affect your credibility as a speaker.

Now that you have identified tech team members, arrange at least two rehearsals with them prior to your speech. If possible, have the rehearsals in the place where you are going to make the presentation so that you can also become familiar with the stage, lights, and sound system.

As your tech team members arrive, shake their hands and tell them how much you appreciate their help with the presentation. Introduce the tech team members to each other and identify their responsibilities during the presentation. After the rehearsals and after your presentation, please make sure to thank each person who helped make your presentation spectacular! Even small details completed on your behalf add up to a big deal on speech day.

Distribute a script to each tech team member. Although you will have one basic script, it is a good idea to highlight and personalize each script so that it is clear what you want each tech team member to do during the presentation.

In the pages that follow, you will see a separate script for each of the three tech team members needed for the informative speech. Notice how each script is designed for the tech team member and highlights the job tasks needed for the speech.

EXAMPLE

SCRIPT: PowerPoint Presentation–Tech Team Member 1

Penny J. Waddell
Toastmasters International Meeting
30 June 2017

Speech Category: Informative Speech
Title: How to Dress for an Interview
Purpose: The purpose of this speech is to inform my audience how to dress for an interview.

Introduction: As speaker is introduced, please have Slide 1 up.
Attention Step: (Show pictures on a PowerPoint Slide of different people dressed in different ways. One person is dressed in jeans, flip-flops, and a T-shirt; another is dressed in a short minidress with tattoos showing on her arms and legs; another is dressed business casual.) Take a look at the pictures of these three candidates who are about to interview for a job position at a Fortune 500 Company. Which candidate do you think will get the job?

Establish Need/Relevance: The truth is that any one of these candidates MAY get the job. The secret is knowing with which company the candidate is interviewing? If interviewing for a position at GOOGLE, the jeans and T-shirt may be appropriate. If interviewing for a position with The Coca Cola Company in Atlanta, the candidate dressed business casual may get the job. Before interviewing for a job position, be sure to know what type of dress is expected.

Establish Speaker Credibility: I am credible to speak to you today about dressing for an interview because I have recently interviewed for a job position and got the job! For the position, I needed to dress in an upscale suit, very little jewelry, and I needed to project extreme professionalism.

Thesis: Today, I will cover three points to inform you how to dress for an interview. (1) Research the company, (2) Understand the culture of the company, and (3) Put your best foot forward.

Body: During the transition sentence, please go to Slide 2—Research the Company.
Transition/Link: Let's begin with the first point, research the company.

    I. Research the Company
        A. What type of business does this company do?
        B. What type of work responsibilities are expected?

Transition/Link: I've shared the importance of researching the company with you, now I'd like to tell you how to understand the culture of the company. During the transition sentence, please go to Slide 3— Understand the Culture of the Company.

    II. Understand the Culture of the Company
        A. Make a trip to the company prior to the Interview (Quast).
        B. Watch to see how other employees dress.

Transition/Link: You've heard how to research the company and how to understand its culture, now I want to show you how to put your best foot forward. During the transition sentence, please go to Slide 4—Put Your Best Foot Forward.

    III. Put Your Best Foot Forward
        A. Choose clothing, shoes, and accessories that mirror how other employees in this company dress.
        B. Err on the conservative side, but don't forget to show your personality.
Transition/Link: Now you should understand a little more about how to dress for an interview.

Conclusion: During the transition sentence, please go to Slide 5—Quote.
Summary: Today, I shared with you three points: (1) Research the company, (2) Understand the culture of the company, and (3) Put your best foot forward.
Appeal to Action: As you interview for what might very well be the most important interview of your life, be sure to remember that "You never get a second chance to make a first impression" (Quast). With this quote, I want to challenge you to dress for success and make sure this interview is the one that will help you get your dream job!
Following the Appeal to Action, please go to slide 6—Blank Slide. After speaker leaves the stage, please take down the PowerPoint.

(Note: The Works Cited page should be added as a separate page following the Outline.)

Works Cited

Quast, Lisa. "8 Tips to Dress for Interview Success." *Forbes.* 2014. Accessed 12 March 2017.

(Note: The Visual Aids Explanation page is a separate page from the Outline and the Works Cited page.)

Visual Aids Explanation Page

PowerPoint Presentation:
Slide 1:   Title of Speech—**How to Dress for an Interview**
            Pictures of Three People Dressed Differently
Slide 2:   (Point 1): **Research the Company**
            Bullet Points:
            • Type of Business
            • Type of Work Responsibilities
Slide 3:   (Point 2): **Understand the Culture of the Company**
            Picture of Business with Employees Entering the Door
Slide 4:   (Point 3): **Put Your Best Foot Forward**
            Picture of Professionally Dressed Employee
Slide 5:   **"You Never Get a Second Chance to Make a First Impression" (Quast)**
            Picture of a Group of Professionally Dressed Employees

EXAMPLE

SCRIPT: Table Display—Tech Team Member 2

Penny J. Waddell
Toastmasters International Meeting
30 June 2017

Speech Category: Informative Speech
Title: How to Dress for an Interview
Purpose: The purpose of this speech is to inform my audience how to dress for an interview.

Introduction: Prior to introduction, please set up the Table Display—Table Cloth, Books/mannequin with suit and tie

Attention Step: (Show pictures on a PowerPoint Slide of different people dressed in different ways. One person is dressed in jeans, flip-flops, and a T-shirt; another is dressed in a short minidress with tattoos showing on her arms and legs; another is dressed business casual). Take a look at the pictures of these three candidates who are about to interview for a job position at a Fortune 500 Company. Which candidate do you think will get the job?

Establish Need/Relevance: The truth is that any one of these candidates MAY get the job. The secret is knowing with which company the candidate is interviewing? If interviewing for a position at GOOGLE, the jeans and T-shirt may be appropriate. If interviewing for a position with The Coca Cola Company in Atlanta, the candidate dressed business casual may get the job. Before interviewing for a job position, be sure to know what type of dress is expected.

Establish Speaker Credibility: I am credible to speak to you today about dressing for an interview because I have recently interviewed for a job position and got the job! For the position, I needed to dress in an upscale suit, very little jewelry, and I needed to project extreme professionalism.

Thesis: Today, I will cover three points to inform you how to dress for an interview. (1) Research the company, (2) Understand the culture of the company, and (3) Put your best foot forward.

Body:
Transition/Link: Let's begin with the first point, research the company.
   I. Research the Company
      A. What type of business does this company do?
      B. What type of work responsibilities are expected?
Transition/Link: I've shared the importance of researching the company with you, now I'd like to tell you how to understand the culture of the company.
   II. Understand the Culture of the Company
      A. Make a trip to the company prior to the Interview (Quast).
      B. Watch to see how other employees dress.

Transition/Link: You've heard how to research the company and how to understand its culture, now I want to show you how to put your best foot forward.
   III. Put Your Best Foot Forward
      A. Choose clothing, shoes, and accessories that mirror how other employees in this company dress.
      B. Err on the conservative side, but don't forget to show your personality.

Transition/Link: Now you should understand a little more about how to dress for an interview.
Conclusion:
Summary: Today, I shared with you three points: (1) Research the company, (2) Understand the culture of the company, and (3) Put your best foot forward.
Appeal to Action: As you interview for what might very well be the most important interview of your life, be sure to remember that "You never get a second chance to make a first impression" (Quast). With this quote, I want to challenge you to dress for success and make sure this interview is the one that will help you get your dream job!

(Note: The Works Cited page should be added as a separate page following the Outline.)

Works Cited

Quast, Lisa. "8 Tips to Dress for Interview Success." *Forbes.* 2014. Accessed 12 March 2017.

(Note: The Visual Aids Explanation page is a separate page from the Outline and the Works Cited page).

Visual Aids Explanation Page

PowerPoint Presentation:
Slide 1:   Title of Speech—**How to Dress for an Interview**
              Pictures of Three People Dressed Differently
Slide 2:   (Point 1): **Research the Company**
              Bullet Points:
                 • Type of Business
                 • Type of Work Responsibilities
Slide 3:   (Point 2): **Understand the Culture of the Company**
              Picture of Business with Employees Entering the Door
Slide 4:   (Point 3): **Put Your Best Foot Forward**
              Picture of Professionally Dressed Employee
Slide 5:   **"You Never Get a Second Chance to Make a First Impression" (Quast)**
              Picture of a Group of Professionally Dressed Employees

EXAMPLE

SCRIPT: Handout Distribution–Tech Team Member 3

Penny J. Waddell
Toastmasters International Meeting
30 June 2017

Speech Category: Informative Speech
Title: How to Dress for an Interview
Purpose: The purpose of this speech is to inform my audience how to dress for an interview.

Introduction:
Attention Step: (Show pictures on a PowerPoint Slide of different people dressed in different ways. One person is dressed in jeans, flip-flops, and a T-shirt; another is dressed in a short minidress with tattoos showing on her arms and legs; another is dressed business casual.) Take a look at the pictures of these three candidates who are about to interview for a job position at a Fortune 500 Company. Which candidate do you think will get the job?
Establish Need/Relevance: The truth is that any one of these candidates MAY get the job. The secret is knowing with which company the candidate is interviewing. If interviewing for a position at GOOGLE, the jeans and T-shirt may be appropriate. If interviewing for a position with The Coca Cola Company in Atlanta, the candidate dressed business casual may get the job. Before interviewing for a job position, be sure to know what type of dress is expected.
Establish Speaker Credibility: I am credible to speak to you today about dressing for an interview because I have recently interviewed for a job position and got the job! For the position, I needed to dress in an upscale suit, very little jewelry, and I needed to project extreme professionalism.
Thesis: Today, I will cover three points to inform you how to dress for an interview. (1) Research the company, (2) Understand the culture of the company, and (3) Put your best foot forward.

Body:
Transition/Link: Let's begin with the first point, research the company.
    I. Research the Company
        A. What type of business does this company do?
        B. What type of work responsibilities are expected?

Transition/Link: I've shared the importance of researching the company with you, now I'd like to tell you how to understand the culture of the company.
    II. Understand the Culture of the Company
        A. Make a trip to the company prior to the Interview (Quast).
        B. Watch to see how other employees dress.

Transition/Link: You've heard how to research the company and how to understand its culture, now I want to show you how to put your best foot forward.
    III. Put Your Best Foot Forward
        A. Choose clothing, shoes, and accessories that mirror how other employees in this company dress.
        B. Err on the conservative side, but don't forget to show your personality.

Transition/Link: Now you should understand a little more about how to dress for an interview.
Conclusion:
Summary: Today, I shared with you three points: (1) Research the company, (2) Understand the culture of the company, and (3) Put your best foot forward.
Appeal to Action: As you interview for what might very well be the most important interview of your life, be sure to remember that "You never get a second chance to make a first impression" (Quast). With this quote, I want to challenge you to dress for success and make sure this interview is the one that will help you get your dream job!

Following the speech, please distribute the handouts. Make sure the instructor and each person in the audience receives one.

(Note: The Works Cited page should be added as a separate page following the Outline.)

Works Cited

Quast, Lisa. "8 Tips to Dress for Interview Success." *Forbes.* 2014. Accessed 12 March 2017.

(Note: The Visual Aids Explanation page is a separate page from the Outline and the Works Cited page.)

Visual Aids Explanation Page

PowerPoint Presentation:
Slide 1:   Title of Speech—**How to Dress for an Interview**
            Pictures of Three People Dressed Differently
Slide 2:   (Point 1): **Research the Company**
            Bullet Points:
            * Type of Business
            * Type of Work Responsibilities
Slide 3:   (Point 2): **Understand the Culture of the Company**
            Picture of Business with Employees Entering the Door
Slide 4:   (Point 3): **Put Your Best Foot Forward**
            Picture of Professionally Dressed Employee
Slide 5:   **"You Never Get a Second Chance to Make a First Impression" (Quast)**
            Picture of a Group of Professionally Dressed Employees

Working with a Tech Team

After you read this chapter, you will be able to answer the following questions:

1. What are the responsibilities of a tech team? _____

   _____

   _____

2. What should you provide to your tech team so they can complete the assigned tasks?

   _____

   _____

3. What will you need to do to plan a rehearsal with a tech team? _____

   _____

   _____

4. How many basic scripts are necessary? _____

   _____

   _____

5. What will you need to do to personalize each script?_____

   _____

   _____

6. How many tech team members are needed for a presentation? _____

_____

_____

7. Your next speech is coming up soon, what aspects are you including in your speech that may require a tech team? _____

_____

_____

8. What time will your tech team need to arrive? _____

_____

_____

9. What will you need to do to make sure your tech team is prepared? _____

_____

_____

10. Whose responsibility is it to make sure your tech team is prepared? _____

_____

_____

Shark Bites

BUILDING YOUR TECH TEAM

List the visual aids and technical assistance that you will need for your speech. Assign a tech team member to each duty and set up a rehearsal schedule with them. Create the script for each tech team member.

Tech Team Member's Name:	Duty Assigned	Rehearsal Date Scheduled
	PowerPoint	
	Stage Setup	
	Lights	
	Sound/Microphone	
	Distribute Handouts	
	Stage Breakdown	

SpeechSHARK™

Unit 5
Presenting the Speech

Presentation Skills

Rehearsing the Speech and Creating a Speech Day Checklist

Evaluating the Speech

Key Terms to Know

Chapter 14—Presentation Skills

- Albert Mehrabian
- Aromatherapy
- Body Language Cues
- Breathing
- Chronemics
- Color
- Dialects
- Eye Contact
- Facial Expressions
- Filler Words
- Gestures
- Haptics
- Head Tilting and Head Nodding
- Intimate Space
- Larynx
- Meditation
- Movement
- Nonverbal Communication
- Pace
- Paralanguage
- Personal Space
- Physical Appearance
- Pitch
- Poise
- Posture
- Proxemics
- Public Space Rate
- Smiling
- Social Space
- Speech Anxiety
- Verbal Communication
- Volume

Chapter 15—Rehearsing the Speech and Creating a Speech Day Checklist

- Presentation
- Rehearse

Chapter 16—Evaluating the Speech

- Oral Evaluations
- Peer Evaluations
- Self-Evaluations
- Written Evaluations

Chapter Fourteen
Presentation Skills

ARE YOU WAITING FOR YOUR SHIP TO COME IN?

If you are sitting around waiting for your ship to come in, then you really should take another look at details involved with achieving success.

Some people think they will find success as they sit in their sturdy little rowboat, master of their own ship, and armed with a strong work ethic and perhaps a few well-chosen tools (oars would be helpful). These people believe that they will row, row, row the boat toward their goals and ultimately find success! And, they may find success eventually and with a great deal of effort! But, that is not YOU!

Other people think they can sit back on their rickety old raft in a nice comfortable lounge chair with a glass of sweet Georgia tea close by and just follow the wind until, hopefully, success finds them! These dreamers believe they are so wonderful that sooner or later someone will notice how great they are and will drag them and their raft directly into the success stream! But, that is not YOU, either!

On the other hand, YOU stand at the helm of your stately sailboat with well-chosen officers on either side and a crew of qualified mates helping you to chart a course and carefully follow the route toward success. YOU have the vision to see what is beyond the horizon. Your loyal officers are paying attention to all details required to set manageable goals and your crew is determined to help you reach those goals. Yet, all of you realize that without the "wind in the sails," your sailboat will go nowhere. The wind is the motivation that comes from within! This is the force that will move this stately sailboat toward the goal. This is the catalyst that is needed to propel you, your officers, your crew, and passengers to success! Yes, this is YOU!

How did you arrive at this type of thinking? How do we know this is YOU? We know this because YOU are the person who sees the value in making good choices regarding your support staff! YOU are the kind of person who chooses to use a great app like SpeechShark to help draft and create speeches intended to reach your goals. YOU are the kind of person who reads a speech textbook to learn about extra tools needed to help you become the speaker you want to be.

You are the captain of your ship and you don't have to "wait for your ship to come in" because YOU are the one who is navigating the ship toward success! Whether you are making a point during a speech presentation with an audience or with your co-workers and colleagues, SpeechShark can help you verbally express your dreams and share enthusiasm for things that motivate and move you! Yes, this is YOU!

Questions? Yes, you will have lots of questions, but we have the answers. In the pages to follow, we have listed your questions about presentation skills and SpeechShark answers!

QUESTIONS AND ANSWERS ABOUT PRESENTATION SKILLS

What do you need to know about Verbal and Nonverbal Communication Skills?

Verbal language transmits words and thoughts. Nonverbal language transmits feelings. Whether you realize it or not, your body is speaking volumes. What you DO speaks so loudly that I cannot hear what you say! Because of this, it is important to be aware of what you don't say. Body language is unconscious and it is the most honest form of communication we use. Our body language communicates true feelings even while we may be using words that communicate something entirely different!

In the communication field, Albert Mehrabian is a name often mentioned as we explore nonverbal communication skills. Mehrabian is a scholar who conducted nonverbal research and reported his findings in a book entitled *Silent Messages*. These findings were reported again in *Communication Theory*, edited by C. David Mortensen. Mehrabian's first findings were reported and tested again to show the very same results. In *Communication Theory*, published almost thirty years later, Mehrabian's findings are reported in a formula that many people are still trying to refute: "Total Impact 100% = .07 verbal + .38 vocal + .55 facial" (193).

Let me explain this in another way.

There are three primary areas of communication: verbal, vocal, and visual. 7% of our communication involves words (verbal), 38% of our communication involves how you say the words (vocal), and 55% of our communication is what others see (visual) while we are speaking. In other words, Mehrabian's findings suggest that 93% of all communication is actually nonverbal. Your body is speaking volumes!

Body language cues are communication signals that we send nonverbally. These cues help us to read the speaker's thoughts and feelings. While we are not mind readers, we do learn to read the cues sent to us. Here are five areas to consider about nonverbal communication: **paralanguage, kinesics, proxemics, chronemics, and haptics**. We'll discuss these areas one at a time.

What vocal cues are important for public speaking?

Paralanguage is the vocal part of speech and involves volume, rate, pitch, pace, and color. To have vocal variance, you will want to incorporate varying degrees of all these aspects. To create more emphasis or effects for your speech topic, you might choose to say some words louder or softer, some faster and others slower, and some words with more emphasis showing energy for the topic, anger, or any other emotion.

Volume is the level at which a sound is heard. While it is important for the audience to hear your voice, your volume does not need to be so loud that it appears you are shouting. Speak at a volume that will allow everyone in the room to hear your message. You control this by the volume of air you project using your **larynx** or voice box. More air = louder volume. Less air = softer volume. If you normally have a softer voice, you might require a microphone to be heard comfortably by your audience. If this is the case, be sure to rehearse using the microphone prior to your speech so that you understand how to use it correctly.

Rate is the method we use to determine how fast or slow someone is speaking. Many speakers tend to speed up because their nerves often push them into overdrive. This is a normal result of adrenaline pumping through your body and causing your heart rate to rev up; resulting in faster speech. While this is not always a problem, it can cause your audience to have trouble following your message because they will not have time to comprehend everything that you say. What can you do to make sure your speech is presented at a comfortable rate? Rehearse your speech, video or audio record your rehearsal, and evaluate the rate at which you speak. Try to take notes of your speech as you listen to the recording. Do you have time to make notes? If not, then your speech rate may be too fast. Consciously make an effort to slow down your rate of speech. Is your rate too slow? Plan to speed up the speech to keep your audience sitting on the edge of their seats!

Pitch is determined by sounds produced by vocal cord vibrations. Faster vibrations result in higher pitches. Slower vibrations result in lower pitches. Typically, women and children have a higher pitch. Men normally have a lower pitch. While this is typical, it is not absolute. Women and children can slow the vocal cord vibrations to achieve a lower pitch and men can speed vocal cord vibrations to achieve a higher pitch when needed. Varying pitch is important to having good vocal variance. A constant pitch results in a monotone voice and this is truly one sure way to lose your audience. A monotone voice lacks interest, variety, and energy like the monotone teacher in Charlie Brown cartoons, "Mwa, mwa, mwa, mwa, mwa, mwa!"

Pace is the rate at which you say syllables in a word. For example, people from the southern states in America usually add a couple of extra syllables in words that folks from the northern states do not. Southerners tend to say the word, well, in two syllables. Here is an example of a typical slower pace to say, "Well, I don't think so!":

Wha-ell, I don't think so!

Pause and Rhythm

A skillfully inserted **pause** in the speech can be a powerful public speaking tool. Dr. Martin Luther King, Jr. was a master with inserting pauses and using rhythm to impact the message of his speech. Listen again to the "I Have a Dream" speech and pay close attention to the long and powerful pause inserted directly following his initial opening statement and following each time he says, "I have a dream." Notice also, the **rhythm** in his speech that carries the audience's attention along with his poetic placement of words. Pauses strategically used provide audiences the opportunity to stop and focus on the last word said. This dramatic use of pauses must be timed and used in such a way that it creates more impact for the message.

Color involves the energy, enthusiasm, feelings, and attitudes that are included in our message. It may have negative or positive implications and can extend to what we see as much as what we hear. Our voice can show color when we tell a story that describes our exhilaration about a new game or fear of the unknown. Color can also be added as we discuss our customs, habits, or describe a place or a person. We love to hear color in a speech. It is how a speaker can add a little spark to the speech!

Dialects often surface as we discuss paralanguage. Dialects are a form of language heard from people living in a particular region, but this term can also be used as we discuss language indigenous to people from specific social or cultural groups. You will hear dialects referred to as local speech, regional speech patterns, languages, linguistics, vernacular, or accents. Dialects may include variations of grammar, vocabulary, and pronunciations. For example, if someone described the man at the store as having a French accent, they would be describing the man's regional speech patterns that would lead the listener to think the man was from a French-speaking part of our world. A phonetic and/or cultural analysis can result in identifying the continent or region where the dialect is most often spoken.

Effective language skills also surface as we discuss paralanguage. It is not enough to have a great topic with research and stories to support the topic, speakers also need to use effective language skills to be a good communicator. In other words, make sure your language skills are clear, concise, and constructive! Here are some tips for using effective language skills:

- Use standard English grammar, mechanics, and language.
- Use concrete and specific language and avoid using vague or abstract language.
- Avoid using acronyms or descriptions that only select audience members will grasp. If you need to use an acronym, identify the full meaning of the acronym before going into detail.
- Create images using adjectives to describe situations or people.
- Eliminate filler words that do not serve a purpose.
- Use vocabulary and grammar that is easily understood by your audience to establish a sense of commonality with the audience.
- Use language that is on the educational level of audience members. Do not talk "above" or "below" your audience's level of understanding.

Pronunciation and Articulation

How do you pronounce pecan? Do you pronounce it as pe-kan or pekahn? Do you pronounce tomato as tu-may-toe or tu-mah-toe? How do you pronounce aunt? Is she an "ant" or an "ahnt"? Although it is the very same word and the same meaning, we find that our pronunciations of these words can be quite different. Often, our **pronunciation** of words will stem from how the word was pronounced as we were growing up and is a product of our culture.

When giving a speech, you might stumble upon words that cause you to be unsure of the pronunciation. If this is the case, always consult with a dictionary which will show the phonetic pronunciations of a word. It is also important to pronounce people's names or the names of cities and states correctly. Incorrect pronunciations of words can distract an audience from hearing the message because they will dwell on incorrectly pronounced words.

Last week, I was coaching a student for an upcoming speech competition and noticed that every time she said the word "asked," she would say "axed." I asked her about this and she said that she didn't know why she pronounced the word that way when she clearly knew how the word was spelled and should be pronounced as written. We talked about it a few minutes and decided that the pronunciation of this one word stemmed from the dialect that was used in her culture. From this example you can tell that pronunciations and articulation of words can be determined from habit, from getting lazy with our speaking skills, or from learned behaviors. I'm happy to report that the student worked very hard to change the way she pronounced the word and during her speech competition, she pronounced it correctly and won 1st place in the state! Now, that's a SpeechShark!

Articulation is the process by which the speaker sounds out words so that the audience can understand what is being said. Speaking too fast will cause words to become slurred or will mean that the end of one word is omitted as the next word begins. Most speakers find that by slowing their speech, they are better able to articulate the content to the audience.

Since this is the case, we should identify words or phrases that we have a habit of saying incorrectly and then work to correct them. Bad habits in pronunciations and articulation can distract audiences from hearing our message, but it can also tarnish our speaker credibility.

For the purpose of a basic speech class, please make sure you are always using Standard English. In other words, slang or off-color words are not acceptable. Also avoid using contractions during a speech as these can often become slurred or chopped to the point that they are hard to comprehend.

Vocal Self-Assessment

Now that we've spent time learning about volume, rate, pitch, pace, pauses and rhythm, color, dialects and effective language skills, let's explore your personal vocal skills. Are you concerned with the quality of your own voice? Did you know that your voice reflects your personality and intelligence? If you want to improve your vocal skills, it can be done, but it takes effort. Practicing vocal skills is much the same as practicing a physical skill. Set your goals, determine the best method for achieving the results, and get to work! Consistently working toward creating stronger vocal skills will help you to gain results you would like to see.

What are the vocal aspects of speaking that you would like to improve? Are you concerned about your vocal quality? Is your voice nasal or monotone? Do you run out of breath as you are speaking? Do people constantly ask you to repeat what you just said?

Using your phone, record yourself speaking or reading a paragraph from a book and play it back to critically listen to your voice. Take your time during the recording, but try to speak as you normally speak in order to create a more accurate evaluation. After you've completed the recording, play it back and complete the following worksheet to get a good idea of your strengths and weaknesses:

EVALUATE YOUR VOICE
Rate your voice using this self-evaluation. Check characteristics that apply to you.

Voice Description—Desirable Traits	Voice Description—Undesirable Traits
My voice sounds pleasant.	My voice sounds nasal.
My voice has pitch variations.	My voice sounds monotone.
My voice is light.	My voice sounds throaty or raspy.
My voice has a pleasant rhythm.	My pitch is too high or too low.
My pitch is appealing.	My voice is too soft or too loud.
I articulate words clearly as I speak.	I do not articulate words clearly.
I sound like I am smiling.	I sound bored with myself.
My vocal quality is clear.	My voice squeaks or cracks when I talk.
My voice sounds confident.	My voice sounds weak.
My accent is not distinguishable.	My accent is heavy and hard to understand.
I like hearing my voice.	I do not like hearing my voice.
I control my breathing well.	I sound like I am gasping for breath.

What would you like to change?

How can you plan to change it?

How do I avoid using "Filler Words"?

Well, you know, it is uhm, like, well, like totally the most annoying thing you can hear, you know, in somebody's well, uh, you know, their speech presentation. It's uhm, the words that people, uhm, well, you know, they add them to what they are uhm, trying to say, when well, you know what I mean, they are so darn aggravating, and you like, well you hear them literally all of the time. You know?

You are in good company because about six million other people have asked this question. **Filler words** are the types of phrases, sounds, or words that speakers use to fill in an awkward pause when trying to communicate a thought or make a speech presentation. Filler words are contagious and socio-linguistically, can be a tribal form of bonding. Filler words are heard in formal speeches and in social conversations. They are "like" everywhere and add no value to the sentence or thought being communicated.

Do you use filler words? Many people use these words without ever realizing how often they use them and how distracting they might be. Once you realize you are using them, you might discover that sometimes you use them more than other times. Often people use them as a filler when they can't think of the word or thought they are trying to share. We feel that the sound helps to soften the pause while we search for the right word. Truthfully, the sound distracts the listener from hearing the full meaning we are attempting to communicate.

Speakers use filler words when:

1. Searching for the right words
2. Filling an awkward pause
3. Making a sentence sound more passive
4. Making a sentence sound more active
5. Sharing what you are thinking
6. Bonding with a friend that speaks with fillers
7. Expanding the sentence to take more time
8. Sharing the idea/experience with the listener

While it is acceptable to use an occasional filler word, it is important that you do not overuse them. Pausing to think of an answer or to remember your next point is a much better option than uhm, well, you know, throwing in a word or two that well uhm, like basically stretches out the moment but not the meaning.

Here are the filler words that you hear most often: Like, ya know, okay, uhm, uh, er, hmmm, so, well, literally, totally, clearly, actually, basically, seriously, really, like, I mean, just, whatever, I guess or I suppose, very, right, but, sorry, anyway, and, uh huh, uh uh, and any combinations of the above. Whew, I'll bet you thought that sentence would never end!

So, well, like, what can do you do to like, totally, get rid of all the well, you know what I mean, those annoying filler words?

Become aware of your filler word habit! Prepare and practice before speaking opportunities. Video or audio-record your speech rehearsals. Count the number of filler words you have in your presentation, speech, audition, pitch, toast, and so forth, and keep working until you eliminate as many filler words as possible.

My friend, Audrey Mann Cronin, is an acknowledged and long-time communication expert in the technology industry. She is on a mission to help us all become better speakers and created *LikeSo: Your Personal Speech Coach,* a mobile app that helps you to talk your way to success. Using voice recognition technology, *LikeSo* is a fun and effective way to practice being a more confident and articulate speaker. Speak into the microphone of your smartphone and LikeSo captures your words and helps you train and remove all of those filler words that undermine your speech, weaken your meaning, and distract your listeners. *LikeSo* also measures pacing (150 wpm considered optimal) and allows you to set goals, reminders, and track your progress over time (day/week/month/year). It is like a "Fitbit for your speech."

I have the app and enjoy using it with students and speakers that I coach. It is so easy! Just choose "Free-Style," your open mic for any upcoming speaking opportunity, or "TalkAbout" a conversation game to practice speaking on the fly with topics including "The Job Interview," "Debate Team," and "Small Talk." Choose your talk time, the filler words you want to train against, and receive a Speech Fitness Report. You can also follow her on Facebook, Twitter, and Instagram at @LikeSoApp. Here is a picture so that you will recognize it in the Apple Store:

Now that we know how to avoid distracting fillers, let's take a look at other important nonverbal cues.

Kinesics are physical cues we see. Following Mehrabian's research, 55% of nonverbal communication is visual and covers the majority of cues we use to read a situation. We begin evaluating and making judgments based upon what we see from the moment the speaker enters the stage area. These judgments continue until the speaker leaves the stage. As we watch the speaker, we evaluate the credibility of the speaker using his physical appearance, posture, poise, gestures, facial expressions, eye contact, smiling, and body movements. Often, we establish a judgment about the speaker before the speaker ever utters the first word. Although we would like to argue that we are not quite so petty, Albert Mehrabian's research findings prove the opposite. So, what do we need to learn from this? Take care that you are putting your best foot forward. Plan to show positive physical cues for your audience.

What type of appearance is expected during a speech?

Appearance is a nonverbal cue. Whether you are in a public speaking environment or a social arena, be very aware of the cues you are sending. The clothes and shoes you wear, the jewelry you choose, the type briefcase or bag you carry all speak to your brand. Take a look at the way you see yourself. Does your appearance reflect your own self-awareness? Do you understand your conscious and unconscious nonverbal cues through your choice of clothing and accessories?

Truthfully, there are many sides of you. There is the playful and casual side that is evident in the way you dress and behave when you are with your family and close friends. When at work, you may dress a bit more conservatively and more in keeping with the culture of the workplace. There is a romantic side when you are with the love of your life. Attitudes, beliefs, and values are often reflected in the type clothing we choose. It is appropriate to change appearances for different occasions and circumstances, but it is equally important to realize when to dress and groom in a particular manner.

Appearance is not just about the clothing, shoes, jewelry, and accessories that you choose, but also about grooming. Ask yourself the following questions:

- How does your clothing fit?
- Are your shoes polished?
- What colors do you choose?
- What styles appeal to you?
- What type hairstyle do you have?
- Are your clothes ironed or wrinkled?

- Does your clothing complement your accessories?
- Is your hair clean and styled?
- Are your fingernails manicured?

A few months ago, I had the pleasure of interviewing the Director of Talent Procurement for a Fortune 500 Company. During the interview, I asked if she looked for a particular type of clothing when she was scouting for new employees. She told me that she looks for candidates who are well-groomed and conservative and not for a particular clothing type. Different businesses reflect the culture of the business through the type clothing worn. She mentioned that for her organization, the most expensive suit was not always a bonus; however, she did want to see candidates wear clothing that was clean, ironed, and tailored to fit. As far as accessories, she said that haircuts, jewelry, and accessories often tell a great deal about the personality of the candidate. The most interesting thing she told me had to do with what the candidate was carrying! She shared that candidates who walked in with huge bags bulging with papers gave her the impression of an employee who was unorganized and messy. Instead, she preferred to see candidates walk in with a simple black folder or an iPad or tablet for note-taking. In today's technological world, anything that the employer may require can be sent with the touch of a key on the iPad or tablet. In other words, less is more!

As people prepare to make a speech presentation, they often wonder what they should wear. As a speech coach, I suggest that speakers dress according to the audience to which they will be speaking. Is it a casual or formal event? Are you speaking to people in your community or to the board of directors for your organization? In any speaking situation, it is always advisable to dress a bit more formally than the people who will be attending your presentation. Business casual or dressy business is always in good taste.

Using the SpeechShark app, you can write your speech and use the note cards available on your device. Consequently, you will not walk to the stage with a fistful of papers; instead, you can take your device and with a well-timed swipe of the screen, you can move to your next card to stay on target with your presentation. Again, less is more!

Physical appearance sends a positive or negative message about the speaker's credibility. For most speaking occasions, it is important to dress as if you are going to a job interview. Business casual dressing for a speech is always preferred. Occasionally, speakers may dress according to the topic they are presenting. For example, if you are giving a speech about cooking, you might wear a chef's hat and apron. But for the most part, your audience will appreciate the fact that you took time to dress professionally for the speech. Blue jeans and a t-shirt that says, "BITE ME," may not be the best choice if you want your audience to take you seriously. Overly bright outfits, unusual styles or garments that do not fit properly can also be distracting. While it may be appropriate to show tattoos or piercings if your speech topic is about tattoos or piercings, it is a better idea to avoid clothing that flaunt these. Have you ever heard "You only get one chance to make a first impression"? What message are you trying to send? Dress the part, SpeechShark!

Posture sends a nonverbal cue about how you feel about yourself and your speech. Not only will good posture show self-confidence, but it has a positive effect on your breathing patterns and the way you project your message. Good posture also lends itself to effective movements and gesturing during the speech. Have you ever heard someone tell you to "Stand tall"? Hold your chin up, keep your eyes focused on your audience, and take your place among great speakers who know what it takes to deliver a strong message. As you are introduced to the stage, walk with a positive purpose to let your audience know that you are ready and prepared.

Poise is displayed with how you carry your body. Are you comfortable in your own skin? Shoulders should be up and eyes looking at your audience to display positive self-confidence. Speakers who walk to the stage looking at the floor and with shoulders drooping will send a negative nonverbal cue about themselves and their speech topic. When giving a speech, walk confidently to the lectern and pan the audience with your eyes, smiling at them and letting them know you are happy to be speaking to them. When you get on stage, avoid leaning on the lectern, shifting from one foot to the other, adjusting your clothing or hair, handling notes, or putting your hands in your pocket. All of these negative behaviors will send negative nonverbal cues to your audience and will be evidence of a poor self-image and lack of confidence in yourself and your topic. Yes, all eyes will be on you. Make sure you are showing them cues that will increase your credibility.

Gestures are the ways you use your hands, body, and facial expressions during the speech to communicate points. I've often had students ask me, "What should I do with my hands during the speech?" My advice is to get immersed in your topic and in your audience so that you do not think about your hands and body. When you do this, you will have more natural and meaningful gestures. Don't put your hands in your pockets, clench them in front of you, or hold them behind you. These movements send a negative nonverbal cue. Gestures should not seem rehearsed, but should enhance your delivery and make visual points about things you are describing. They should be natural movements. The important thing is to make sure your gestures mirror the message you are sending.

Facial expressions include eye contact, smiling, head nodding, and head tilting to send a nonverbal cue to the audience during communication. When rehearsing a speech, consider standing in front of a mirror or video recording your rehearsal so that you can observe your facial expressions. Thoughts, emotions, and attitudes are often seen through facial expressions. Since many of our nonverbal cues include what people see, you can be assured that facial expressions are communicating to your audience things you are not saying verbally.

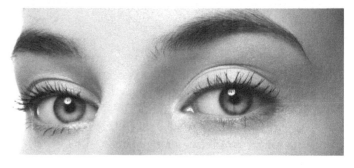

Eye contact promotes goodwill and a connection with the audience. It also helps the speaker appear more credible and knowledgeable about the topic. As you enter the stage, establish strong eye contact and keep strong eye contact throughout the speech. I've heard people suggest looking at the back wall if you get nervous with all eyes on you; however, that will only help you to establish a connection with the back wall. Take a deep breath and establish direct eye contact to develop a connection with the audience. Believe it or not, but the smiles and head nods of audience members will give you the strength and self-confidence to complete your speech in a positive manner. You need them and they need you.

When you have a large audience, you may find it hard to establish eye contact with each member. In this case, start with looking toward one side of your audience and pan the entire side with your strong eye contact as you move your gaze to the other side of the audience. Looking at the entire audience will help them to feel valued and included in your speech. This is how you connect with them and have them invest in your topic. Avoid gazing at any one person or group of people for too long of a time. Share your eye contact and your attention with all audience members.

Smiling is a nonverbal cue that says, "I am happy to be here!" A genuine smile will send a positive message to your audience. As you smile, you will be pleased to notice that they will also smile at you. This reciprocal smile will help you not be as nervous as you might be without positive audience cues.

Head tilting and head nodding is a nonverbal cue which lets you know if your audience comprehends your point or if they still might have questions.

Proxemics is the study of space and how we use it. We send spatial cues to show whether we are comfortable or uncomfortable with the space placed between us and the person speaking. Have you ever noticed a person back up when you move in to speak to them? If they do this, you might be moving into their personal space. When speaking to a small audience, you will need to keep a distance between yourself and the first row of audience members.

There are four different designations for space that we use when discussing communication: public space, social space, personal space, and intimate space. Different cultures and different people will be more comfortable in the different types of spaces. Here are designations to help you understand this better.

Public space is the space designated for speakers and usually twelve to twenty-five feet away from audience members. It is appropriate to move closer to your audience when making a particular point, but advisable not to stay too close to any one audience member for too long of a period. If you do, you will notice that it will make the audience members nervous. If there is a table in front and you move closer to the table, the audience member may move their personal items closer to them and away from the speaker. If you see then, take the cue that you are too close and back away.

Social space allows you to get just a little closer. This is the space that others are most comfortable with when working with a co-worker or customer and is usually about four to twelve feet.

Personal space allows someone to get closer, but not closer than one to four feet. This area is usually reserved for meeting with friends or family members.

Intimate space is the closest and is usually one foot or less away and usually involves touching the person next to you. This area is reserved for very close family members and also a romantic partner. With intimate space, we usually allow someone there for a short period of time, but will expect that same person to move to the personal space area at a certain point. We often will allow someone in the intimate space for a quick hug or to bid farewell, but also expect them to move back to the personal or social space once the hug is over.

As we conclude this section about proxemics, remember these designated spaces are the standards we recognize most often in the United States; however, they can change due to diverse cultures and circumstances. In all cases, whether speaking to an audience or speaking one-on-one to another person, be sure to read carefully the nonverbal cues being sent. Space distances with one person or a group of people may be altered according to that person or group's comfort level.

Sharks are known for their uncanny way of maneuvering gracefully through murky waters. You can do this, too. The only difference is that SpeechSharks will be maneuvering gracefully across the stage—no murky waters for you! **Movement** during a presentation involves the use of space on stage. For a speaking arena, most stages will have a lectern in the center of the stage. Even though a lectern is there, it isn't a good idea to go immediately to a lectern and stand behind the lectern the entire time you are speaking. Standing behind the lectern creates a barrier between the speaker and the audience. Nervous speakers tend to hold on to the lectern causing them to have poor gestures. In fact, I suggest using the lectern as a speaking tool to place notes and not resort to standing behind the lectern. Placing notes on the lectern will allow the speaker to use both hands for gesturing instead of holding notes.

What do you need to know about entering and exiting the stage area?

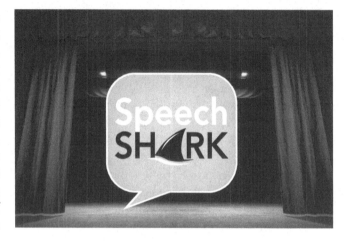

Whether you know it or not, your speech begins the moment you stand and enter the stage and does not end until you have been seated or exit the stage. Audience members watch you from the very first indication that you are going to be the speaker. It is for this reason that speakers need to enter the stage confidently, acknowledging the audience while approaching the lectern. If you are using notes, place them carefully on the lectern and then move away from the lectern toward the center of the stage. Avoid standing at the lectern and spending valuable time arranging and rearranging pages of notes. Notes should be in order before you enter the stage.

Once the speech is completed, take your notes from the lectern and again make eye contact and acknowledge your audience as you move back to your seat. BIG smiles and strong eye contact will convey the nonverbal cue that you are confident to give the speech and proud of the results once the speech is completed.

Using movement during a speech will improve the audience's retention and understanding of the message as long as the movement is natural. Pacing back and forth on the stage during a presentation is not an effective use of movement because this becomes distracting. Be aware of barriers or obstruction for movement: speakers, microphone stands, wires, chairs, tables, desks, or visual aids. Using well-planned movement during a presentation serves a purpose and can help the audience feel connected.

SpeechSharks know ways to orchestrate movements that are effective and carefully placed during the speech. It is called movement with a purpose. Use the letter W in the alphabet to help you visualize movement during your speech. There are five points in a W. Here is a numbered diagram and movements to help you walk your way to success.

WALK YOUR WAY TO SUCCESS!

- Imagine a giant W in the middle of the stage area. Move from 1,2,3,2,1 and then from 1,4,5,4,1. This helps you move to the left side of your stage and to the right side of your stage equally.

- Begin your speech at area 1. While you are front and center of the stage area, this is where you should stand to deliver the attention step, establish relevance for the topic, establish credibility, and clearly state your thesis.

- Take two steps back and away from the middle front of the stage to area 2 as you transition to the first point.

- Then move to area 3 as you cover the first point. Use this area of the stage to cover point one.

- As you transition to the second point, take two steps back to area 2 of the diagram. Stay in this area during the transition. Move to area 1 as you cover the second point.

- After the second point has been covered and as you transition to the third point, move directly to area 4. As you lead into the third point, take two steps up to area 5. Stay in this area while you cover the third point.

- As you transition to the conclusion, move back to area 4.
- Following the transition move back to area 1 to complete the summary of three main points.
- Stay in area 1 to deliver the final Appeal to Action and end with a BANG while standing center of the stage area and close to your audience.

Chronemics is the study of how we use time to communicate. If you arrive early or if you arrive late, you are sending a nonverbal cue about your time and the time of those who are expecting you.

I'm sure all of you have a friend who is constantly arriving late for all functions. In fact, you might even find yourself telling this friend the event begins thirty minutes to an hour prior to the time it actually begins, just so they will arrive in time. If your friend constantly arrives late, they are sending you a message that their time is more valuable to them than your time. This is true for personal events and for professional events. They are being rude to you. Don't forget it!

If someone always arrives a few minutes early or on time, this means that they honor your time and they value you and the event. This is a nonverbal form of communication that many people dismiss, but the way you handle this will determine how others consider you in the long run.

Why are time restraints important when presenting a speech?

When asked to present a speech, always ask the host about the time limit for your speech. Often other points of interest are included during the gathering and your speech will be just one portion of the event. Whether you are the key note speaker or a support speaker, timing is extremely important so that the event planner can keep the event moving according to a planned schedule. If your speech is longer than needed, the entire event may run overtime.

A good rule to follow is to meet the minimum time limit, but not go over the maximum time limit. A four- to six-minute speech should last five minutes. A twenty to thirty minute speech should last twenty-five minutes. It is always preferred to end your speech just short of the maximum time limit to keep your event host happy!

Your SpeechShark app has a built-in timer to help you stay on time! Just dial in the time that you have been asked to speak and the app will give you a visual reminder of the time left! The screenshot to the right will show what this looks like in your app. If a speech is designed to last eight to ten minutes we suggest you dial in nine minutes as your max time. This gives you a little cushion to make sure you do not go over time.

Haptics is the study of communicating through touch. This happens when we shake hands with a colleague, share a friendly pat on the back, or hug a family member. We send nonverbal communication through touch. Culture also plays an important part with touch and we should always be mindful of cues the recipient sends to us to let us know if the touch is welcomed or not.

During a speech, the audience is able to evaluate the speaker's confidence by observing if the speaker is adjusting clothing, touching hair, crossing arms, hands in pockets, wringing hands, scratching, fidgeting, touching head or face, and licking lips. All of these touching examples are negative cues and will communicate the speaker's lack of confidence to the audience. Be aware if you are sending negative cues by video recording a rehearsal. Watch the video and make notes of ways you might be sending unfavorable nonverbal cues.

SPEAK WITH CONFIDENCE: TAKING A "BITE" OUT OF THE FEAR OF PUBLIC SPEAKING

Just as a shark swims boldly forward to pursue his goal, you can also walk toward the stage with confidence and deliver your speech without hesitation! The first thing that you will want to do is to examine your own confidence level when speaking to an audience.

Unsure of whether your speaking anxiety level is low or high? Take this self-evaluation from **George L. Grice and John F. Skinner's** *Mastering Public Speaking.*

Directions: This instrument is composed of thirty-four statements concerning feelings about communicating with other people. Indicate the degree to which the statements apply to you by marking whether you **(1) strongly agree, (2) agree, (3) undecided, (4) disagree, or (5) strongly disagree** with each statement. Work quickly and record your first impression.

PERSONAL REPORT OF PUBLIC SPEAKING ANXIETY

1	2	3	4	5	Statements Concerning Feelings about Communicating with Other People
					1. While preparing for giving a speech, I feel tense and nervous.
					2. I feel tense when I see the words Speech and Public Speaking on a course outline when studying or on a job description.
					3. My thoughts become confused and jumbled when I am giving a speech.
					4. Right after giving a speech, I feel that I have had a pleasant experience.
					5. I get anxious when I think about a speech coming up.
					6. I have no fear of giving a speech.
					7. Although I am nervous just before starting a speech, I soon settle down after starting and feel calm and comfortable.
					8. I look forward to giving a speech.
					9. When the instructor announces a speaking assignment in class, I can feel myself getting tense.
					10. My hands tremble when I am giving a speech.
					11. I feel relaxed when I am giving a speech.
					12. I enjoy preparing for a speech.
					13. I am in constant fear of forgetting what I prepared to say.
					14. I get anxious if someone asks me something about my topic that I do not know.
					15. I face the prospect of giving a speech with confidence.
					16. I feel that I am in complete possession of myself while giving a speech.
					17. My mind is clear when giving a speech.
					18. I do not dread giving a speech.

continued

1	2	3	4	5	Statements Concerning Feelings about Communicating with Other People
					19. I perspire just before starting a speech.
					20. My heart beats very fast just as I start a speech.
					21. I experience considerable anxiety while sitting in the room just before my speech starts.
					22. Certain parts of my body feel very tense and rigid while giving a speech.
					23. Realizing that only a little time remains before a speech makes me very anxious.
					24. While giving a speech, I know I can control my feelings of tension and stress.
					25. I breathe faster just before starting a speech.
					26. I feel comfortable and relaxed in the hour or so just before giving a speech.
					27. I do poorer on speeches because I am anxious.
					28. I feel anxious when I hear an announcement of a speaking assignment.
					29. When I make a mistake while giving a speech, I find it hard to concentrate on the parts that follow.
					30. During an important speech, I experience a feeling of helplessness building up inside me.
					31. I have trouble falling asleep the night before a speech.
					32. My heart beats very fast while I present a speech.
					33. I feel anxious while waiting to give my speech.
					34. While giving a speech, I get so nervous I forget facts I really know.
					TOTAL Points

To determine Your Score on the PRPSA, Complete the Following Steps:

1. Add the scores for items in purple (1,2,3,5,9,10,13,14,19,20,21,22,23,25,27,28,28,30,31,32,33,34).
2. Add the scores for items in peach (4,6,7,8,11,12,15,16,17,18,24,26).
3. Complete the following formula: PRPSA = 132 – (total points from step 1) + (total points from step 2).
4. What is your score? _____

NOTE: Your score can range between 34 and 170. There is no right or wrong answer because this report just helps you to understand if you do have speaker anxiety and the level of speaker anxiety that you may have. Understanding Your Score:

- 34–84—Very low anxiety about public speaking
- 85–92—Moderately low level of anxiety about public speaking
- 93–110—Moderate anxiety in most public speaking situations, but not too severe that the individual cannot cope and be a successful speaker
- 111–119—Moderately high anxiety about public speaking. People with this score usually tend to avoid public speaking situations.
- 120–170—Very high anxiety about public speaking. People with these scores will go to considerable lengths to avoid all types of public speaking situations.

Whether your level is low or high, it is good to realize that we ALL get nervous when speaking in public; even sharks get nervous, especially when they are swimming in waters teaming with other sharks! So, that means you are normal! Yes, I said it—you are NORMAL!

Some people like to use **breathing exercises** before the speech to help channel the adrenaline running through their bodies. Slowing down their heart beat will also slow down the flow of adrenaline and will help calm nerves. Here are some breathing exercises to try before your next speech.

BREATHING EXERCISES

Before the Speech—Meditate:

- Sit straight with both feet on the floor.
- Close your eyes.
- Focus your attention on this thought, "I am a good speaker", "I am confident", "I will do a good job", and "My audience wants me to succeed."
- Place one hand on your stomach.
- Take a deep breath and recite the positive thought as you exhale.
- Dismiss any distracting or negative thoughts.
- Repeat this exercise for ten minutes prior to going into the room to speak.

While Waiting for the Speech:

- Sit with shoulders touching the back of the chair.
- Make sure your legs are not crossed and your feet are flat on the floor.
- Hang hands loosely to the side.
- Close your eyes and inhale slowly and deeply.
- Fill your chest with air and count four seconds to yourself.
- Hold your breath for another four seconds.
- Exhale air slowly through your mouth for four seconds.
- Imagine the tension flowing out of you and dropping from fingertips onto the floor.
- Feel yourself relaxing as you exhale.
- Continue this until called to present the speech.

After the Speech—Decompress:

- Place a warm heat wrap around your neck and shoulders for ten minutes.
- Close your eyes and relax your face, neck, upper chest, and back muscles.
- Breath deeply and exhale slowly as you relax.
- Remind yourself of the good things you did during your speech.
- Dismiss any distracting or negative thoughts.

Learning to deal with stress associated with public speaking will be your key to speaking with confidence. We all get nervous, so the best thing to know right now is that you are normal! See, doesn't that make you feel better? As you speak, you will experience good stress and bad stress.

Audiences WANT speakers to succeed. Audiences WANT speakers to be amazing and to wow us with their presentations! Why? Because the audience is investing their time to hear your speech. They don't want to waste time, but want to hear a message that is relevant and riveting! You can be the SpeechShark that provides what the audience WANTS!

Using the SpeechShark app will help you to do just that! The app is designed to create a speech that is geared toward your audience and is designed to satisfy the purpose for which you have been asked to speak! SpeechShark provides you with prompts that will help you maneuver through murky waters so that you, too, can swim easily and confidently toward your goal and deliver a crowd-pleasing presentation without hesitation or FEAR!

Dealing with Speech Anxiety

How do you cope with speech anxiety? What is stage fright? Stage fright is different for everyone and speakers compensate for stage fright by using techniques that work for them.

The feeling of stress is produced as adrenaline rushes through your body. **Adrenaline** is physiological and involves increased heart and respiration rate as a result of a situation perceived to be frightening or exciting. With this adrenaline rush, you may feel more energetic, excited, sometimes stronger and happier. This is good stress and will help you to rise to the challenge. Bad stress will cause you to feel fear and anxiety. Fear is a negative emotion which truly does not help the situation at all. With this in mind, I want to show you ways to focus on the good stress and alleviate the bad stress. Try all of these different strategies and you will soon discover the strategy that works best for you.

I've discovered that the people who have stage fright the most are the people who enter the stage unprepared. The best remedy for stage fright is again—**Plan, Prepare, and Persevere!** Know what you are going to say and most of the stage fright will disappear.

We've heard from lots of speakers who say that using the SpeechShark app helps them to be less anxious because it helps them to know what they should say during the speech. The app also provides note cards for presenting the speech.

PLAN

KNOW your audience, understand your purpose, and know what you need to say. If you can do that, you will have less stage fright and will be a more effective communicator! The **SECRET** is to do everything and anything that will help you be more confident. It is a confidence factor, not a personality or knowledge factor.

Here is what SpeechSharks do BEFORE the speech:

- **Walk around the room before the speech.**
- **Stand by the lectern and rehearse in the room where you will be giving the speech.**
- **Rehearse with people listening to you instead of rehearsing to an empty room.**
- **Rehearse by audio or video taping yourself.**
- **Rehearse in front of a mirror.**
- **Exercise positive self-talk.**

Rehearse, rehearse, rehearse—and rehearse some more. Change wording to make sure the words are coming to you comfortably. Believe in yourself! Feel comfortable with yourself, your location, and your content. As a result, you will be more confident and you will be happier with your presentation.

PREPARE

How do you cope with speech anxiety? Here is what SpeechSharks do BEFORE the speech:

- **Walk around the room before the speech**, instead of sitting in a chair and waiting to be called up front. It will help you to work off some of the nervous energy, and you can greet audience members as you move around the room waiting for the event to begin.
- **Stand by the lectern and rehearse in the room where you will be giving the speech.** This is difficult when the room is full, so arrive early and spend time rehearsing in the SAME PLACE where you will be giving the speech.
- **Rehearse with people listening to you** instead of rehearsing to an empty room. Having a rehearsal audience will give you a similar experience as having the presentation audience. That will help you to feel more confident because you can see how the audience will react to certain points that you make.
- **Rehearse by audio or video taping yourself.** Be AWARE of words that you tend to "chew" up. It may mean changing the wording so that your message will have a smoother delivery.
- **Rehearse in front of a mirror.** This is awkward, but it will help you see your gestures and facial expressions as you make the presentation. It will also give you a chance to check your appearance before you meet your audience.
- **Exercise positive self-talk.** Don't let anything negative come into your brain—tell yourself, "I am going to do a GREAT job!" "This will be my BEST speech!" "The audience is really going to LOVE my topic!" "Nobody in this room KNOWS this topic like I do!" "I am an EXPERT!"

PERSEVERE

Ultimately, the main thing you can do is rehearse, rehearse, rehearse—and rehearse some more. Don't quit. Move forward. Keep your goal in mind. Change wording to make sure the words are coming to you comfortably. Believe in yourself! Feel comfortable with yourself, your location, and your content. As a result, you will be more confident and happier with your presentation.

Look forward to your next speech!

Knock out stress using the **BAM** Approach:

B = Breathing exercises can help affect your state of mind, lower heart rate, and bring stress under control. The trick to this is to use controlled breathing exercises. As you follow the breathing exercises, you will notice that your muscle tension will relax when providing your body with much needed oxygen. The result will have a positive effect on your thoughts and feelings. The Internet is packed with breathing exercises to use before your next speech!

A = Aromatherapy involves the sense of smell and uses scents to overcome stress and improve overall mental health. Certain scents may help you to feel more calm than others, so it is important to find the scent that helps you to feel "ahhhh!"

Some popular scents used to calm stress are lavender, chamomile, lemongrass, and peppermint. Diffusers are readily available online and in department stores along with vials of essential oils. There are also mixtures of various essential oils designed to bring a sense of calmness to the user. Experiment to find the oil/scent which works best for you. Diffuse the oil as you sit in your home or desk prior to giving the speech. Dab a tiny bit of oil on the inside of your wrists before a speech. There are even diffusers available that plug in to your car so that you can experience the calming scents while driving to your speech location.

M = Meditation enhanced with music will calm stress. Use imagery and positive visualization to think your way to success! Positive self-talk and imagining a successful speech are achieved as you concentrate on feeling successful while communicating to others. First, imagine yourself walking confidently to the stage, delivering the best speech of your life, and then hearing the welcomed applause of audience members! Tell yourself, "I can do this! I know my topic. I am prepared for this speech. I have a message my audience needs to hear. I am the best person to share this topic to my audience. I will do a great job and my audience will

be glad they heard this speech." Do not allow negative thoughts or feelings to enter this moment. Only concentrate on positive thoughts and visualize your success. Using calm music or sounds of nature while meditating can intensify this effect and will help you feel composed and ready to meet the challenge.

There are several strategies available, but as with anything, it is important to do what works for you and understand your stress triggers and indicators. Be sure to review the chapter covering the Speech Day Checklist. Following a checklist will help you arrive feeling prepared and ready to take the stage!

Presentation Skills

After reading this chapter, you will be able to answer the following questions:

1. What is the definition of verbal language? _____

    _____

    _____

2. What is the definition of nonverbal language? _____

    _____

    _____

3. What is the formula for Albert Mehrabian's communication theory? ___

    _____

    _____

4. What are the three primary areas of communication? _____

    _____

    _____

5. What are five areas of nonverbal communication? _____

    _____

    _____

6. What is the definition of paralanguage? _____

_____

_____

7. What is the definition of volume? _____

_____

_____

8. What is a larynx? _____

_____

_____

9. What is the definition of rate? _____

_____

_____

10. What is the definition of pitch? _____

_____

_____

11. What is the definition of pace? _____

_____

_____

12. What is the definition of color as used to describe a voice? _____

_____

_____

13. What type dialect do YOU have? _____

_____

_____

14. What are filler words? Do you use them? _____

_____

_____

15. What are kinesics? _____

_____

_____

16. What nonverbal cues do you send about yourself with your posture and poise? _____

_____

_____

17. What gestures send negative nonverbal cues? _____

_____

_____

18. What is a benefit of using strong eye contact throughout the speech? _____

_____

_____

19. What is the definition of proxemics? _____

_____

_____

20. Define the difference between public, social, personal, and intimate space? _____

_____

_____

21. What is the definition of chronemics? _____

_____

_____

22. What is the definition of haptics? _____

_____

_____

23. What is the definition of adrenaline? _____

_____

_____

24. What is the BAM Approach for speaking with confidence? _____

_____

_____

25. What strategy works best for you when you need to deal with speech anxiety? _____

_____

_____

26. Why do most of us experience speech anxiety in some form? _____

_____

_____

27. What symptoms are evident with speech anxiety? _____

_____

_____

28. Does the audience want you to succeed? _____

_____

_____

29. How do breathing exercises help with speech anxiety? _____

_____

_____

30. What can you do before the speech to calm your nerves? _____

_____

_____

Shark Bites

IMPROVING PRESENTATION SKILLS

Practice Eye Contact: Work in a group of four or five people. Put your chairs in a circle. Take turns speaking impromptu (Suggested Topic: Your favorite vacation). As you speak, make sure you are making direct eye contact with each person in your group. Spend two or three seconds looking directly at each person and then move your gaze to the next person. Continue doing this until your story is finished and you have held direct eye contact with each person in the group.

Practice Good Posture: Stand next to your chair. Place an object on your head (iPad or phone). Count to twenty slowly and keep your head balanced so that your device does not fall off your head. Now, practice walking across the room with the object on your head. Can you keep it steady or does it fall? If it falls, try it again.

Practice Good Gestures: Using your arms, hands, head, and face, practice gestures for the following: saying "no," saying "yes," showing how many numbers, showing how large or small something is, showing locations, showing you understand, and showing you do not understand.

Practice Using Note Cards: If you are using the SpeechShark app, note cards will be on your phone or tablet. Practice using them and swiping to move from one point to the next point.

Practice Using Different Verbal and Nonverbal Cues: Make up hypothetical situations with a friend and respond using the following:

1. Angry response
2. Happy response
3. Confused response
4. Submissive response
5. Assertive response

Peer Evaluate each other to make sure verbal words and the responses aligned with nonverbal cues. Are there things you need to improve? What are they?

Shark Bites

TAKING A BITE OUT OF THE FEAR OF PUBLIC SPEAKING

List five things that cause you to have presentation anxiety:

1.

2.

3.

4.

5.

Rank these fears from 1–5. Assign 1 to the fear that causes the most anxiety.

Draw a line through the fear and add a positive thought beside each one.

Use BREATHING Exercises to help you feel calm:

Sit in a chair with both feet on the floor and your hands in your lap. Close your eyes. Breathe in and count 1, 2, 3, 4 and out 1, 2, 3, 4. Do this for one full minute (timing yourself with the timer on your phone).

Do this exercise again, but this time try to take only six to ten breaths per minute.

Take your hands out of your lap and let them hang loosely by your sides. Shake your hands as hard as you can for three seconds. Then drop your hands by your side and imagine all of your anxiety dripping out from your fingertips and landing on the floor. Stay in this position for ten seconds.

Return your hands to your lap. Again repeat breathing in and count 1, 2, 3, 4 and breath out 1, 2, 3, 4.

Think positive thoughts and tell yourself—I've got this! I'm a SpeechShark!

Chapter Fifteen

Rehearsing the Speech and Creating a Speech Day Checklist

In this chapter:

How do I rehearse my speech?

Why should I plan to rehearse using presentation aids?

What is a Speech Day Checklist?

What are some communication tips to remember?

REHEARSING THE SPEECH

You have heard it said that practice makes perfect. This is true, but only if you practice properly. You will do little to improve your speech delivery unless you practice the right things in the right ways. **Here is a five-step method that works well for presenters:**

1. Go through your outline to see what you have written.
   - Are the main points clear?
   - Do you have supporting materials?
   - Does your introduction and conclusion come across well?
2. Prepare your speaking notes. In doing so, be sure to follow the guidelines. Use the same framework as in the preparation outline. Make sure your speaking notes are easy to read. Give yourself cues on the note cards for delivering the speech.
3. Practice the speech aloud several times using only the speaking outline. Be sure to "talk through" all examples and to recite quotations and statistics. If your speech includes visual aids, utilize those as you practice. The first couple of times, you will probably forget something or make a mistake, but don't worry. Keep going and complete the speech as best as you can. Concentrate on gaining control of the ideas; don't try to learn the speech word for word. After a few tries you should be able to get through the speech extemporaneously with surprising ease.
4. Polish and refine your delivery. Practice the speech in front of a mirror to check for eye contact and distracting mannerisms. Record the speech to gauge volume, pitch, rate, pauses, and vocal variety. Most important, try it out on friends, roommates, family members—anyone who will listen and give you honest feedback. Because your speech is designed for an audience you need to find out ahead of time how it goes over with people.
5. Finally, give your speech a dress rehearsal under conditions as close as possible to those you will face in class. Some students like to try the speech a couple times in an empty classroom the day before they actually present the speech. No matter where you hold your last practice session, you should leave it feeling confident and looking forward to speaking in your class.

If this or any practice method is to work, you must start early. Don't wait until the night before your speech to begin working on delivery. A single practice session—no matter how long—is rarely enough. Allow yourself at least a couple of days, preferably more, to gain command of the speech and its presentation.

PRACTICE WITH YOUR VISUAL AIDS

We have mentioned several times the need to rehearse using your visual aids, but the point bears repeating. No matter what kind of visual aid you choose, be sure to employ it when you rehearse. Go through the speech multiple times, rehearsing how you will show your aids, the gestures you will make, and the timing of each move. In using visual aids, as in other aspects of speechmaking, there is no substitute for preparation.

If you are using presentation technology, don't just click through casually or rush quickly over your words when you practice. Make sure you know exactly when you want each slide to appear and disappear, and what you will say while each is on-screen. Mark your speaking notes with cues that will remind you when to display each slide and when to remove it.

Rehearse with the mouse, remote, keyboard, or iPad until you can use them without looking down for more than an instant when advancing your slides. Also concentrate on presenting the speech without looking back at the screen to see what is being projected. Rehearse with your tech team, if you need one!

Given all the things you have to work on when practicing a speech with any kind of presentation technology, you need to allow extra time for rehearsal. So, get an early start and give yourself plenty of time to ensure that your delivery is as impressive as your slides.

Practicing Visual Aids Checklist	Yes	No
• Have I checked the speech room to decide where I can display my visual aids most effectively?		
• Have I practiced presenting my visual aids so they will be clearly visible to everyone in the audience?		
• Have I practiced presenting my visual aids so they are perfectly timed with my words and actions?		
• Have I practiced keeping eye contact with my audience while presenting my visual aids?		
• Have I practiced explaining my visual aids clearly and concisely in terms my audience will understand?		
• If I am using handouts, have I planned to distribute them after the speech rather than during it?		
• Have I double-checked all equipment to make sure it works properly?		
• If I am using PowerPoint, do I have a backup of my slides that I can take to the speech with me?		

CHECK THE ROOM AND EQUIPMENT

For classroom speeches, you will already be familiar with the room and equipment. Even if you have used PowerPoint on previous occasions, you need to check the setup in the room where you will be presenting.

If you are using a computer that is installed in the room, bring your slides on a flash drive so you can see how they work with that computer. If your presentation includes audio or video, double-check them using the room's audiovisual system.

Sometimes, of course, it is not possible to visit the room before the day of your speech. Never assume that everything will be "just fine." Instead, assume that things will not be fine and that they need to be checked ahead of time.

Finally, always bring a backup of your slides on a flash drive. This may seem like a lot of fuss and bother, but anyone who has given speeches with PowerPoint—or any other kind of visual aid—will tell you that it is absolutely essential.

Have a Backup Plan

No matter how much time presenters invest in mastering the technology, they can still be undermined by technological glitches. This is why experts recommend that you always have a backup plan in case the technology fails. Because we have all encountered sabotage by technology at one time or another, audiences usually have sympathy for a presenter who encounters such problems. When in doubt, be prepared to present without technology.

SPEECH DAY CHECK LIST

- Plan, Prepare, Persevere! The more planning and preparation you do before the speech, the more confident you will be.
- Think positively—YOU can do this!
- Understand what is expected of you for the speech.
- Pack all materials you need the day before your speech. Have a checklist planned to keep you on target.
- Take care of you!
  - Get a good night's sleep before the speech.
  - Eat a healthy high protein meal.
  - Stay away from milk products which can coat your throat.
  - Drink plenty of fluids before your speech, but avoid caffeine and sugar which can make you feel jittery.
- Rehearse with your tech team so they know what you need.
- Arrive early to become familiar with the speaking area.
- Rehearse using a microphone, if you need to use one.
- Rehearse using a remote for your PowerPoint, if you choose to use one.
- Visit with people as they arrive for the speech. It helps to create a bond with the audience prior to your presentation.

Consider these areas carefully and pre-pack for your presentation. Begin to pack a bag of things you will need to carry for the speech. If you need visual aids, you will also need to work with a tech team and have them rehearse with you to make sure they understand all that you will require them to do for your presentation. This means providing a script so they will know when to set up your table display for props or so they will know when to advance the slides of your PowerPoint presentation. Preparation also includes rehearsal.

First, rehearse *without* your tech team to smooth out the rough edges and to make decisions regarding the point in your speech when visual aids, sound, light changes, or PowerPoint slides should be introduced. Once you have worked through these details, then bring in the tech team.

CHECKLIST FOR A GREAT SPEECH

Before each presentation, follow this checklist to make sure every detail is in shipshape!

The Outline:
- ☐ Typed
  - ○ Correct outline format
  - ○ Header (name, company name/class name/date)
  - ○ Headings for each item is in bold letters
- ☐ Speech Category
- ☐ Title
- ☐ General Purpose
- ☐ Specific Purpose

Introduction:
- ☐ Full sentence format
- ☐ Attention Step
- ☐ Establish Need/Relevance
- ☐ Establish Speaker Credibility
- ☐ Thesis/Preview Statement (clearly states main points)

Body:
- ☐ Roman numerals (I., II., III.) Capitalized letters for sub-points (A., B., C.) and numbers for sub-sub-points (1., 2., 3.)
- ☐ Three main points (using key words or phrases)
- ☐ Transition sentences between the introduction step to the main points, between each main point, and between the last main point and the conclusion
- ☐ Each main point is covered equally

Conclusion:
- ☐ Full sentence format
- ☐ Signal to let your audience know you are concluding the speech
- ☐ Summary restates all main points clearly
- ☐ Final appeal keeps the audience thinking about the speech

Visual Aids:
- ☐ Visual aid explanation page is included with the outline
- ☐ PowerPoint/Prezi slides follow outline
- ☐ PowerPoint follows design requirements
- ☐ Handout is usable, designed by the speaker, and supplies one for each person
- ☐ Rehearse using visual aids with tech team

Research:

- ☐ Follow citation guidelines for the topic
- ☐ Include credible research sources
- ☐ Include the minimum number of sources required
- ☐ Vary types of research used
- ☐ Parenthetically cite research in the document
- ☐ Include a separate page for the Works Cited

Presentation:

- ☐ Rehearse using presentation notes
- ☐ Rehearse with the tech team
- ☐ Place a water bottle on the lectern
- ☐ Check EVERYTHING—lights, sound, computer, PowerPoint, notes folder

TECH TEAM CHECKLIST

Complete this form as you plan the use of visual aids so you are prepared for the speech. Speakers who use visual aids will need to make use of a tech team. It is the speaker's responsibility to meet with tech team members ahead of time, provide a script, and rehearse with the tech team to make sure they understand what is needed. Visual aids are an important part of the speech and a direct reflection of your credibility as a speaker.

Speaker's Name: _____ **Date:** _____

Time of Speech: _____ **Type of Speech:** _____

Description of Visual Aids:

_____

_____

_____

_____

Note: In the area below, please list each tech team member's name and their assigned duties. Be sure to assign a member for the PowerPoint, sound, lights, setup, breakdown, and distribution of handouts. All duties may not be needed for all speeches.

Tech Team Member's Name: _____

Duties Assigned: _____

Tech Team Member's Name: _____

Duties Assigned: _____

Tech Team Member's Name: _____

Duties Assigned: _____

Tech Team Member's Name: _____

Duties Assigned: _____

_____

_____

COMMUNICATION TIPS FROM THE EXPERTS AT SPEECHSHARK

What is the worst thing that a person can do when trying to make a speech presentation?

If a speaker knows that a speaking engagement is approaching, the worst thing the speaker can do is to be so overly confident that he does not prepare for the event! Preparation includes knowing to whom you will be speaking and making sure you provide content that the audience needs. It also includes researching the topic to add support for your points and rehearsing the presentation several times.

How can you prevent a failed presentation?

To prevent a failed presentation, the key is over-preparation. For example, if you are speaking to specific groups, learn the names of the directors and interject their names into the speech at an appropriate moment. Include projects or plans the group is making so they know you cared enough about the group to learn about them. Plan, prepare, and practice so your presentation will be perfect!

What are the characteristics of effective speakers?

- Effective speakers are great listeners. They listen to find out what is needed and then go the extra mile to research main points within the content and provide the audiences with credible information.
- Effective speakers are detail oriented and are planners. They LOVE using speech checklists! Once they have the content of the speech covered, they are effective in the delivery of the information.
- Effective speakers use energy to captivate their audiences so that enthusiasm and excitement for the topic is "caught" and not "bought"!
- Effective speakers learn to calm their nerves so they always appear confident and competent.

In a socially awkward situation like meeting someone for the first time, what is the best way to break the ice?

Let's face it, meeting someone for the first time can be very awkward. Understanding that there will be a short period of awkwardness before the relationship begins is a realistic way of approaching the situation. From a communicator's point of view, it is important to know your audience before speaking to them. What can you learn about this person before the meeting? What common ground might you have with this person? Do your homework before the meeting and the period of time between "Hello!" and "I'll look forward to seeing you again!" will be less awkward and more productive!

What sort of approach is best to avoid?

If you know your audience before the meeting, it will be easier to instigate conversation that is mutually satisfying. Stay away from topics and points that would cause a conflict. I am not saying that you should never speak about controversial matters, but that is a subject for another meeting once your relationship has progressed to the point where you can speak candidly about your thoughts.

   "Do unto others as you would have them do unto you!" I know you have heard that a million times, but as you meet someone for the very first time, treat your new friend the way that you

would like to be treated. Be open to them and be a good listener. The awkwardness will soon pass and you will be the master of conversation before the meeting is over!

What can good communication skills do for someone?

Having good verbal and nonverbal communications skills are crucial to success in life! Effective communication skills will foster relationships, solve problems, promote teamwork, motivate and influence others, achieve goals, and the list goes on!

Nonverbal skills are just as important as verbal skills. Have you ever heard someone say, "What you do speaks so loudly that I can't hear what you are saying"? The truth is that people believe what they see before they believe what they hear. If you are going for a job interview, ask yourself the following questions:

- What will my potential employer see when I walk through the door?
- How are you dressed?
- What are you carrying with you?
- How is your poise and confidence?
- How is your handshake?
- Are you wearing a big smile?
- Are you demonstrating enthusiasm in your walk and the way that you carry yourself?

If all of these are positive, then you could very well get the job as long as your resume is as impressive as you are! If they are negative, then you will need to keep job searching, but please work on nonverbal skills before going to another interview.

I was speaking to a businessman the other day who shared with me that he likes to hire people who belong to Toastmasters International Clubs. He said that people who actively work on their images by improving their communication skills are also going to be conscious of improving the image of the business they represent. None of us are perfect communicators. Learning effective communication skills is not a destination, but a journey and something that we continue to improve as we move toward success!

Why do you think so many people fear public speaking?

It is no secret that most people fear public speaking more than they fear death. The truth is, everyone gets nervous when they need to speak in public. The good news is, no one has ever died from public speaking! Now, I know that the fear of public speaking is no laughing matter; however, if we realize we are perfectly normal and that everyone gets nervous, then we do not enter the stage feeling like we are the only nervous speaker in the world! We simply need to learn how to handle our own fears so that we can be effective speakers.

Usually people fear public speaking because they think everyone in the audience will be judging them—judging their appearance, voice, accent, body movements, content of speech, and the list goes on and on. Truthfully, people do not judge negatively and "take the speaker apart piece by piece." Instead, they want the speaker to be successful. After all, they are investing their time to hear this person speak and they don't want to waste their time. So, the audience is hoping for a knock-you-out-of-your-chair speech.

The question is not so much, "Why do so many people fear public speaking," but "How do I overcome my own fear of public speaking?" The answer to that is:

- Conduct an audience analysis prior to giving a speech.
- Choose a topic that is relevant for the audience.
- Conduct research to make sure you are covering points the audience wants to hear.

- Plan visual aids that support points.

- Craft a speech outline that includes an introduction, body, and conclusion. Let the first words you say grab your audience's attention. Establish why the audience needs to hear your speech. Establish why you are the person credible to speak to them. Clearly state the three points you will cover. Plan effective transitions between each main point. In the conclusion, clearly restate the three main points you covered. Finally, end with a BANG! Make sure your last words are something that will keep your audience thinking about your topic and about your speech.

- Rehearse, rehearse, rehearse! I say this three times because a speaker should rehearse speeches a minimum of three times before making the presentation.

- Positive self-talk will take you from "I can't do this" to "I can do this and I will do a great job!"

- Breathe! That's right, breathing exercises prior to the presentation can help you calm your heart rate and slow the flow of adrenaline in your body.

- Walk confidently to the stage realizing that you have earned the right to be the speaker of this particular event. Establish strong eye contact with your audience as you move toward the lectern, smile at them, and send nonverbal cues that send the message of your confidence and competence to speak!

- Do your best, but understand that you will never give a perfect speech. There will always be that one thing you forgot to say or there may be a time when you trip over your own words. Remind yourself that you are human—just like everyone in your audience—and do not beat yourself up over mistakes. Instead, dwell on all of the great things that you do!

- Be proud of yourself! Pat yourself on the back! Get ready for the next speech.

I am a SpeechShark! What is your super power?

Rehearsing the Presentation

After reading this chapter, you will be able to answer the following questions:

1. What are keys for preparing to rehearse your presentation?

_____

_____

2. What are the guidelines provided for a checklist for rehearsing with visual aids?

_____

_____

3. Why is it important to check the room and equipment prior to your presentation?

_____

_____

4. What will help you to be more confident the day of your speech? _____

_____

_____

5. When should you pack your speech materials? _____

_____

_____

6. What should you do before the speech to take care of YOU? _____

_____

_____

7. When should you arrive for your presentation? _____

_____

_____

8. What should your outline include? _____

_____

_____

9. What are research requirements to include? _____

_____

_____

10. What should you check prior to the presentation? _____

_____

_____

11. How many tech team members will you need? _____

_____

_____

12. What is the worst thing you can do when preparing for a speech? _____

_____

_____

13. What are the characteristics of effective speakers? _____

_____

_____

14. Why does the audience want YOU to succeed? _____

_____

_____

15. What are the benefits of good communication skills? _____

_____

_____

16. Why do people fear public speaking? _____

_____

_____

17. What strategies do you use to overcome the fear of public speaking? _____

_____

_____

18. Are you ready for your next speech? If not, what do you need to do in order to be prepared? _____

_____

_____

Shark Bites

GETTING READY FOR THE BIG DAY!

Complete the following Outline Checklist:

The Task (Outline)	Completed	Needs More Work
☐ Typed ☐ Uses Standard Outline ☐ Header (name/company/date) ☐ Headings for Each Item ☐ Speech Category ☐ Title ☐ General Purpose ☐ Specific Purpose		
Introduction Step: ☐ Full Sentence Format ☐ Attention Step ☐ Establish Need/Relevance ☐ Establish Credibility ☐ Thesis/Preview Statement		
Body: ☐ Roman Numerals I., II., III. ☐ ABCs for Sub-Points ☐ Three Main Points ☐ Transition Sentences		
Conclusion: ☐ Full Sentence Format ☐ Signal to Conclude Speech ☐ Summarize Main Points ☐ Appeal/Closing Statement		

Shark Bites

CHECKLIST FOR THE VISUAL AIDS AND RESEARCH!

Complete the following Task Checklist:

The Task	Completed	Needs More Work
Visual Aid ☐ Include a Visual Aid Explanation Page with Outline ☐ PowerPoint/Prezi Follows Outline ☐ Handout is Usable ☐ Handout is Designed by Speaker ☐ One Handout for Each Audience Member ☐ Rehearse Visual Aids with Tech Team		
Research ☐ Follow Citation Guidelines for the Subject ☐ Use Credible Sources ☐ Include Minimum Required ☐ Vary Types of Research ☐ Parenthetically Cite Sources in the Outline ☐ Include a Works Cited or Bibliography Page with the Full Citation		
Presentation ☐ Rehearse, Rehearse, Rehearse ☐ Rehearse Using Presentation Notes ☐ Rehearse with Tech Team ☐ Double-Check EVERYTHING—Lights, Sound, Computer, PPT, Notes, Water		

Chapter Sixteen
Evaluating the Speech

In this chapter:

What do I need to know about self-evaluations?

How do I conduct a peer evaluation?

How will I be evaluated during my speech?

How will my outline be evaluated?

SPEECHSHARKS HAVE THICK SKIN

It's no secret, SpeechSharks have thick skin and will often ask others to evaluate or critique their speeches. As speakers work to improve stage presence, they will often video and audio record presentations then play the recordings over and over again searching for ways to improve. You need thick skin for this!

Speakers welcome evaluations and critiques that recognize their strengths, but also evaluations that offer specific suggestions and tips for overcoming weaknesses. **The purpose of an evaluation is to coach, help, build, mold, and encourage.** ALL of us can improve. Not only do SpeechSharks understand this concept, but they need thick skin to welcome feedback in all types of forms. Evaluations of presentations allow speakers to recognize and be prepared to capitalize on strengths and identify areas for improvement.

Generally, a one-page document is sufficient to evaluate overall speaking strengths and areas in need of improvement. In a learning environment, speakers may be asked to offer written or oral speech evaluations of their peers. **Written evaluations** are conducted during the presentation in the form of a rubric or guidelines. **Oral evaluations** are presented immediately following the speech and may be delivered by a member of the audience or by the speech coach. In any case, evaluations are an excellent tool to help us become better speakers.

Consider asking a friend or colleague to video record your speech. Plan to watch the video twice before completing a **self-evaluation**. The first time, watch the video without sound so that you pay careful attention to nonverbal cues that you may send: the way you are dressed, movements, gestures, eye contact, facial expressions, handling of visual aids, and referring to speech notes. The second time, watch the video with sound and pay careful attention to your vocal skills and to the content delivered. How was the attention step? Were your three main points supported by examples or research? Did you cite sources of research used? How was the conclusion of your speech? Did you use vocal variance? Could you hear passion for the topic in your voice?

Everyone benefits from speech evaluations. Obviously, the speaker benefits as he becomes aware of strengths and areas for improvement. The evaluator benefits and becomes a better speaker because the areas needed in a speech are accentuated by an evaluation. Not only is the evaluator reinforcing knowledge of areas needed in a speech, but is also using that knowledge to guide others. Audiences also benefit from hearing an evaluation because they are able to apply the lessons learned to their own speech presentations.

Before **peer-evaluating** a speaker, consider the skill level of the speaker. Is the speaker a novice or experienced speaker? Take advantage of evaluation tools in the form of rubrics or templates. Use audio or video recordings to play back and show the speaker as you offer a suggestion or praise. Be kind, but truthful with evaluations and be specific with areas that demonstrate speaking strengths or weaknesses. Here are explanations of things to consider.

SKILL LEVEL

If new to public speaking, the evaluator should use a less critical and more encouraging strategy for the evaluation, especially if the speaker is trying to overcome a fear of public speaking. First, compliment the speaker for stepping up to the stage to deliver a speech and then proceed with supportive and positive comments. Ask questions of the speaker. How did you feel as the speech was beginning? What strategies did you use to power through? What were you most proud of? What areas do you feel need to be improved? By having the speaker look inward, you might find their answers are delivered with less stress than the actual delivery of the speech.

If that is the case, be sure to compliment their ease in speaking about the speech. It never hurts to offer evaluations that focus on the positive aspects of a speech for beginning speakers. It helps them to develop enough self-confidence to speak again. For a more experienced speaker, consider using some of the techniques and tips shown below.

EVALUATION TOOLS

Using evaluation tools will help evaluators to do a more thorough job, which will be beneficial for the speaker and for those listening to the evaluation. In this chapter, you'll find rubrics, forms, and suggestions for evaluating a speech. Recordings are excellent tools. Whether you are using audio or video recordings, it is a great idea to play back sections of the speech as you offer evaluations. Not only are you telling the speaker about their strengths or weaknesses with presentations, but you can also show clips which add credibility to your evaluation.

BE KIND, BUT TRUTHFUL

Speakers usually know how they did and will know if it was a successful speech or if it wasn't successful at all. Be kind with your statements, but be truthful. Speakers can spot a dishonest evaluation a mile away and this will damage your credibility as an evaluator. In other words, don't say you liked something in their speech if you really did not like it at all. Preface the critique with, "It is my opinion that . . ." This allows the speaker to know that what you are sharing is your own perceptions of the performance. Kindness goes a long way when evaluating someone else's speech. Avoid being accusatory, rude, or insensitive with comments. Damaging the speaker's confidence and your own relationship with the speaker is not the purpose of an evaluation.

BE SPECIFIC

It takes skill to build an evaluation that motivates, encourages, and highlights areas to improve without making the new speaker feel defeated. Because of this, evaluators should provide specific examples and then offer suggestions for ways to improve. Avoid simply saying, "I liked your speech." Instead, tell the speaker why you liked the speech and give specific details regarding the areas you thought were outstanding. When offering critiques, avoid being vague. Give specific details regarding what areas need to be improved and provide suggestions for improving.

Sure, SpeechSharks have thick skin, but evaluators also need thick skin. With time and experience, evaluations can be delivered as a tender morsel to be savored, enjoyed, and appreciated! In the pages to follow, you will find explanations of the various methods and also rubrics that will help with the process. You'll find a rubric to give to the speech instructor prior to each speech, a self-evaluation rubric to be completed by you following each speech, and a series of peer evaluations that can be used as you evaluate the speeches of your classmates. Please be sure to check with your instructor to see which type rubric you are expected to use in the speech class.

SPEECH EVALUATION WORKSHEET
Instructor's Copy for Grading the Speech

Speaker's Name: _____   Title of Speech: _____

Time of Speech: _____   Date: _____

Grade: _____

Speech Performance 100 possible points	Excellent 5 points	Good 4 points	Average 3 points	Fair 2 points	Poor 1 point	N/A 0 points
Introduction Step Attention Step Establish Need/Relevance Establish Credibility Thesis (Preview 3 Points)						
Body: Point 1 Direct Support of Point						
Body: Point 2 Direct Support of Point						
Body: Point 3 Direct Support of Point						
Transitions (4) To First Point To Second Point To Third Point To Conclusion						
Conclusion Summary (Review 3 Points) Closing Statements						
Language Skills Vocabulary Filler Words Sentence Structure Grammar Usage						
Vocal Delivery Skills Voice Volume Rate Vocal Variance						
Enthusiasm for Topic Passion/Energy						
Gestures						
Eye Contact						
Poise and Confidence						
Professional Appearance						

Speech Performance 100 possible points	Excellent 5 points	Good 4 points	Average 3 points	Fair 2 points	Poor 1 point	N/A 0 points
Movement Entrance to Stage Exit from Stage Movement on Stage						
Research (If Required) Number of Sources Verbally Cited ❏ ❏ ❏						
Research (If Required) Verbal Citations Supported Topic ❏ ❏ ❏						
Visual Aids (If Required) Types Used: _____ Setting up Visual Aids Handling Visual Aids Design of Visual Aids Visibility of Visual Aids Management of Tech Team						
Handout (If Required) Type Design Distribution of Handout						
Time of Speech Meets Minimum Time Exceeds Maximum Time						
Handling of Notes/Note Cards						
Note to Instructor If research, visual aids, and handouts are not required, divide the Introduction Step and Conclusion Step into multiple sections to accommodate.						

Suggestions/Comments

SPEECH OUTLINE WORKSHEET
Instructor's Copy for Grading the Speech

Speaker's Name: _____   Title of Speech: _____

Time of Speech: _____   Date: _____

Outline Details	Possible Points	Points Earned
Standard Outline Format	20 points	
Typed	5	
Roman Numerals I, II, III	5	
ABCs	5	
123s	5	
Introduction	20 points	
Attention Step	5	
Establish Need/Relevance	5	
Establish Credibility	5	
Thesis (Previews Main Points)	5	
Body	15 points	
Point 1	5	
Point 2	5	
Point 3	5	
Transitions/Links (4)	10 points	
Leads to Point 1	2.5	
Leads to Point 2	2.5	
Leads to Point 3	2.5	
Leads to Conclusion	2.5	
Conclusion	10 points	
Summary	5	
Closing Statement (Appeal)	5	
Research	25 points	
Required Sources Used	5	
Parenthetical Citations	5	
Works Cited Page	5	
Follows Citation Guidelines	5	
Copy of Research Included	5	

SPEAKER'S SELF-EVALUATION
This is an opportunity to evaluate YOUR speech.

Speaker's Name: _____   Date of Speech: _____

Speech Category: _____   Title of Speech: _____

After viewing the speech video twice, once to observe your nonverbal message and a second time to listen to the verbal message, please complete the self-evaluation worksheet. Be objective with responses and answer the questions asked with YES or NO.

Introduction Step:

When introducing the speech, did you:

_____ 1. Begin with an attention step?

_____ 2. Establish relevance for the topic?

_____ 3. Establish credibility by sharing your own experience with the topic?

_____ 4. Clearly state thesis and preview the main points?

Body:

In developing the body of the speech, did the speaker:

_____ 1. Identify and organize three main points?

_____ 2. Use well-chosen examples?

_____ 3. Effectively use research support materials such as statistics and quotations?

_____ 4. Properly cite sources (verbal citations)? How many sources did you hear? _____

_____ 5. Use transitions between each main point?

Conclusion:

When moving to finish the speech, did the speaker:

_____ 1. Signal the speech was concluding?

_____ 2. Review three main points?

_____ 3. End the speech with a BANG? How was this achieved? _____

Presentation and Visual Aids:

When using visual aids, did you:

_____ 1. Incorporate relevant and well-designed visual aids?

_____ 2. Effectively handle visual aids?

Delivery:

During the speech, did you:

_____ 1. Use voice appropriately by varying inflection, tone, and volume?

_____ 2. Speak words clearly with proper grammar and pronunciation?

_____ 3. Physically move and gesture with purpose?

_____ 4. Establish and maintain eye contact?

_____ 5. Appear confident, poised, and in control?

_____ 6. Dress professionally?

Overall Evaluation:

Considering the speech as a whole, did you:

_____ 1. Choose an appropriate topic?

_____ 2. Meet the assignment requirements, including time limits?

Add Specific Details and Comments:

BASIC PEER EVALUATION
Use a separate copy to evaluate each speaker.

Speaker's Name: _____ Evaluator: _____

Title of Speech: _____ Date: _____

Truthfully answer all areas with a simple YES, NO, or short answer.

Introduction Step:

When beginning the speech, did the speaker:

_____ 1. Use an effective attention step? What was used? _____

_____ 2. Establish relevance for the topic?

_____ 3. Establish credibility by establishing speaker's own experience with the topic?

_____ 4. Clearly state thesis and preview main points?

Body:

When covering the three main points, did the speaker:

_____ 1. Transition from the introduction step to the body of the speech?

_____ 2. Introduce each main point and provide adequate support (research, examples, testimonials) for each one?

_____ 3. Offer transitions between each main point?

_____ 4. Verbally cite research or testimonials?

_____ 5. Transition to the conclusion?

Conclusion:

When moving to finish the speech, did you:

_____ 1. Signal the speech was concluding?

_____ 2. Summarize three main points?

_____ 3. End the speech with a BANG?

Presentation and Visual Aids:

When using visual aids, did the speaker:

_____ 1. Incorporate relevant and well-designed visual aids?

_____ 2. Effectively handle presentation aids?

Delivery:

During the speech, did the speaker:

_____ 1. Use voice appropriately by varying inflection, tone, and volume?

_____ 2. Speak words clearly with proper grammar and pronunciation?

_____ 3. Physically move and gesture with a purpose?

_____ 4. Establish and maintain eye contact?

_____ 5. Appear confident, poised, and in control of the presentation?

_____ 6. Dress professionally?

_____ 7. Speak passionately about the topic?

Overall Evaluation:

Considering the speech as a whole, did the speaker:

_____ 1. Choose an appropriate topic and purpose statement?

_____ 2. Meet the assignment requirements, including time limits?

_____ 3. Handle speech notes effectively?

Use the back of this page to add feedback/comments for the speaker.

GROUP PRESENTATION PEER EVALUATION
Use a separate copy to evaluate each speaker.

Speaker's Name: _____   **Evaluator:** _____

Title of Speech: _____   **Date:** _____

Truthfully answer all areas with a simple YES, NO, or short answer.

Introduction Step:

When beginning the speech, did the speaker:

_____ 1. Use an effective attention step? What was used? _____
_____ 2. Establish relevance for the topic?
_____ 3. Establish credibility by establishing speaker's own experience with the topic?
_____ 4. Clearly state thesis and preview main points?

Body:

In developing the body of the speech, did the speaker:

_____ 1. Identify and organize three main points?
_____ 2. Use well-chosen examples?
_____ 3. Effectively use research support materials such as statistics and quotations?
_____ 4. Properly cite sources (verbal citations)? How many sources did you hear? _____
_____ 5. Use transitions between each main point?

Conclusion:

When moving to finish the speech, did the speaker:

_____ 1. Signal the speech was ending?
_____ 2. Review three main points?
_____ 3. End the speech with a BANG? How was this achieved? _____

Presentation and Visual Aids:

When using visual aids, did the speaker:

_____ 1. Incorporate relevant and well-designed visual aids?
_____ 2. Effectively handle presentation aids?

Delivery:

During the speech, did the speaker:

_____ 1. Use voice appropriately by varying inflection, tone, and volume?
_____ 2. Speak words clearly with proper grammar and pronunciation?
_____ 3. Physically move and gesture with a purpose?
_____ 4. Establish and maintain eye contact?
_____ 5. Appear confident, poised, and in control of the presentation?
_____ 6. Dress professionally?
_____ 7. Speak passionately about the topic?

Overall Evaluation:

Considering the speech as a whole, did the speaker:

_____ 1. Choose an appropriate topic and purpose statement?
_____ 2. Meet the assignment requirements, including time limits?
_____ 3. Handle speech notes effectively?

Use the back of this page to add feedback/comments for the speaker.

PEER EVALUATION—FABULOUS FEEDBACK
Use a separate copy to evaluate each speaker.

Speaker's Name: _____   Evaluator: _____

Title of Speech: _____   Date: _____

> Feedback is the opportunity to share information about perceptions of a speaker's performance and is used as a basis for improvement. It is an opportunity for evaluators to emphasize positive aspects found with new speakers, to evaluate how well the message was delivered, and to keep comments focused on the presentation instead of the presenter.

Introduction Step:
What were the highlights of the Introduction Step?

Body:
What three points did the speaker use to detail the topic?

1.

2.

3.

Were transitions used?

Conclusion:
What did the speaker do to close the speech?

Presentation and Visual Aids:
List ways the visual aids enhanced the speech:

Delivery:
What delivery techniques did the speaker use to make the speech memorable?

Overall Evaluation:
How did the speaker expand your knowledge of the topic?

Use the back of this page to add feedback/comments for the speaker.

PEER EVALUATION—THE SANDWICH APPROACH
Use a separate copy to evaluate each speaker.

Speaker's Name: _____   Evaluator: _____

Title of Speech: _____   Date: _____

The Sandwich Approach: This strategy involves building an evaluation the way that you would build a sandwich. The best part of any sandwich is the bread, but without the meat and cheese, it's just a piece of bread—a snack, but not a meal. The same is true with an evaluation. Consider the two slices of bread as the (1) Introduction Step and the (2) Conclusion Step. Consider the meat and cheese as the Body of the speech.

Introduction:

Start the evaluation with the first piece of bread. Do this by complementing the speaker's strengths noticed during the speech.

Body:

Now, it is time to evaluate the message delivered. This is the meat and cheese of the sandwich and includes the content and purpose of the speech. The condiments are the transitions that blend nicely with the main points, but transitions or connects to the next point.

Were the points clear?

Did they make sense?

Did the speaker use research or personal experience to clarify the points?

How were the transitions?

Share any issues you noticed that the speaker should strengthen. Give examples and offer suggestions.

Conclusion:

Finally, it's time for the last slice of bread and an opportunity to end strong with a final positive message for the speaker.

What is one more thing that you noticed the speaker do that was really over the top?

Leave the speaker with a positive word that keeps the speaker motivated to continue working on communication skills.

PEER EVALUATION—HIGH/LOW EVALUATION
Use a separate copy to evaluate each speaker.

Speaker's Name: _____   Evaluator: _____

Title of Speech: _____   Date: _____

This type of evaluation presents the highs and lows of a speech presentation. This needs to be delivered as a straightforward evaluation that stays away from the message, but focuses on the delivery.

Introduction:

How did the speaker get your attention?

What did the speaker do or say to show passion for the topic?

Body:

What was the HIGH POINT of the speech?

Was the speaker organized and in control of the stage?

How was the speaker's vocal skills?

What sources did the speaker verbally cite?

What was the speaker wearing for the speech? Was he professionally dressed?

What type of visual aids were used for this speech?

Where did the speaker stand during the speech?

What was a LOW POINT of the speech?

Conclusion:

As the speaker was ending the speech, what signal words did you hear?

Did the speaker keep you thinking about the speech topic after the speech was over?

PEER EVALUATION—ANALYSIS ANGLE
Use a separate copy to evaluate each speaker.

Speaker's Name: _____   Evaluator: _____

Title of Speech: _____   Date: _____

The purpose of this type of peer evaluation is to analyze the content of the speech. Answer the following questions for the speaker:

Introduction Step:

What were the highlights of the Introduction Step?

How did the speaker explain relevance for the topic?

How did the speaker explain credibility for the topic?

Did you hear a clear thesis stating the three main points?

Body:

What three points did the speaker cover?

1.

2.

3.

What sources of research did you hear the speaker cite?

Were the research sources good choices to support the three main points?

Were transitions used to lead from the Introduction Step to the Body, between each main point, and then to lead to the Conclusion?

Conclusion:

What did the speaker do to close the speech?

Why were the speaker's closing statements in line with the topic?

Overall Evaluation:

How did the speaker expand your knowledge of the topic?

What suggestions would you give the speaker if he were to present this same speech again?

Use the back of this page to add feedback/comments for the speaker.

PEER EVALUATION—SENSORY SENSATIONS
Use a separate copy to evaluate each speaker.

Speaker's Name: _____   Evaluator: _____

Title of Speech: _____   Date: _____

This type of evaluation will involve sharing the senses that were evoked during the speech. It is a simple type of evaluation, but can carry a BIG punch. Be sure to provide details regarding each answer that can cover content or delivery or content in combination with delivery.

Introduction:

What I saw:

What I felt:

What I heard:

Body:

What I saw:

What I felt:

What I heard:

Conclusion:

What I saw:

What I felt:

What I heard:

End the evaluation with: What I liked and would like to see again:

PEER EVALUATION—COACHING CRITIQUES
Use a separate copy to evaluate each speaker.

Speaker's Name:_____   Evaluator: _____

Title of Speech: _____   Date: _____

To take on the role as a coach, make sure constructive criticism doesn't outweigh praise. Be specific with comments, because positive or negative comments will be more meaningful than generic. Avoid saying, "I liked your speech," because that really doesn't say anything. Explain what you did like about the speech. Use examples. Explain why.

Introduction Step:

What are some things the speaker did in the Introduction Step that was effective?

What are some different strategies the speaker can do to get the audience's attention?

What can the speaker do to let the audience know the topic is relevant?

How can the speaker make sure the audience knows he is credible to speak about the topic?

Was the thesis crystal clear? If not, give suggestions for previewing the main points.

Body:

How can the speaker add examples and research to support main points?

Are there other main points that might make the speech more effective?

Could you suggest a better way to transition from one step to the next?

Conclusion:

How can the speaker signal the speech is ending?

What other way can the speaker use to end with a BANG?

Presentation and Visual Aids:

When using visual aids, what tips can you share to make the speaker's visual aids more effective?

Delivery:

What are specific delivery strategies that would improve the speaker's presentation?

Use the back of this page to add feedback/comments for the speaker.

PEER EVALUATION—123 EVALUATION
Use a separate copy to evaluate each speaker.

Speaker's Name: _____   Evaluator: _____

Title of Speech: _____   Date: _____

The 123 method of presenting a peer evaluation is to offer 3 positives, 2 suggestions for improvement, and 1 explanation of an area that was over-the-top. Finish the evaluation by suggesting why the speaker should keep the over-the-top in all future speeches.

One explanation of an area that was over-the-top:

Two suggestions for Improvement (details):

1.

2.

Three positives:

1.

2.

3.

Conclusion:

Explain why the speaker should keep the over-the-top area in all future speeches.

PEER EVALUATION—MONDAY MORNING QUARTERBACK EVALUATION
Use a separate copy to evaluate each speaker.

Speaker's Name: _____   Evaluator: _____

Title of Speech: _____   Date: _____

Cover each aspect of the speech truthfully answering all areas as a sports commentator might.

Introduction Step:

When beginning the speech:

1. What was used as the attention step? _____

2. How did the speaker establish relevance? _____

3. What was the speaker's own experience with the topic? _____

4. What were the three main points? _____

Body:

In developing the body of the speech:

1. Did the speaker use well-chosen examples? _____

2. How many research sources were verbally cited? _____

3. How did the speaker explain how the research supported the topic? _____

4. How many transitions did you hear? _____

Conclusion:

When ending the speech:

1. Did the speaker signal the speech was ending?

2. Did the speaker review three main points?

3. Did the speaker end the speech with a BANG? How was this achieved? _____

Presentation and Visual Aids:

When using visual aids, how did the speaker use visual aids? _____

Delivery:

During the speech:

1. What vocal qualities did the speaker have? _____

2. Were the speaker's gestures, eye contact, and movement effective? _____

3. Did the speaker establish and maintain eye contact?

4. Did the speaker appear confident, poised, and in control of the presentation?

5. Was the speaker dressed professionally?

Overall Evaluation:

1. How did the speaker handle the use of note cards (coin toss, fumble, forward progress, false start, holder, pass, possession, safety)?

2. Would the speaker make it to the play-offs? _____

Use the back of this page to add feedback/comments for the speaker.

PEER EVALUATION—AIRPLANE EVALUATION
Use a separate copy to evaluate each speaker.

Speaker's Name: _____   Evaluator: _____

Title of Speech: _____   Date: _____

The evaluator should use metaphors aligned with air travel. First the speaker starts the engine and taxis onto the runway—we are in the air—in flight—movies—turbulence—arrive at destination—smooth landing? Include what happens to baggage (fear, stress, poor speaking habits).

Introduction Step:

When beginning the speech:

How did the speaker "start the engine"?

How did the speaker "taxi onto the runway"?

How did the speaker get us "in the air"?

Body:

For the body of the speech—in flight:

What movies did we see?

Was there turbulence?

What was the destination?

Conclusion:

When ending the speech:

Was it a smooth landing?

Did we arrive at the destination?

Overall Evaluation:

Was there a problem with baggage (Fear of speaking? Stress? Speaking Habits?)?

Would you take this trip again?

Use the back of this page to add feedback/comments for the speaker.

PEER EVALUATION—HOUSEWARMING EVALUATION
Use a separate copy to evaluate each speaker.

Speaker's Name: _____   Evaluator: _____

Title of Speech: _____   Date: _____

Approach this evaluation as if you are entering a house for the first time. Answer the questions as a guest and let us know if you feel welcomed. Walk into the front door, move to the front living room, get comfortable in the house, visit the different rooms for each point, and then exit out of the back door.

Introduction Step:

When beginning the speech, how did you enter the house?

Were you greeted at the front door?

Did you feel welcomed to come in?

Did the homeowner give you an introduction to the rooms you would see?

Body:

For the body of the speech, how many rooms of the house did you visit?

1:

2:

3:

Conclusion:

When ending the speech, were you able to exit the house as a happy guest?

Overall Evaluation:

Would you visit this house again?

Evaluating Presentations

After reading this chapter, you will be able to answer the following questions:

1. Why is it important to evaluate your own presentation?

   _____

   _____

2. How many elements are generally assessed when conducting a self-evaluation?

   _____

   _____

3. What are some suggested guidelines to follow when assessing a peer's presentation?

   _____

   _____

Shark Bites

It is a good idea to offer various types of evaluations when peer evaluating speakers. Ask your instructor before each speech to identify which of the Peer Evaluation worksheets you should use. If the instructor does not have a preference, try alternating with the different options for each of the speech types shown below.

Introduction Speech

- Basic Peer Evaluation
- Peer Evaluation—Fabulous Feedback
- Peer Evaluation—The Sandwich Approach
- Peer Evaluation—Sensory Sensations
- Peer Evaluation—Coaching Critiques
- Peer Evaluation—123 Evaluation
- Peer Evaluation—Airplane Evaluation

Informative Speech

- Speech Evaluation Worksheet
- Peer Evaluation—The Sandwich Approach
- Peer Evaluation—The High/Low Evaluation
- Peer Evaluation—The Analysis Angle
- Peer Evaluation—Airplane Evaluation

Persuasion Speech

- Speech Evaluation Worksheet
- Peer Evaluation—The Sandwich Approach
- Peer Evaluation—The High/Low Evaluation
- Peer Evaluation—The Analysis Angle
- Peer Evaluation—Sensory Sensations
- Peer Evaluation—Monday Morning Quarterback Evaluation

Group Presentation

- Group Presentation Peer Evaluation
- Peer Evaluation - Fabulous Feedback
- Peer Evaluation—The Sandwich Approach
- Peer Evaluation—The High/Low Evaluation
- Peer Evaluation—Sensory Sensations
- Peer Evaluation—123 Evaluation
- Peer Evaluation—Airplane Evaluation

Special Occasion Speech

- Basic Peer Evaluation
- Peer Evaluation—Fabulous Feedback
- Peer Evaluation—The Sandwich Approach
- Peer Evaluation—The High/Low Evaluation
- Peer Evaluation—Sensory Sensations
- Peer Evaluation—Coaching Critiques
- Peer Evaluation—123 Evaluation
- Peer Evaluation—Airplane Evaluation

Sales Presentation

- Speech Evaluation Worksheet
- Basic Peer Evaluation
- Peer Evaluation—Fabulous Feedback
- Peer Evaluation—The Sandwich Approach
- Peer Evaluation—The High/Low Evaluation
- Peer Evaluation—The Analysis Angle
- Peer Evaluation—Sensory Sensations
- Peer Evaluation—Coaching Critiques
- Peer Evaluation—123 Evaluation

Glossary

Active Listening: listening to understand

Adrenaline: is physiological and involves increased heart and respiration rate as a result of a situation perceived to be frightening or exciting

APA: the American Psychological Association style of citing research

Appreciative Listening: showing enjoyment of a speaker and the content exhibits appreciative listening

Aromatherapy: a strategy by which the user engages scents/smells to bring about a feeling of calmness

Articulation: the process by which the speaker sounds out words so that the audience can understand what is being said

Asynchronous Meetings: meetings that happen on your own time and are accessed through a video recording, e-mail, letters, text messaging, or direct messaging

Attention Step: a step in the Introduction of the speech which gets the attention of the audience

Attitudes: to look at a topic with a favorable or unfavorable manner

Bar Graph: a diagram used to show comparisons among two or more items

Behaviors: a combination of personal values, beliefs, and attitudes, which causes us to behave a certain way when reacting to these three different areas

Beliefs: involves a perception of something to be true or false

Bibliography: itemized list of sources used for presentations that follow APA guidelines

Block Indentions: a method for showing quotes in a written document that are over four lines long

Blogs: a written view of a person or organization, but not necessarily a credible source

Body Language Cues: communication signals that we send non-verbally

Breathing: a strategy whereby the speaker can breathe in managed, steady breaths in order to bring about a calming effect and to relieve speech anxiety

Causal Order: an ordering strategy in which the writer arranges information according to cause and effect

Category: a step for narrowing a topic

Central Idea Speech: a speech that begins with one general informative topic, but is narrowed down to one key/central idea

Ceremonial Speeches: include installation, presenting an award, accepting an award, dedication, eulogy, commemorative, and commencement speeches

Chart: a visual aid effective for summarizing large blocks of information

Chronemics: is the study of how we use time to communicate

Chronological Order: an ordering strategy in which the writer arranges information according to time

Citation: the written or verbal posting of credentials to give credit for an author's thoughts or ideas

Closed Questions: limit the amount of information that can be gathered about a topic. Closed questions are usually answered with a simple "yes" or "no"

Clustering and Webbing: a type of brainstorming strategy to help determine a writing plan

CMS: the Chicago Manual of Style for research citations

Color: a way to describe a voice that shows passion, energy, and enthusiasm

Communication: a process in which ideas or information are transmitted, shared, and exchanged

Connective: a term used to indicate a transition or link within an outline and used to help tie a speech together

Connectors: another term used for transitions/links

Conversational tone: a preferred tone for speakers to use because it causes the audience to feel like the speaker is engaged in a direct conversation with them and helps the speaker to connect with the audience in a more intimate manner

Conversational Quality: maintaining a prepared, yet spontaneous element to a presentation

Credibility: implies how the audience perceives a speaker's ability to present information about a particular topic

Critical Listening: resisting outside noises and distractions

CSE: the Council of Science Editors guidelines for research citations

Decoding: a process by which we translate or interpret the content into meaning

Debate: a presentation in which two sides, affirmative and negative, are argued and resolved

Delivery Cues: items to consider when presenting the speech

Demonstration Speech: an opportunity to demonstrate a process or procedure needed to complete a task

Dialects: a form of language used by people living in a particular region. Dialects are often referred to as local speech, regional speech patterns, languages, linguistics, vernacular or accents

Empathetic listening: trying to see the speaker's point of view, even if you do not share the speaker's views

Empathy: is the act of seeing another person's point of view

Encoding: a process by which a person derives meaning and understanding

ESOL Translation Features: English Speakers of Other Language participants enjoy virtual meetings that use translation features that transcribe the message content into translated subtitles

Entertaining Speech: speeches with a purpose to invoke laughter, humor, and happiness

Establish Credibility: this is a step within the Introduction of a speech in which the speaker shares his own experience with the topic and establishes himself as a credible speaker

Establish Relevance: this is a step within the introduction of a speech in which the speaker shares the relevance of the topic with the audience

Ethos: an appeal to ethics

Extemporaneous Speech: a presentation carefully planned, rehearsed in advanced, usually containing visual aids, research to support points, and includes brief notes

Eye contact: promotes goodwill and a connection with the audience and helps the speaker to appear more credible and knowledgeable about the topic

Facial Expressions: include eye contact, smiling, head nodding, and head tilting to send a non-verbal cue to the audience during communication

Feedback: helps the speaker to know if the content delivered has been effectively decoded and received

Filler Words: types of phrases, sounds, or words that speakers use to fill in silence when trying to communicate a thought or make a speech presentation

Font: imagery to ensure your presentation technology can be seen

GALILEO: Georgia Library Learning Online—an Internet-based virtual library

General Purpose: the purpose of the speech is to inform, entertain, or motivate

Gestures: ways we use our hands, body, and facial expressions during the speech to communicate points

Goodwill: measures a speaker's intent

Graph: a visual aid diagram used to illustrate complex series of numbers

Group Presentations: presentations made with three or more people

Hanging Indentions: the indention of a research source citation with more than one typed line of content

Haptics: a non-verbal cue that involves touch

Head Tilting and Head Nodding: a non-verbal cue from your audience to indicate comprehension of message delivered

Humorous speech: a presentation designed to warm up the audience, make them laugh, and then keep them laughing!

Hybrid: meetings that include virtual and face-to-face at the same time

HyFlex: meetings where the participant can choose to attend in person or attend at a time that is best for their own personal schedule

Imagery: this is the act of painting a visual picture for audience members during a speech

Impromptu: presentation delivered with little preparation and no rehearsal

Improvisational Speaking: a method which combines several elements to include movement, technology, imagination, and discussion on a stage or in a classroom setting

Information gathering interviews: conducted with many people responding to a question asked

Informative Listening: taking notes during a speech will incorporate informative listening skills

Informative Speech: an opportunity to share something of value with your audience

Internal Summary: an opportunity to clarify and reinforce main points to be covered in a speech

Interview: the asking of specific questions with the intent to gather information from the person being interviewed

Intimate Space: is the closest and is usually one foot or less away and usually involves touching the person next to you

Job interviews: structured conversations with a goal to discover if a person is suitable for an open position within a company

Key Idea/Central Idea Speech: a speech that begins with one general informative topic, but is narrowed down to one key/central idea

Key Words: words used for the purpose of gathering information

Kinesics: physical cues that we see as we evaluate physical appearance, posture, poise, gestures, facial expressions, eye contact, smiling, and body movements

Larynx: voice box which produces sound

Logos: an appeal to logic

Main Points: identifies key points to be covered in a speech

Manuscript Speech: presenting a crafted speech reading a script word-for-word

Meditation: a strategy used to relieve speech anxiety in which the participant finds a quiet place to intently focus on a calming place or thought to bring a feeling of peace and tranquility

Mehrabian, Albert: a scholar who conducted non-verbal research and reported his findings in a book entitled *Silent Messages*

Memorized Speech: committing a presentation to memory

MLA: the Modern Language Association style of citing research

Moderator: the lead speaker of a group presentation

Monotone: a constant pitch results in a monotone voice

Motivational Speech: a speech delivered with the purpose to motivate the audience to action

Movement: calculated movement from one place to another while onstage presenting a speech

Narrow: a step to break down a large topic into a more manageable topic

Noise: distractions in the speaking environment including preconceived notions, opinions, and ideas

Non-Verbal Communication: the act of communicating without words

Open Question: broad questions that cannot be answered with a simple "yes" or "no" answer

Oral Interpretation: involves making careful material selections and using interpretive or dramatic readings of prose, poetry, drama, plays, or oratorical speeches

Pace: is the rate at which you say syllables in a word

Paralanguage: is the vocal part of speech and involves volume, rate, pitch, pace, and color

Paraphrasing: the sharing of research without offering a direct quote; in this case, the author's name, title of the publication, publisher, and published date are also provided either in written format or verbally

Parenthetical Citation: an in-text citation of a source of research which will show the author's last name and/or the page number of the document

Pathos: an appeal to emotion

Pause: a strategically planned break in speech to allow the audience to process a delivered point

PechaKucha: a presentation that uses twenty slides shown for twenty seconds each

Performance reviews: considered interviews and are initiated by management authorities in a company to review the performance of employees

Personal Space: one- to four-foot area usually reserved for meeting with friends or family members

Persuasion Speech: a type of speech in which the speaker provides useful information and supporting research that will motivate the listener to action

Pie Graph: a visual aid diagram used to show the parts of a whole

Pitch: is determined by sounds produced by vocal cord vibrations

Physical Appearance: sends a positive or negative message about the speaker's credibility

Plagiarism: the act of using someone else's ideas or work as if they are your own

Poise: a term used to describe a speaker who has good posture and exhibits self-confidence while speaking

Posture: sends a non-verbal cue about your self-confidence

Preparation Outline: an outline created to assist with organizing the speech

Presentation: a speech, whether impromptu or extemporaneous, with the intent of informing, entertaining, or motivating

Preview Points: presentation of points to be covered in the body. This is also called a thesis

Problem-Solution Order: a strategy for arranging information addressing the problem and following it up with a solution

Problem-Solving Interviews: designed to bring peace or solve grievances between two parties. A mediator is usually present in the event of a problem-solving interview

Probing Questions: encourage the interviewee to elaborate about the topic

Pronunciation: the way that words are pronounced

Proxemics: is the study of space and how we use it

Public Domain: property not protected by copyrights laws and available for the general public to use

Public Space is the space designated for speakers and are usually twelve to twenty-five feet away from their audience members

Public Speaking: a communication process in which speakers and listeners participate together

Question and Answer Session: also known as a Q&A Session is a point in a group presentation in which the audience members can ask questions of the group and receive answers not covered in the group presentation

Questions of Fact: point delivered during a persuasion speech that covers fact by using credible research to support points

Questions of Policy: point delivered during a persuasion speech that offers solutions which involve changing laws, enforcing existing laws, or revising procedures

Questions of Value: point delivered during a persuasion speech that covers questions of value—whether something is moral or immoral, just or unjust, good or bad

Rate: the method we use to determine how fast or slow someone is speaking

Rehearse: an opportunity to practice a speech prior to making the presentation

Research: the process for finding support materials, data, and credible information

Rhetorical Question: a question posed without a verbal response

Rhythm: a speaking pattern than involves a cadence that keeps the audience interested

Sales Presentation: a type of speech in which the speaker's purpose is to sell a product or service to the listener

Scripts: copy of speech outlines highlighted to show tech team member responsibilities

Shark-o-licious Treat: a way to describe a great speech to a group of soon to be SpeechSharks

Signpost: signals offered by the speaker to indicate points covered and points yet to cover

Smiling: a non-verbal cue that says "I am happy to be here!"

Social Space: the space that others are most comfortable with when working with a co-worker or customer and is usually about four to twelve feet

Spatial Order: a strategy for arranging information according to geographical location

Speaking Outline: an outline created with brief notes to jog memory during a speech presentation. This can also be called a presentation outline

Special Occasion Speeches: speeches given during events that are work-related, social, or ceremonial

Specialty Speeches: presentations which involve situations that may require unique preparation strategies and varying delivery skills

Specific Purpose: a purpose statement made that details the topic and the speaker's purpose for presenting the topic

Speech Anxiety: a feeling of stress felt by some speakers when faced with the duty of making a presentation in public

Startling Statement: a strategy used to get the audience's attention in the beginning of the speech

Storytelling: the process of sharing stories to educate, inform, and entertain

Strategic Organization: an organizational skill critical to outlining speech content

Supporting Materials: items used to enhance content of the speech

SWOT Analysis: a strategy in which the user determines strengths, weaknesses, opportunities, and threats and makes a plan based upon these four areas

Synchronous Meetings: scheduled meetings that happen through real-time interactions by phone, video conference, or in person

Tech Team: a group of people qualified to help you complete your speech presentation by setting up or breaking down, managing the PowerPoint/Prezi slides, managing lighting and/or sound requirements, and distributing handouts

TED Talks: began as a method for delivering brief speeches (talks) about great ideas. The name, TED, is an acronym taken from the words **T**echnology, **E**ntertainment, and **D**esign

Teleconferencing: is the simplest form of virtual meeting because it only involves audio

Thesis: the point in the introduction step of a speech in which the speaker details the three main points that will be covered

Topical Order: a strategy used to arrange information according to topic

Transitions: sentences used as a bridge/connector/link between one main point and another main point in a speech

Verbal Communication: a form of communication using words

Video Conferencing: a popular form of meeting which allows participants to see and hear each other, observe body language, facial expressions, and other nonverbal cues that help encourage collaboration

Virtual Meeting Etiquette: an expectation of how meeting leaders and participants should behave during virtual meetings

Virtual Meetings: a method that allows people in various locations to use Internet devices to meet in a virtual space

Virtual Meeting Platforms: applications and software designed so that we can meet remotely online

Vocal variance: incorporates varying degrees of volume, rate, pitch, pace, and color

Volume: is the level at which a sound is heard

Webinars: a virtual seminar with hosts, speakers, or panelists which can be held synchronously, asynchronously, hybrid, or HyFlex and offers meeting options that accommodate more attendees

Wikis: an Internet source of research not always deemed credible

Works Cited: itemized list of sources used for presentations that follow MLA guidelines

Shark Bites

UNDERSTANDING SPEECH TERMS

Do you know the terms to the words found in your glossary? Find a partner and make a game of asking the term and responding with the correct definition.

Works Cited Page

Adichie, Chimamanda Ngozi. "The Danger of a Single Story." *Chimamanda Ngozi Adichie: The Danger of a Single Story.* TED Talks. Accessed 28 May 2017. <https://www.ted.com/talks/chimamanda_adichie_the_danger_of_a_single_story>.

"APA Central." American Psychological Association. 2017. Accessed 8 Feb. 2017. www.apastyle.org/.

"Benjamin Franklin Quotes." Your Dictionary. 2017. Accessed 12 March 2017. Lovetoknow.com

Berry, Richard J. "A practical way to help the homeless find work and safety". TED Talks. 2017. Accessed 15 Sept. 2017. www.ted.com/talk/richard_j_berry_a_practical_way_to_help_the_homeless_find_work_and_safety/up-next.

Blanton, Becky. "The year I was homeless." TED Talk. 2017. Accessed 15 Sept. 2017. www.ted.com/talks/becky_blanton_the_year_i_was_homeless/up-next.

Chicago-Style Citation Quick Guide. The Chicago Manual of Style. 2017. Accessed 15 March 2017. http://www.chicagomanualofstyle.org/tools_citationguide.html.

Frequently Asked Questions. PechaKucha 20X20. Klein Dytham Architecture. 2017. Accessed 15 Sept. 2017. www.pechakucha.org.

Frymier, Ann Bainbridge, and Gary M. Shulman. "What's in it for me?" *Communication Education Journal,* vol. 44, no. 1, May 22, 2009.

Grice, George L., and John F. Skinner. "Personal Report of Public Speaking Anxiety (PRPSA)." *Mastering Public Speaking.* 6th ed., Allyn & Bacon, 2007.

Mehrabian, Albert. *Silent Messages: Implicit Communication of Emotions and Attitudes.* 2nd ed.,

Wadsworth Publishing Company, 1980.

"MLA Style Manual." Modern Language Association. 2017. Accessed 4 March, 2017. https://www.mla.org/.

Mortensen, C. David, Ed. *Communication Theory.* 2nd ed., Transaction Publishers, 2008.

Pollan, Michael. *Cooked.* The Penguin Press, 2013.

"Public Domain." Merriam-Webster. 2017. Accessed 6 April 2017.

Quast, Lisa. "8 Tips to Dress for Interview Success." *Forbes.* 2014. Accessed 12 March 2017.

"Scientific Style and Format." Council of Science Editors. 2017. Accessed 4 March, 2017.

www.councilscienceeditors.org/ publications/scientific-style-and-format/.

Smith, Chris. "Dress to Impress: what to wear for a job interview." *The Guardian.* Guardian Careers. 2017.

Accessed 12 March 2017.

"Zig Ziglar Quotes." 2016. Accessed 12 March 2017. AZQuotes.com.

Shark Bites

FEATURES FOUND IN SPEECHSHARK, THE BOOK:

SpeechShark is a guide book to public speaking and offers sixteen chapters of content to help as you begin your public speaking journey. Within each chapter, you will find instructional materials, tips, and tools for speaking.

Following each chapter, you will find **Shark Attack**. This is a list of questions so that you can test your understanding of the subject matter. In a college or university course, speech instructors may use this list as an assignment to be graded following each of the chapter readings.

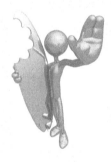
The last section of each chapter has a helpful section that we named **Shark Bites**. This section will help you to sharpen your skills and practice your newfound speech strategies by actively completing the exercises and suggestions found in Shark Bites.

This public speaking guide book is unique from other speech texts because it was written as a companion book for the SpeechShark app.

Let us know how you enjoy using it!

Index

Photo Credits